Soldiers, Spies,
and the Rat Line

Soldiers, Spies, and the Rat Line

America's Undeclared War Against the Soviets

Col. James V. Milano, USA (Ret.)

and

Patrick Brogan

BRASSEY'S
Washington   London

First paperback edition 2000

Library of Congress Cataloging-in-Publication Data

Milano, James V.
    Soldiers, spies, and the rat line: America's undeclared war against the Soviets/Col. James V. Milano, USA (Ret.) and Patrick Brogan.
        p.   cm.
    Includes index.
    ISBN 1-57488-050-0
    1. Espionage, American—Austria—Vienna. 2. United States—Foreign relations—Soviet Union. 3. Soviet Union—Foreign relations—United States. 4. Milano, James V. I. Brogan, Patrick. II. Title.
E183.8.S65M54 1995
327.73047—dc20   95-20382

10 9 8 7 6 5 4 3 2 1

Paperback ISBN 1-57488-304-6

Printed in Canada

This book is dedicated to the members of the intelligence community who served with the U.S. Army in Austria following World War II. They were a group of talented and dedicated people who lived and worked under the growing cloud of the cold war. Their contributions greatly aided the American government's understanding of the Soviet threat that led to more than four decades of global confrontation and conflict.

Contents

Acknowledgments

I would like to thank my son, James, for his valuable assistance in planning and organizing the initial phase of the project. Also, John B. Burkel, former agent in charge of the Counter-Intelligence Corps in Salzburg, Austria, during those exciting days. John was most helpful in recalling many of the details of those times.

I am most grateful for the clerical assistance extended by Anna Amato, our office coordinator at Pfizer Aviation.

Last, special thanks to my wife, Ann, for her patience and understanding. We spent those years together in Salzburg when, due to security restrictions, she had virtually no knowledge of what I was doing. Fellow workers came to the house after office hours, and she was never included in the conversations. Telephone calls to report to the code room often came in the middle of the night, and she endured many lonesome hours due to my extensive meetings after work.

—James V. Milano

Preface

This is a story of the secret beginnings of the cold war in Europe. It concerns intelligence operations carried out for the U.S. Army in Austria immediately after World War II—before the CIA came on the scene—and the "Rat Line" that was used to smuggle Soviet deserters to South America. The operation was kept secret from civil officials of the U.S. government, and from most military officers, and remained hidden for nearly forty years.

It is Jim Milano's story. He was a young intelligence officer with the American army in Italy that fought its way from Sicily to the Alps and then undertook the occupation of Austria. He directed American military intelligence against Soviet targets from 1945 to 1950, and established the Rat Line. The line's existence, and Milano's role in it, emerged in 1983 when the public learned of the case of Klaus Barbie. Barbie was a Nazi war criminal who had been smuggled out of Germany in 1951 by American officers there and who used the escape route that had been set up by their colleagues in Austria. Milano had left Europe by then and never heard of Barbie until the case became public decades later. The Rat Line, while he operated it, was never used by war criminals; it was reserved exclusively for Soviet defectors and their families. His successors in Austria, at the bidding of their associates in Germany, broke that rule. There was a great outcry in the United States when the public learned that U.S. Intelligence had employed Barbie and had then sent him to safety in South America to escape prosecution for war crimes. The Justice Department held an inquiry. Jim Milano was interviewed and gave an account of his activities in the postwar period and a history of the Rat Line. The inquiry concluded that between 1945 and 1950 the Rat Line may have acted with dubious legality, but did not help war criminals. Milano and his team had nothing to do with Klaus Barbie.

Now Jim Milano has told his own story of those dramatic events. No files survive of the Rat Line or any of the other operations he directed. After forty-five years, a great many of those who had a part to play have died, and very many details of their secret campaigns, their triumphs and failures, have been lost for good. Old men forget, but he offers his imperfect recollections as the best record still available of this corner of modern history. He gave these and his papers to Patrick Brogan, a writer living in Washington. These are Jim

Milano's memoirs as recounted by Patrick Brogan, which is why the book is cast in the third person. The authors did not want a "ghost-written" book like the memoirs of politicians, film stars, or prominent businessmen in which the purported author puts his name to someone else's work.

In writing the story for Milano, Brogan has checked whatever details can still be confirmed after such a long interval, and has added some background as well as details of the Barbie case, which all appear in their appropriate place. The conversations are obviously reconstructions based upon Milano's best recollection. Some of the incidents recounted were only partly to be recovered, but nothing was invented, nothing added. Jim Milano was no James Bond, but this is a true story of the real world of intelligence during the most dangerous period of the cold war.

James V. Milano
Patrick Brogan

1

The Chilean Connection

In the fall of 1948, a dilapidated Italian freighter made the long, slow voyage from Genoa in Italy to Valparaiso in Chile. It was a sign, one of many, that life and trade were reviving after the bloody interruption of the war. The ship was in no other way significant, the general goods she carried were not at all remarkable, and all the world's governments and intelligence services ignored her. But there were also passengers on board, refugees or emigrants who were ready to put up with the great discomforts and delays of the cargo line. It was the cheapest and least conspicuous way to escape from the grim reality of postwar Europe to the peaceful, different, and vaguely exotic world across the oceans. It had been autumn when they had left Italy, with its promise of another cold, uncertain winter, but they would arrive in the spring of the southern hemisphere to blue skies, a new life, and renewed hopes.

If the intelligence services of the United States or the Soviet Union had paid closer attention, they would have found two of those passengers particularly interesting. They carried immigrant visas for Chile, provided by the Vatican Office for Refugees. The documents stated that they were good Catholics from Central Europe, plumbers, qualified artisans, just the sort of immigrants Chile needed. They had appeared on the dock in Genoa on the morning the ship sailed, their tickets and documents all in order, and had been hustled aboard at the last moment by Italian police officials, closely watched by silent men in civilian clothing whose nationality and intentions were never revealed. The two spoke no Italian, Spanish, or English, conversing together in some incomprehensible Slavic

1

tongue, and kept themselves to themselves throughout the long voyage west. People traveling the world on their own business in those days were jealous of their privacy. They often had their own, excellent reasons for discretion and did not concern themselves with the identities and business of any strangers they might encounter. It was a prudence greatly appreciated by the two travelers.

They could have told an extraordinary story, even for those exceptional times. They were refugees from the Soviet Union, deserters from the Red Army, whose names and histories had been wiped away by American intelligence agents in Austria. The Americans had recruited them and had spirited them away from the vengeance of the Soviet security service, the MGB (later known as the KGB). They had been hidden in obscure farmhouses in the Alps and in apartments in small towns in Austria for months while they were thoroughly and laboriously interrogated to discover everything they knew about the Soviet army. They were taught the rudiments of a useful trade, in this case plumbing, and the Americans had bought new identities and passports for them from a corrupt Yugoslav priest in the Vatican. They had been given tickets on that anonymous freighter. They had been taken secretly from Austria to Genoa, with the complicity of senior officers in the Italian Security Police, and hustled on board before any of the emigration or port authorities could examine their papers too closely. The whole operation had been conceived and executed by a group of young Americans working for Army Intelligence but acting wholly outside the normal Army chain of command. They called the operation the Rat Line. It was a method of getting Soviet deserters out of Europe secretly, away from the danger of being kidnapped or killed by the KGB.

The group of Americans who controlled the Rat Line was commanded by Major James Milano, chief of operations of the intelligence staff of the U.S. Army in Austria, who protected his own identity and his operations as closely as did the refugees. His headquarters was in Salzburg, far from the spotlight that illuminated army command in Vienna. Secrecy, anonymity, and discretion were the rule. The refugees were never to draw attention to themselves. They were to merge silently into their new lives, leaving no trace behind them.

The Americans had given the two the cosy code names Patsy and Pete, and, when they sailed from Genoa, their hosts hoped they had heard the last of them. But six weeks later, as they stepped into the immigration hall in Valparaiso, all the nightmares returned. Standing before them, in the uniform of a Chilean customs official, was a German SS lieutenant, a war criminal and murderer, who had killed Patsy's brother in a concentration camp in Germany.

The brothers had been captured by the Wehrmacht during the siege of Leningrad in 1943 and shipped with tens of thousands of other prisoners in cattle trucks a thousand miles west to a camp in Germany. The prisoners were to be worked to death, and Patsy and his brother had been put on a gang laying railroad track. One day, as they were being driven to the site, one of the SS guards had beaten Patsy's brother with a whip. The brother had tried to defend himself, grabbing the whip from the man's hand—and the guard had shot him dead. Patsy had been powerless to help. Other prisoners had seized him by the arms to keep him from interfering: otherwise he would certainly have been shot beside his brother. But the guard's face, the face of a killer, had been forever seared into his memory. He saw him again, four years later, in Chile.

There was no doubt of his identity. South America was the favorite refuge of war criminals who could escape: Adolf Eichmann, Josef Mengele, and Klaus Barbie were merely the most famous. There were many rat lines out of Europe after 1945. Many German police and military officers escaped to Chile and naturally offered their services and a sanitized version of their experience to the local police authorities, who gave some of them employment. A cruel accident had brought this killer face to face with one of his victims. The SS man transformed into a Chilean customs official was suddenly confronted by the refugee whose brother he had murdered.

Patsy was a Russian officer. He had survived the horrors of the Nazi death camps, where nine out of ten Soviet prisoners had died. At the end of the war, the camp had been liberated by the Red Army, in the spring of 1945. Patsy had concealed his identity from the commissars and had made his way to a displaced persons camp near Linz in Austria. There he had met Pete, another Soviet deserter, and the two had been discovered by American interrogators examining the thousands of people in the camps. During his travels after his defection, Patsy had obtained and hidden an Italian Beretta 9mm pistol. He had acquired a few bottles of a fine German wine and used them to buy the pistol from an Italian soldier, stranded in Austria and trying to get home, who knew that he would have to part with his gun when he presented himself to the authorities and preferred to sell it instead.

Now, in Valparaiso, Patsy saw his enemy before him in uniform. Immediately, though he was surrounded by other refugees and the police and officials of the country he had hoped to make his home, he pulled out his pistol and hurled himself onto the Nazi, firing the pistol and shouting that he was avenging his brother.

The man was shot in the stomach and fell screaming to the floor, in a widening pool of blood. There was pandemonium in the cus-

toms hall as passengers and civilians dived for cover while uniformed police pulled out their guns and rushed to the scene.
Miraculously, the Nazi was not killed, though he was seriously
wounded, and Patsy was seized and thrown to the ground before he
could finish the job. He was arrested and interrogated, and the
Chilean authorities discovered immediately that he and his compan-
ion were not at all the simple plumbers they claimed to be. They may
also have learned something of the true history of their new customs
official.

The incident was potentially a catastrophe for American intelligence operations in Europe, which depended on defectors from the
East for information on the Soviet armed forces and the situation
behind the Iron Curtain. The shooting in Valparaiso occurred at the
most dangerous moment of the cold war, during the Berlin Airlift
and soon after the Communists had seized power in Czechoslovakia.
It was essential to continue gathering intelligence on the strength
and intentions of the Soviet army and therefore equally important to
keep the Rat Line open, so that the deserters and refugees could be
made to disappear when they had told their tales. Now the whole
Rat Line might be unraveled and one of the U.S. Army's best hidden
intelligence operations revealed. The danger was not only from the
Soviet secret service, the KGB. As ever, the various departments of
the U.S. government were at odds with one another, competing for
power and reputation. The State Department and other bureaucra-
cies barely accepted the necessity for clandestine operations, and if
they were to find out about the Rat Line, which was altogether illegal and unofficial, they might also discover all the other secret operations conducted by Milano and his friends, and an invaluable
source of intelligence would be compromised. There were high officials in Washington who were quite capable of closing down a major
intelligence source, just because they had never been told about it,
and others who would insist on shutting down the Rat Line because
it could embarrass the U.S. government. Patsy and Pete had to be
saved, and every trace of their passage across Europe and the
Atlantic had to be erased.

The Chilean police quickly decided that this was an international
affair, a question involving the secret services of several countries
and an echo of the war in Europe that had ended three years before.
They wanted none of it. They decided to save themselves the trouble
of a trial and simply deported Patsy and Pete back to Italy—and
informed the U.S. and Italian governments. Jim Milano and his colleagues would have to deal with them and salvage the Rat Line.

As soon as news of the Chilean disaster reached him, Milano convened his staff to decide how to limit the damage. They sat and mar-
veled at the malign coincidence that had brought Patsy face to face

with his enemy. He had often told his American interrogators about his brother's murder, how he had missed being killed himself, how clearly he remembered the face of the murderer, and how implacably he vowed vengeance. The odds against such an encounter must have been millions to one.

Paul Lyon, the chief operator of the Rat Line, had rushed down to Genoa to speak with his contact in the Italian police there and had returned seriously concerned. Major Mario Anselmo, chief of security for the Border Police branch of the Carabinieri, had been informed by the port police and the Genoa police that the two undesirables were due back in a few days. The Chilean police had held them for a week before their ship had turned around and had doubtless discovered that they were not the simple immigrants they pretended to be. The State Department in Washington had gotten wind of the affair and was putting pressure on the Italians to investigate it thoroughly and to send them a report of their findings. The embassy in Rome had sent two investigators to Genoa, and they were already interrogating the local police. Perhaps the Chilean government had protested directly to Washington, suspecting that the United States was running an illegal rat line out of Europe to South America.

Fortunately, the Genoa police knew nothing. Major Anselmo had seen to that. But when Patsy and Pete came ashore, they would be arrested immediately and the whole saga would be revealed. The group briefly considered reporting the matter to their superiors in Vienna and asking their help. Milano slapped the idea down firmly. That was not the way they did business.

"Those idiots would probably give all sorts of orders that would screw up everything," he said. "They'd have Patsy put on trial out in the open where the Russians could see him, they'd wind up the Rat Line and God knows what else. We'll solve this one ourselves—and if anyone ever asks us about it later, we'll just have to tell them and take our lumps. Until then, not a word to anyone."

That solved that problem. Lyon was a smart operator. He had not spent his time in Genoa wringing his hands. He had already taken the first, essential step toward extricating them all from their difficulties.

"There's going to be real trouble unless we can get hold of Patsy and Pete before anyone else does and keep them out of harm's way," he said. "If the regular police, or the MPs or anyone get hold of them, it'll be horrendously difficult to get them back again. We need to grab them the moment they step off the boat. So I raised the subject, all most delicately, with our friend Mario. He thinks they can be gotten out of the hands of the Genoa police—but it will be expensive."

The group contemplated the further drain on their budget with equanimity. This was an emergency.

"What he needs is a formal, written request from the U.S. Army for these characters. The local police would be delighted to get rid of them, and the embassy has been sniffing around already, so they won't be surprised if we pick them up off the boat. But it has to be a formal document, with plenty of rubber stamps and some impressive signature. The police chief will swallow it whole, and then we can grab those two idiots and have them out of the way before anyone else comes looking."

All eyes turned to Dominic Del Greco. None of them needed to ask how they would get hold of a formal request from the American High Command for the release of two prisoners. They would forge it. Del Greco was the facilitator, the man who organized such things. He could always lay his hands on a general officer's stationery, he could produce official-looking rubber stamps at a moment's notice, and he had some of the best forgers in the business on his staff.

Milano ruled that the signature should be that of the commander of American forces in Austria, Major General Paul Kendall. The intelligence operation was outside his jurisdiction, and he knew little or nothing about it. They did not want to take the name of any of their own superior officers in vain, even though it would probably be easier to do. Milano wanted to keep this matter at several removes from his own place of work. Del Greco was instructed to set to work acquiring a sample of General Kendall's signature and letterhead and then to set his forgers to work. He cheerfully promised that the letter would be ready in two days.

Then Milano turned to the next problem: how to get the letter back again. The Genoa police would certainly agree to a request from an American general for the two prisoners, but they would then file the letter away in their safest archives, ready to produce if anyone came asking questions. It was only too probable that someone would indeed check. The embassy in Rome, or the army command, would eventually discover that Patsy and Pete had disappeared before they could be interrogated and would want to know why. When they were told that a senior American general had made the request formally, in writing, they would demand to see the document—and would immediately discover that it was a fake. Milano had no intention of leaving such an incriminating document anywhere it might be found. Paul Lyon was instructed to return to Genoa for further words with Major Anselmo.

Then they had to decide what to do with the two miscreants. The first step was easy: they would be lodged in a safe house in the countryside, well clear of the Genoa police. But Milano wanted them out of the way as quickly as possible, and most certainly he never wanted them back in Austria. He was lucky. Another pair of Soviet deserters, code-named Isaac and Dieter, had been prepared and trained, this time as mechanics, and given documents and visas to get them to Argentina. Their ship was due to leave a few days after the freighter from Chile returned to port, and the Americans decided on the spot to swap them with Patsy and Pete. Isaac and Dieter would be disappointed: they would have to wait—in a new safe house, as their present landlady, who had been told that the two were due to sail immediately, might get suspicious if they did not leave. Del Greco's team was given another rush job, preparing a new set of papers for Patsy and Pete in the names that had been chosen for their compatriots. They would barely have time to learn their second false identities before they were once again on the seas, heading for South America—this time to the opposite side of the continent from the SS man in Valparaiso. One of the team's best Russian specialists would be sent down to Genoa to explain these matters to Patsy and Pete—and also to grill them thoroughly on every detail of their Chilean adventure. Milano needed to know as precisely as possible just what they had told the police in Valparaiso.

Paul Lyon returned to Genoa, prepared to immerse himself in the complexities of the rival Italian police forces. His contact, Major Anselmo, was head of the security branch in the region. He was the essential link in the chain that ran from Salzburg to the ships sailing from the harbor, but he depended on the head of the Genoa police. Nothing was possible unless these two agreed. On the other hand, if both could be persuaded, the Americans could do anything in Genoa, anything at all.

One of the joys of working in postwar Italy (and things did not change, in this respect, over the next fifty years) was that everyone understood the rules. A certain subtlety was required in the matter of offering bribes or exerting influence, but Paul was very good at that. When he arrived, he found that Major Anselmo had arranged a discreet dinner for three in a quiet but excellent fish restaurant on the port. The third guest was Inspector Giuseppe Salvatore of the Genoa police.

The meal was a great success, the food and wine excellent, the conversation flowing expansively as the three men exchanged war stories, none of them finding it in the least odd that Inspector Salvatore had been working for Benito Mussolini until the end, while Anselmo, who had changed sides with most of Italy in 1943, and Lyon, who had been in the U.S. Army, had tried their best to kill him. By the time the three reached the brandy and cigars, they were the best of friends and could comfortably broach the subject that concerned them.

Lyon explained to Salvatore that the Americans were particularly interested in two refugees who had been sent, mistakenly, to Chile. They had encountered some little trouble there and were about to return to Genoa. Captain Lyon would account it a supreme favor if Inspector Salvatore would hand them over to him upon their arrival. This was a matter wholly official and aboveboard: he would have a formal request, signed by the senior American general in Austria, that the prisoners should be delivered to him.

Salvatore saw no objection. The request was purely routine, though no doubt Captain Lyon would require him to show unusual discretion in the operation.

"There is one further detail," said Major Anselmo. "It would be best if the letter from the American general could be returned to Captain Lyon afterward. If the Signor Inspector could see his way to retrieving the letter from his own office files, perhaps a few days after the two men have been delivered to the Americans, I would take it upon myself to ensure that it was returned to our American friend."

It became apparent to Lyon that this was not the first Salvatore had heard of the proposal. The way had been prepared, the inspector had indicated that he might be willing to oblige, and the question of price had been delicately hinted at. The inspector did not reply directly but started talking about his plans for the future. He was to retire in a year from the Carabinieri and devote himself to cultivating his family's vineyard in the hills above Genoa. There was a little house there, out in the country, where he planned to live. It sounded like an idyllic existence. The three men talked about wine, grape growing, and the difficulties of getting modern equipment in these difficult times. "I was particularly impressed," said Inspector Salvatore, turning to Anselmo, "by your jeep. You are indeed a fortunate man to have been allocated such a marvelous vehicle for your personal use."

The jeep was, in fact, the price Lyon had paid for Anselmo's cooperation when he had first organized the Rat Line through northern Italy. Jeeps were the legendary vehicles on which the U.S. Army had ridden to victory, and every Italian coveted one. A number of fortunate or well-placed Italian civilians had acquired jeeps quite legitimately, buying them as U.S. Army surplus. Others had been sold as scrap to Italian dealers, who had then rehabilitated them and sold them for exorbitant prices. They were therefore important status symbols in Italy, where there were few cars and fewer reliable ones. For a while the three men discussed the merits of four-wheel-drive vehicles and the difficulties of obtaining such things in postwar Europe.

The conversation returned to the question of retrieving the general's letter. The inspector waxed philosophical. "One hand washes the other," he remarked. In this particular case, perhaps, the washing needed to be particularly thorough. It was rather unusual, he observed, for the Americans to submit a formal request and then to require the letter to be returned. Lyon, of course, had been prepared for this. He made the decision on the spot, on the assumption that Milano would back him up and provide the jeep. It was clear that this was Salvatore's price and that if Lyon did not accept the offer immediately, the two refugees would fall into the hands of the police as soon as they arrived and never be recovered. He remembered Milano's guiding principle: "Make the damn decision. Success comes from the intelligent manipulation of risk and not from avoiding risk. If you make a good decision, you get a pat on the back. If you make a bad decision, you get your ass chewed out. In all cases, make the damn decision."

"I think," said Captain Lyon, "that if the Signor Inspector were to be cooperative in the little matter of the two refugees and the general's letter, that I could promise some very thorough hand washing. Indeed, I am quite sure that I could find a jeep, brand-new and with its papers in order, which I could turn over to a friend, someone who had made an appropriate contribution to the well-being of the American army."

That was all that needed to be said. The meal ended as happily as it had begun, with many a toast to Italian-American harmony, with warm handshakes and sincere professions of friendship. A few days later, Dominic Del Greco delivered a very impressive official letter, to all appearances signed by General Kendall and countersigned by his chief of staff, requesting the Italian authorities to deliver Patsy and Pete to his representatives. When the ship docked, Milano's men, led by Paul Lyon, in full uniform for once, marched on board accompanied by Inspector Salvatore and hustled the two worried Russians ashore. They were driven twenty miles out of town to a safe house prepared for the occasion, an inn where they were the only guests. They were kept under lock and key until it was time to ship them back through Genoa again with different passports, visas, and identities and a different destination.

They were examined most thoroughly by the Russian expert, John Ustas. They insisted that they had stuck by their story in Chile. They had told the police there that they were Russian refugees who had been fighting in the Resistance behind German lines when they were arrested by the Germans near Leningrad in 1943 and shipped to a labor camp in Germany. That explained Patsy's animosity to the former SS man. They claimed that they had then been sent to a DP camp and that an American church group had provided them with visas and other documents, as well as tickets to start a new life in South America.

All this was part of the cover story they had been given before leaving Austria. They had been told to say nothing about being soldiers in the Red Army or deserters. It was not so much a question of the Chileans believing them completely. What mattered was that there should be no suspicion that the two had been in the hands of a U.S. Intelligence operation and were traveling on a well-established rat line. Naturally, the two men had been told that they were the only deserters the Americans had ever seen and that passage to the far Pacific had been arranged just for them.

Then they were briefed on their new identities and the quite different country to which they were being sent. The Americans made it clear, just in case there was any doubt, that Patsy and Pete had no choice in the matter. They were to become Argentines whether they liked it or not. When their new ship was ready, they were sent on their way with the pressing advice that they be nice to customs officials. They were put aboard at night, just in case anyone was watching. Major Anselmo and Inspector Salvatore were on hand to supervise matters, and the two were sent below and told to stay there until twenty-four hours after the ship sailed.

A few days later, once again dining at the same waterfront restaurant, Inspector Salvatore discreetly slipped Major Anselmo an envelope containing the incriminating letter. If ever the Americans, or anyone else, came looking for it, they would look in vain. It had vanished from the files, and the file clerk would have to explain that he had no idea what had become of it. Inspector Salvatore could swear, with perfect sincerity, that there had been a formal request and that he had of course acceded to it. The letter's disappearance was probably yet another case of Italian inefficiency, a matter for regret, but what could he say more? Alas, he could not remember the name of the general who had signed the letter. These American names were so difficult.

Major Anselmo kept his side of the bargain and returned the missive to Paul Lyon. It was taken back to Salzburg and solemnly burned, with appropriate ceremony, in Milano's office.

A year later, the day after Giuseppe Salvatore retired from the police, he found a fine new jeep outside his apartment. As for Patsy and Pete, as far as anyone knows, they are in Argentina still, elderly men living in peaceful retirement who could tell some interesting stories if they wished.

2

The Cover-up

The saga of Patsy and Pete did not end there. Less than a week after the second ship had sailed from Genoa, bearing them to safety, and while Milano's group was in the midst of arranging transportation for Isaac and Dieter, the other pair of refugees who had been summarily bounced from their own ship to make way for the fugitives, Milano was abruptly called by headquarters in Vienna. The chief of staff, U.S. Forces in Austria, Major General Thomas Hickey, was on the line. Milano was to stand by for a coded message coming over the secure line and was to execute the order immediately. This circuitous route was needed because all telephone lines between Vienna and Salzburg went through the Soviet zone and were certainly tapped. Milano went to the code room, watched the message come over the telex, and waited for it to be decoded. It read:

OPERATIONAL IMMEDIATE STOP STATE DEPARTMENT, WASHINGTON, DC STOP MAJOR JAMES MILANO STOP YOUR COMMAND WILL REPEAT WILL BE PUT ON THE FIRST AVAILABLE AIRCRAFT TO REPORT TO THE STATE DEPARTMENT IN WASHINGTON DC STOP PASSENGER PRIORITY ONE STOP ENDIT

The telegram was signed by an assistant secretary of state, and evidently the department had got wind of Milano and his operations. The Pentagon might have been willing to turn a blind eye to the occasional flagrant illegalities and repeated corner cutting that allowed Milano to produce a steady stream of first-rate intelligence, but the State Department was likely to take a far less benign view. It was quite capable of closing everything down.

General Hickey saw all Milano's reports and forwarded them to the director of intelligence of the Army Staff, General Alexander Bolling, in the Pentagon. Hickey was the man who signed the vouchers allowing

11

Milano to draw on U.S. Army funds for his operations: he never questioned any of the claims. He knew how valuable Milano's reports were and how difficult it would be to replace them if his operations were suspended. Hickey therefore gave him supplementary orders, appended to the message from Washington. He was to set out for Washington immediately, but when he got there he was to present himself first to General Bolling, in the Pentagon, and make a full report. Hickey would inform Bolling that Milano was on his way, and why.

The next day, before dawn, Milano set out on the long drive to the nearest U.S. airbase, at Erding, near Munich. There he picked up a small Army plane to take him to Rhine-Main, at Frankfurt, the main U.S. Air Force base in Germany. He had about an hour to spare. The Air Transport Office was expecting him: he was to report at six in the evening for the flight to the United States. He was in the hands of the great, impersonal machinery of the U.S. Army and had nothing to do but go along with it.

The C-54 left on time, and after a stop to refuel in the Azores it reached Westover Field in Massachusetts in the morning. There was a lieutenant there to meet Milano. He was allowed time to wash up in the officers' mess and have breakfast, and was then flown to Washington in an army C-47. He was the only passenger: evidently something special was being prepared for him. There was a car waiting for him at the Military Terminal at National Airport in Washington, and late in the morning, less than thirty-six hours after getting that ominous telegram in Salzburg, he was ushered into General Bolling's office.

Jim Milano knew nothing of the ways of Washington. He was an intelligence officer whose business was to spy on the Russians, and he only vaguely understood the bureaucratic infighting that made politics in the nation's capital so interesting. He had assumed that because the Pentagon and State Department worked for the same president and the same country, they would cooperate in everything and that he was due for the same frosty reception from Bolling that he expected to get over at State. So he was surprised and delighted when the general welcomed him warmly. Bolling praised his work, assured him that his intelligence reports were the best he knew, and told him that the work he was doing was of vital importance and should be continued and expanded. He could be sure of the general's full support.

Then he asked Milano about Patsy and Pete and what they had been doing in Chile. Though they had stuck rigorously to their cover story when they were interrogated, they had clearly not fooled the Chilean authorities, who had passed their suspicions on to Washington. Milano took a deep breath and began his tale.

He explained who the two men were, what intelligence they had provided, how dangerous it would have been to leave them in Europe. He told the general about the problem of disposing of Soviet defectors in Europe and about the Rat Line. He described the difficulty of obtaining visas and other documents and how he resolved those difficulties: his people forged the documents and bought the visas from a Fascist Yugoslav priest in the Vatican, a war criminal who was certainly providing the same service to other, far less salubrious, clients at the same time.

Milano told the general about Patsy's experiences as a prisoner of war, the death of his brother, and his encounter with the murderer in Valparaiso. He described how the two had been returned to Genoa and the steps that had been taken to spirit them away from the Italian police. He told everything: Bolling was his superior officer, and he would need his full support to escape from his present difficulties. Taking a deep breath he confessed that he had forged the signature of a senior U.S. general and then bribed the Italian chief of police with a stolen jeep to get the incriminating letter back.

The general listened to the story in silence, except for the single comment "Wow!" when Milano told him that Patsy and Pete were now safely on their way to Argentina. When Milano had finished, there was a long silence while the general digested the story. Then he questioned Milano closely on the details: he was particularly concerned to learn how they had covered their tracks, fearing that if the State Department had heard the name James Milano, then perhaps other people in the U.S. government, or beyond, might also have heard of him and might even have heard of the Rat Line.

Milano could not be sure how his name had come to the surface in connection with Patsy's troubles in Chile and could not offer the general any very firm reassurance. He promised, however, that he would look into it and try to find the source of the leak. In his single lapse in candor of the conversation, he refrained from telling Bolling what he planned to do as soon as he got back to Salzburg.

When he had finished, Bolling stood up. "Thank you, Major," he said. "Your briefing has been most illuminating. I don't have to tell you that you are to repeat none of it to anyone. I'm counting on you to continue supplying intelligence on our Soviet friends and being discreet about it. Your plane is waiting for you at National. I will deal with the State Department."

Milano was astonished, grateful, and relieved. Bolling was going to cover for him, and he could return to work. He thanked the general and made a request: "I've not been home for two years," he said. "My parents live in Morgantown, West Virginia, two hours away. Could I go visit them for a couple of days before returning?"

The general's reply was formal: "Permission denied. I want you back on the job immediately—and I don't want anyone to know you've been here. Good-bye, Major, and keep up the good work."

Milano, of course, had no choice but to obey. He said his farewells to the general and then tried one last shot: "General," he asked, "what are you going to tell the State Department?"

General Bolling smiled at him. "Jim, really that's none of your business. Now just go on your way, and have a pleasant trip."

Milano spent a second night on a plane and by midafternoon the next day was back in his office, with his senior staff once more around him to discuss the situation. General Bolling would square the State Department, but they needed to find the source of the leak and stop it. Milano had had plenty of time to reflect on the question and had come to a conclusion.

"It can't have been in Chile," he said. "Patsy and Pete didn't know my name. They're just a pair of ignorant Russian peasants, and even if they'd spilled all the beans they knew they couldn't have compromised us. The leak must come from Genoa: someone there picked up something and passed it on to those two embassy sleuths who were nosing around. That's where the trouble is, in the embassy in Rome."

There was a long, pregnant pause as the group contemplated the situation. Finally, Dominic Del Greco, who was the most innovative and unscrupulous of them all, broke the silence. "So you're going to break into the embassy and steal it," he announced with a mixture of triumph and amusement. There was an explosion of delight from everyone else. Of course, that was what they had all been thinking, and now Del Greco had said it out loud. After forging a general's signature, stealing a jeep, and bribing a chief of police, burglarizing the U.S. Embassy in Rome was just one more step in crime.

Milano glared at them. They were taking it altogether too frivolously.

"Okay, Dominic," he said. "So how do we do it?"

"We need to consult the professionals, of course. This is no job for amateurs, and whatever happens, we've got to keep our fingerprints off it. I think we might have a word with Bill Afano in Trieste. He spent the war in Rome and has a lot of interesting contacts."

Afano was an Italian American who had gone to Italy in the 1930s and stayed there. After the war, the U.S. Army had investigated him for possibly treasonable activities, but he was over military age and had apparently done nothing to help Mussolini. He had, however, acquired a great variety of useful contacts. He was now on the books of Army Intelligence in Italy, with CIC in Trieste.

Milano made the approach himself, driving down to Trieste the next day. Because of its disputed status it was one of the centers of cold war espionage at the time, and Bill Afano was kept busy. He was a professional, he had no sympathy for the bureaucrats at the embassy, and he quite understood Milano's problem. No doubt about it, the file must be stolen and all trace of it removed.

What is more, he knew just the man to arrange it. Evan Goodenof ran a bar just off the Via Veneto near the U.S. Embassy in Rome. He was a Slovenian who had moved to Trieste ahead of Josip Broz Tito's partisans in 1945 and had acquired Italian citizenship. He had made several fortunes on the black market and had a reputation as the one man in Rome who could provide anything, however scarce, at a price. He was certainly well connected, both with the Rome police and with the Mafia, which was beginning to reappear after Mussolini had tried to suppress it—not to mention the other mobs that proliferated in Italy at the time. Some of his closest friends were Italian-American bootleggers and gangsters who had been deported to Italy. What was more, together with his sister he ran one of the best bordellos in Rome. Altogether, thought Milano, a most useful contact.

He prevailed on Afano to go down to Rome to see Goodenof. It turned out that many of the officials at the embassy frequented his bar, which was comfortable and discreet and served American liquor at very reasonable prices. In fact, the prices were so reasonable that several unattached young Americans had run up dangerous bar tabs. Perhaps, Goodenof suggested, one of those middle- or low-level embassy officials might be susceptible to a tactful approach.

This was a delicate question for Jim Milano. He could not make the pitch himself. On the other hand, he could not be sure of Goodenof's tact and discretion. It would be a worse disaster than the Chilean affair itself if the man rejected the suggestion and reported to the ambassador that someone named Major Jim Milano was offering money to have his file stolen. Bill Afano recommended Goodenof highly, saying he was not only wholly reliable but also very discreet, a man of sound judgment who would choose the right man and approach him in the right manner. In the end, Milano heeded his own advice—"Make the damn decision"—and authorized the attempt.

He sent one of his junior men, Jim Alongi, down to Rome as contact man. Alongi was more than willing to leave Salzburg for a lengthy stay in the Eternal City. He was the unit's administrative and supply officer, and he longed to get involved in operations. Besides, he hoped to resume his friendship with a girl he had met in Naples the previous year.

Afano made the introductions to Goodenof, and Alongi stated his case. He was interested in any file anywhere in the embassy that included the name Jim Milano or mention of Chile or a fracas involving two Russian refugees who had gone there from Genoa. He needed every file in this category: leaving anything behind would be worse than leaving them all. What is more, he needed all mention of the files removed from the file locator system, the card indexes. Goodenof understood perfectly and understood why Alongi did not think it necessary to say who Major Milano was or why he was so anxious to retrieve these documents. He said that there was one junior clerk at the embassy who had run up a $900 bar tab and apparently had no hope of paying it off. He was reluctant to demand payment too insistently, since he valued his embassy contacts. Alongi got the impression that Goodenof was thinking of many matters besides liquor. All the same, business was business and the man had been told that his supply might be cut off.

The man was clearly an alcoholic, and this was a serious matter. Goodenof proposed that he should suggest that the bar tab would be canceled and that the man would be offered a line of credit, perhaps a further $100, in exchange for the files. Alongi would, of course, provide the money—and pay Evan Goodenof a fee for his services. Another $1,000 would be acceptable. The total of $2,000 was a large sum, but Alongi agreed at once.

The embassy man was a communications clerk named Archie, and Goodenof offered him the deal. Naturally, he did not spell out what files he wanted until Archie had accepted, which he did immediately. What were a few papers compared to canceling a debt?— and $900 was the equivalent of two months' pay. He claimed that he had access to the file room and could easily go through every index and find anything anywhere in the most confidential files in the embassy.

Alongi had arranged for Goodenof to call a contact number in Salzburg to report on his success and had given him a few code words to use to convey the message. It would not do to discuss it over an open telephone line. Goodenof was delighted at this fragment of the spy business. About two weeks after their conversation in the bar, the call came. Goodenof talked of the weather—and offered the anonymous voice on the end of the phone a turkey sandwich if he were ever in Rome. That was the code for complete success. Archie had found the files, had stolen them, and they were now in Goodenof's safe.

Alongi was sent posthaste back to Rome, to pick up the files and to pay off Goodenof. He took $2,000 with him, even though the bar bill had been run up in lire and Goodenof would no doubt do very well with the exchange. He was indeed delighted and offered Jim Alongi a bonus, a reduction of 50 percent on the services of his finest call girls. His usual price was a hundred dollars a night, but his new American friends could take their pick for a mere fifty. They were scandalized. As Jim Alongi observed, the going rate was a mere two dollars back in Brooklyn, or five dollars for the prettiest girls. Fifty dollars for a whore was outrageous. They declined, but politely. They never could tell when they might need the services of Evan Goodenof again.

Archie had done his job well. He had found that there was only one file that mentioned Major Milano or the Chilean affair, and he had extracted it, together with its locator card. Alongi returned to Salzburg in triumph. Archie was paid off and his bar tab canceled. He soon ran through his $100 credit, and Goodenof was faced with the problem of whether to extend him a further grace period. Fortunately, his drinking habits had been observed by his superiors, and he was sent back to the United States to dry out.

The file that had been acquired with so much trouble and risk proved two things: the embassy sleuths were strikingly incompetent, and the Rat Line had not been seriously compromised. One of the embassy investigators had been told by a port patrolman that he had overheard the name "Major Milano from Austria" mentioned by a police inspector talking to a man in civilian clothes. He could offer no further information and could not say who the civilian was. He had noted Milano's name because it was a familiar, Italian name. The embassy investigator had spoken to the inspector, no doubt Inspector Giuseppe Salvatore, who had stoutly denied knowing anyone of that name. Surely the patrolman was mistaken.

The embassy sleuths had not been able to pursue the matter any further. They had not even discovered that Patsy and Pete had returned to Genoa and had then disappeared. They had merely filed their report and returned to Rome—where their superior had reported to Washington that an American major named Milano, presumably in the Army in Austria, might be involved in the Chilean affair. General Bolling would take care of Washington, and Milano had taken care of Rome and Genoa, so his trail was now covered everywhere and he could resume the serious business of gathering intelligence on the Soviets.

3

A Start in the Business

Jim Milano and his friends were old hands at the game. They had
served a long, hard apprenticeship in the U.S. Army, in North Africa
and Italy during the war and in occupied Austria afterward. By the
time of the Chilean incident, they had had several years' experience
of handling Soviet defectors, Austrian and Italian officials, and their
own superiors. They were not about to let something like this interfere with their long-established procedures.

The United States by its nature has an unequaled advantage over
all other nations in matters of intelligence. It can at any moment
find among its citizens immigrants or the children of immigrants
who are intimately familiar with the language and customs of any
country in the world. As America was sucked toward the Second
World War in 1941, its armed forces reached out to German
Americans, Italian Americans, Japanese Americans, and others
whose families came from all the warring nations of Europe and the
Orient, recruiting from among them cadres of smart, enthusiastic
young men and women to build a formidable intelligence service.
Peacetime conscription was introduced for the first time in
September 1940, passing the House of Representatives by one vote,
and the great expansion of the armed forces began at once.

Jim Milano was then twenty-one, a recent graduate of West
Virginia University. Like so many other young men of his generation, he had seen the war coming and had joined the Army Reserve
during his university years, rising to the rank of lieutenant. His parents were Italian. They had emigrated to the New World, along with
millions of their compatriots, in the decade before World War I.
Milano's father had been brought over by his father, along with a
brother, in 1907, when he was fourteen. Like many immigrants, the
grandfather had found the adjustment too difficult and had returned

to his wife in Italy after two years, but his sons had already adapted to their new country, and they had stayed. Milano's mother had been brought over as a three-year-old by her parents in 1905.

Both immigrant families had joined the large Italian community in West Virginia, working in the coal mines. Milano's father and uncle were miners and farmers. They had married Italian girls, spoke Italian at home, and carried on Italian traditions in Appalachia: they ate pasta, drank wine, and went to Catholic church on Sundays and holy days, quite unlike the Scotch-Irish who peopled the hills and hollows of the region. They had known hard times in Italy, and when the Depression came down upon them in America, they survived on their savings, their lifetime habits of frugality, and their farms. They raised chickens, vegetables, and fruit, including grapes to make their own wine, and were thus protected from the worst calamities that afflicted the miners when the mines closed.

Jim Milano, like the children of so many different immigrants of every nation and creed, had risen in the world through education and hard work. He had kept in touch with his roots, not only his Italian heritage but his recent West Virginian legacy: he had paid his way through college by working down in the mines during the summer vacations. He had studied chemistry at the university, and no doubt that would have been his career if the war had not supervened. In October 1941, he was called to active duty in the Army for a year, a duty that was abruptly extended for the duration plus six months after Pearl Harbor. A few months later, the Army Personnel Department came looking for language specialists, and he offered himself as a bilingual Italian American. After the necessary tests and training, he was taken on as an intelligence officer.

He was to be an interrogator of prisoners of war. He was not to know that in the spring of 1942 a great debate was raging in the Allied High Command over the Americans' first direct contribution to the war in Europe. The Americans wanted to get their armies ashore in France as soon as possible. They accepted, with reluctance, that a landing there in 1942 was out of the question but insisted that the United States must play its part at once. The decision led inexorably to Operation Torch, the Allied landings in North Africa. That meant conflict, perhaps open war, with the Vichy French in Morocco, Algeria, and Tunisia, and it certainly meant war with the German armies, commanded by Erwin Rommel, and the Italians. Jim Milano, though he did not know it, was sure to take part in the American war effort from the start. There were going to be many Italian prisoners to examine.

The U.S. Armed Forces were expanding vertiginously. In 1940, the Army could cope with 300,000 recruits. In two years, it was training 4,360,000. Time was to show the deficiencies of raising a citizens' army from scratch. Milano was assigned to the Military Intelligence Service (MIS). He and other MIS personnel were attached to various units of the Western Task Force that was being assembled at Norfolk, Virginia, and other East Coast ports for the invasion of Morocco. The Eastern Task Force was gathered in the estuary of the River Clyde, in the west of Scotland, and was destined for Algeria and Tunisia. The invasion took place in November 1942. Milano landed on D plus 2, November 10, at Fedala, Morocco, with the combat unit he was attached to. The landings were initially unopposed, but there was some hard fighting with the French before the Vichy commanders concluded, after forty-eight hours, that their duty to Marshal Philippe Pétain had been sufficiently observed and signed an armistice. The Americans and British then occupied the rest of Morocco and Algeria: they had to fight for Tunisia, which the Germans occupied as soon as the Allied invasion began. After the excitement of the landings, therefore, the American forces in Morocco had to regroup and prepare for their next tasks, while the real war rumbled on far to the east, in Tunisia. The British, meanwhile, were fighting their way across Libya after stopping Rommel at El Alamein on the border of Egypt in October 1942. The MIS personnel who participated in the North African landing were formed into the 7769th MIS Battalion.

It was an opportune moment for Milano's unit to complete its training, and a British officer, Lieutenant Colonel Charles Norman Cavendish Boyle, was seconded from the British army to take command. It was an interesting assignment. There were 180 officers and 150 enlisted men, an unusual balance reflecting the unusual mission they were charged with. All the officers and most of the GIs were bilingual: there were eighty-five Italian and eighty-five German specialists among the officers, the balance being French speakers. Ninety-five percent of the officers were university graduates, thirty had master's degrees, and there were seven Ph.D.s and three Rhodes scholars. It was a distinguished group.

It was also undisciplined. Most of them were intelligence officers who had not been subjected overlong to the grueling regime of infantry school, which induces in soldiers a proper respect for the military hierarchy. Boyle asserted his authority with a mixture of tact and firmness that won him lifetime friendship with many of the Americans, including Milano. The training exercises were partly lectures and exams but chiefly consisted of practical experience. The battalion remained at Fedala for four months, and its members were put to work at once censoring all mail from prisoners of war in the North African theater. Prisoners on both sides were allowed to write home, and their mail was collected and delivered by the International Red Cross. Every letter was carefully scrutinized for any clues it might provide to the state of the enemy armies and their morale. MIS teams were sent out to POW camps to interrogate Italian and German prisoners. There were two big camps near Casablanca, and that was where the 7769th first studied the difficult task of questioning POWs to extract as much information as possible within the bounds laid down by the Geneva Conventions. Other teams were sent to the front to join combat divisions to interrogate prisoners as they were captured. This was the most urgent task. The information they gathered was relayed to the order of battle specialists, whose duty was to determine as accurately as possible the strength and position of enemy formations.

The MIS also developed other skills. There was a secret ink laboratory that examined any suspicious mail from POWs that might conceal messages. The Forward Operations Section trained officers who were to be dropped into France for intelligence and resistance work and trained Italian specialists who would work with the Italian Resistance. There was also a section that analyzed aerial photographs.

Another task was examining French civilians who had made their way out of France to reach North Africa and who often had important information of the state of German defenses along the Atlantic. This had nothing to do with the war in North Africa or future operations in Italy: it was part of the immense intelligence effort that went into preparing for the Normandy landings. On one occasion, Milano was introduced to a seventy-eight-year-old schoolteacher who had just arrived in Fedala by way of Portugal. It was an astonishing achievement, and Milano asked him how he had prepared himself mentally for such an arduous journey. The teacher glared at him and replied, "Have you ever seen the Germans in your home country?"

After four months in Fedala, the battalion was moved to Algiers. Soldiers and all their equipment were loaded into boxcars. It was uncomfortable but stimulating: the men had straw pallets to sleep on and were supplied with jerry cans of water. They supplied themselves with a fine selection of local wine to help them on their way and soon established amicable relations with the train crew: the train would stop every three or four hours to allow the men to stretch their legs and inspect the countryside. One stop was at Sidi-bel-Abbès, the fabled headquarters of the French Foreign Legion. The MIS soldiers, intellectuals and college professors though they were, had all been brought up on Hollywood and the legend of Beau Geste and were delighted to discover that the reality far exceeded the Hollywood myth. The Legion was most hospitable and showed the Americans around and served them wine and sweets.

This was a new way to go to war: most of the soldiers had never been abroad before, and after spending Christmas in Morocco they were now crossing half of North Africa, through utterly unfamiliar countryside, meeting people quite out of their experience. Travel, they concluded, broadens the mind. The whole trip took five days, and the unit was soon installed in its new quarters at Maison Blanche outside Algiers, where it remained until it embarked to take part in the Salerno landings in Italy.

When the Germans in Tunis capitulated in May 1943, part of the 7769th MIS moved there to examine and report on the copious archives left behind by the German Army and Luftwaffe. A hundred thousand German soldiers and 150,000 Italians surrendered at the end of that campaign, and there was an immense job to be done sorting them out and analyzing the information they provided.

After the conquest of North Africa, the Allies launched the invasion of Sicily, on July 10, 1943. The 7769th was not part of that operation, but a number of its members were sent over to Seventh Army Headquarters on the island to serve as interrogators, order of battle specialists, and photo interpreters. The battalion, meanwhile, prepared for the invasion of the Italian mainland.

Among the consolations offered by the eclectic way the battalion had been recruited were the varied skills and interests of its members. One of the most popular officers was Lieutenant John Scheering, whose family came from Germany and who was a pianist who had made a living before the war performing in hotels and cafés in New York. He had been recruited as an intelligence officer because he was bilingual in German, but his chief contribution to the war effort in the early days was entertaining the troops with an upright piano he had acquired in Morocco. The transportation officer would never have allowed the piano to be shipped from Fedala to Algiers, so the troops had simply loaded it into the train without bothering to ask permission, concealing it in their other baggage. It survived the journey undetected and undamaged and was soon established in the mess. Scheering resumed his regular performances. If Colonel Boyle ever noticed that his men had miraculously produced a new piano so soon after supposedly leaving the old one behind in Morocco, he never commented on his observation.

Getting the instrument to Italy was much more difficult. The 7769th was due to go over the beaches when the invasion took place and anticipated some rough fighting. They could hardly take the instrument with them on a landing craft under enemy fire. A committee was formed under Jim Milano's direction to consider the problem and concluded that the piano was an essential weapon of war and therefore had to be conveyed to Italy by any means, fair or foul. The MIS, by its nature and functions, had a wide circle of acquaintances throughout the Army, and the committee soon made a deal with members of a sympathetic ordnance maintenance unit. The sympathy was nourished with booze, cigarettes, and the universal desire of GIs to get the better of the system. The piano was boxed up, marked "spare parts," and confided to the transport unit to be picked up in Italy.

The climax of the war in the Mediterranean was upon them. The Italian people and government, all but the die-hard Fascists, were desperate to escape from the war and Adolf Hitler's embrace. The government finally summoned its courage and deposed Mussolini on July 25, then opened negotiations to surrender to the Allies. The British and Americans were taken by surprise, even though the event had been anticipated. They did not react immediately, and Hitler was given time to make ready the occupation of Italy, Operation Axis, while the Allies busied themselves with completing the liberation of Sicily and preparing their next move. At last, on September 3, the British Eighth Army landed in Calabria, on the toe of the Italian boot. Italy surrendered on the eighth, and the next day the Americans and British landed at Salerno, thirty miles south of Naples. But the Germans were ready, and in the next few days, they occupied the whole of northern Italy and Rome and rushed troops down to Naples and beyond, bottling up the Americans in Salerno. Four days after the invasion, they almost succeeded in driving the Americans back into the sea. There was heavy fighting for a month before the Fifth Army broke out from its bridgehead and linked up with the Eighth Army, which was fighting its way up the peninsula. By then the Germans had constructed a series of fortifications across the peninsula they called the Gustav Line, which held the Allies for the next nine months.

The 7769th MIS was in the thick of the fighting after the Salerno landings, though not all together. Milano and others landed a week after D-Day, an interval they spent at sea, waiting for the infantry to clear the beaches. The whole unit did not follow until a month later, after the liberation of Naples on October 1. Milano and his colleagues were busy from the start at their task of collecting intelligence and interpreting it for the generals. By this time, the neophytes who had landed in Morocco a year earlier were hardened professionals. Like the rest of the Army, they had learned their trade the hard way. In due course their heavy equipment caught up with them—and with the help of a lavish use of Italian wine the unit had liberated in its travels, John Scheering recovered his piano. It stayed with the 7769th for the duration of the war, as they moved up Italy through Rome, Caserta, and, eventually, Milan. When the Germans surrendered and the 7769th moved on to Austria, Scheering donated the instrument to an Italian orphanage. He assumed, correctly, that he would have no trouble finding a replacement in his new assignment.

In the meantime, wherever the 7769th set up its camp, Scheering and his piano were installed in the mess, and every evening he would entertain his colleagues with Cole Porter, Duke Ellington, or Irving Berlin. It was a long, difficult campaign, and Milano never had any doubt that he had been right in designating the piano an essential weapon of war.

The fighting in Italy lasted from the first Allied landings on the mainland, in September 1943, until the end of the war. The Wehrmacht held its line across the peninsula between Rome and Naples for nine months, until it was finally forced back by a huge British assault on Monte Cassino. After the retreat from Rome, the Germans formed a new line north of Florence and held it almost until the end of the war. The chief Allied effort shifted to France, first with the Normandy landings on June 6, 1944, then with the landings on the French Riviera, Operation Anvil, on August 15. The Italian front stabilized for the next ten months until the general German collapse in April 1945.

Milano and his colleagues spent their time interrogating prisoners and civilians, censoring POWs' mail, tapping telephones in the occupied areas, and performing all the other tasks of Army Intelligence. The enemy order of battle was the unit's central concern. Tactical information came from prisoners, patrol leaders, aerial photography, and constant feedback from combat units on such matters as "sound and flash" reports and the sightings of artillery spotters. For several months, Milano was a member of a task force that supported partisans fighting the Germans and the Fascists behind the lines in northern Italy. The Allied intelligence teams debriefed partisans who came through the lines and prepared airdrops of supplies. This involved choosing which forces to support, selecting drop zones, coordinating the timing of the drops, and then getting together the weapons, ammunition, and other supplies that were to be sent over. The planes were then loaded and their crews briefed. The most important of all these functions was ensuring that the supplies went to the right group. Even at that early stage, the U.S. Army had no wish to send supplies to the Communist Resistance.

By the end of 1944, the Army was planning for the postwar occupation of Austria. Milano's unit was designated to participate in intelligence activities in the proposed American zone of that country, and he spent a great deal of time preparing for his new task. He attended training courses at Castellammare di Stabia, near Naples, including one directed by his old friend Lieutenant Colonel Boyle of British Intelligence, and studied such matters as telephone surveillance. The equipment arrived from the United States and was installed at the central telephone exchange in Naples to keep watch on any surviving Fascists and also to prepare the Americans for their future duties in Austria.

The 7769th, as we have seen, started its war with eighty-five Italian-speaking officers. More joined later, and there were thousands of other Italian Americans in the U.S. armies that fought up the length of Italy. There was never any doubt of their loyalty: they were Americans, not Italians; but, all the same, fighting across their parents' or grandparents' homeland was a painful task for them. Fortunately, there was never any doubt whose side the Italians were on: the Allied troops were met everywhere with flowers and cheers. The Allies came as liberators and noted sardonically how difficult it was to find anyone in Italy who had ever supported Mussolini.

Milano, like many of his comrades in arms, had come to Italy with a personal objective. In the summer of 1942, when he was in training at Fort Myer, Virginia, it was obvious that he was due to be shipped overseas, though he was not officially warned of the transfer, nor of his destination. However, he was being trained to interrogate Italian prisoners of war and had no trouble imagining that his unit would soon find itself in Italy. His only error was in timing: he did not anticipate the detour through North Africa. Then came the unmistakable signs that his departure was imminent: he was vaccinated and issued with a sidearm and a gas mask. He therefore took a weekend pass for a last visit to his parents in Morgantown, where he told them they would probably not see him again for a considerable period.

His father was not surprised and later that evening summoned him to the living room. He produced five hundred-dollar bills and told him, "I've no idea where you'll wind up, but I hope it's Italy. If you get there, go and see your grandmother. This is for her: you're to put it away safely and not to touch it. Don't get tempted by poker or craps or some lady of the evening. It's for my mother, and she'll need it. I've no idea what the situation is like in the *paese*, but it can't be any too bright after three years of war. So go find her and do what you can for her."

Milano naturally promised that he would keep the money safe for his grandmother and that, if the course of war took him anywhere near her village, he would go looking for her. He had never been to Italy. Indeed, he had never left the United States, but he had been brought up on stories of his father's native village in Aquila and had seen many pictures of it. His grandfather had died just before the war, but Milano had many relatives there, besides his grandmother. When he finally reached Italy, more than a year after saying farewell to his parents, he began planning for his return to his ancestral village.

Aquila is northeast of Rome, and it was months before the Allied armies reached it. The front had stabilized on the Gustav Line, whose key position was a network of fortifications at the celebrated Benedictine monastery at Monte Cassino. The Americans attempted to turn the line by a second landing, at Anzio, south of Rome, on January 22, 1944, but failed to exploit their initial success and were contained in their beachhead. Rome finally fell on June 5, 1944, the day before D-Day in Normandy.

During those long months of war, from the Salerno landings to the capture of Rome, Jim Milano watched the pins showing the front line in the situation room. For weeks they never moved, but at last, as the Germans withdrew to their new lines north of the capital, he saw that the British had liberated Avezzano, the capital of Aquila. His father's village, Collelongo, was about twelve miles away. The moment had come for him to set out. By that time he had collected several duffel bags full of medicine, candy rations, and other goodies from the PX and a selection of supplies for his grandmother, as well as letters from home. His was by no means the only family from Aquila in West Virginia, and many of his friends, knowing what he was planning to do, had given him mail to deliver. Finally he gave himself a leave of absence and set out on his quest.

He took his driver, Sergeant Porter, and set out from Caserta, where the Allied Forces Headquarters were located. They drove north into territory just liberated by the British army, passing the ruins of Cassino and the monastery on its cliff top. It was an extraordinary and depressing sight. Monte Cassino had been one of the citadels of Western civilization, and its destruction had been one of the most controversial acts of war carried out by the Allies, certainly the most debatable in Italy. The two Americans pressed ahead, confronting all the difficulties of transport in the rear of an army fighting a major battle. They went through Sora, where Milano's grandfather had been born, but they did not stop. Their objective was Collelongo, and they reached the village in the afternoon.

It had not been damaged by the fighting. Jim Milano left his jeep in the piazza and looked about him. It was an unremarkable Italian village with its church, village square, and houses huddled together under the blazing summer sun. This was the home his father had left at the age of fourteen, and these unknown people, looking curiously and nervously at the Americans, were his own father's contemporaries, friends, and relatives. One middle-aged woman approached and looked intently at him—then screamed in recognition and threw her arms around his neck, kissed him, and began to cry. Milano was more than astonished. An old man came up and seized him by the hand: "You're Jim, aren't you?" and he replied, *"Si, io sono Jim."* Then the woman identified herself. She was his Aunt Marietta, his father's sister, and she had recognized him from the graduation photograph from West Virginia University that his parents had sent to Collelongo and that was displayed proudly on the family's fireplace mantel.

His first question was to ask where his grandmother was. His aunt pointed to an old lady dressed all in black, standing in a doorway three houses down the street from the piazza. He walked briskly down to meet her, put his arms around her, and said, "How are you, Grandma?" She, too, recognized him at once. After a moment she looked up at him and said, "You know, almost every day the American bombers fly over, going north. Often I wondered if you were up there."

4

Austrian Beginnings

Major Jim Milano and his driver, Sergeant Porter, drove over the Brenner Pass into Austria on May 9, 1945, the day after the war in Europe ended. They were following in the footsteps of the U.S. Army, which had occupied western Austria, unopposed, a few days earlier. The rest of the unit was to follow Milano to Innsbruck, their temporary headquarters. These were the interrogators, the censorship group, the technical staff with all their paraphernalia for tapping telephones, and the headquarters staff. Other members of the intelligence team had accompanied the Army across the Alps and had already arrived in Salzburg. They were the Intelligence Task Forces, whose role was to secure post offices, telephone exchanges, banks, local government offices, and any other buildings and facilities that might be of interest to intelligence operations.

Milano and his driver had loaded a jeep and trailer with their personal belongings, C rations and a large supply of cigars. They had their sidearms, of course, and took the precaution of bringing a good quantity of ammunition in case of need. Their first encounter with the Austrians occurred high in the Alps and proved entirely pacific. They stopped for a picnic lunch in an orchard near a small cottage. Two little girls came out to observe them, and the Americans promptly waved them over and started sharing their rations. The children were delighted at the novelty of American army food, but the al fresco idyll was interrupted by a sudden scream from the cottage: the girls' mother had emerged and was horrified at the sight of her daughters quietly eating with uniformed foreigners. She shouted and gestured at them to return. They ignored her; they were having too much fun. The Americans waved at the woman to join the picnic, but she stayed back, paralyzed with apprehension. Finally Milano took pity on her, loaded the children with spare C rations, and sent them back to their mother. As Milano and Porter left, they waved at her and the girls, who waved back: their first meeting with civilian Austrians had gone well.

Perhaps they did not know it, but their kind gesture had been strictly illegal. For the first few weeks of the occupation, the High Command tried to impose a policy of "nonfraternization" on the Allied troops, who were not allowed to talk to Austrian civilians. The order failed from the start and was soon abandoned. American soldiers, like Jim Milano and Sergeant Porter on the Brenner Pass, instantly started handing out candy and chewing gum and other goodies to children, out of pure altruism, and cigarettes and food to adults, for various and different reasons. Tobacco was the first, universally recognized unit of currency in liberated Europe, and American soldiers discovered at once that many Austrian women, like the Italian women they had encountered in their march north, were quite ready to exchange their favors for a pack of Camels. And not only Austrians: the American zone was awash with other refugees, fleeing the Soviets.

Milano and Porter reached Innsbruck that evening and drove on to Salzburg in the morning. An officer had gone ahead to requisition quarters for the unit, which was to arrive later in the day. A villa had been commandeered for the officers and a hotel for the rest of the troops. Milano installed himself, for the first night, in the Münchnerhof Hotel, while the troops moved into the Stein Hotel. There were about fifty of them, and at four in the morning, Milano was awakened by military police and told that there was serious trouble. He hurried into his uniform and rushed over to the Stein, where he found the place in an uproar. The billeting officers had failed to notice that two floors of the hotel were still occupied by women in the German Army. They were drivers, stenographers, secretaries, and telegraphists who had been gathered together to await their discharge. Milano's men had been delighted to make their acquaintance. They had brought large supplies of Italian wine and spirits, not to mention American cigarettes, C rations, and more enticing goodies from the PX. The German women had seen nothing of the sort for years. In no time at all, and in flagrant disregard of the rules on nonfraternization, the American (male) and German (female) soldiers had established the ground rules, and a party was under way. The military police had arrived and, after attempting to separate the two groups and bring the party under control, had concluded that discretion was the better part of discipline. Milano's men were armed, drunk, and not at all inclined to miss this heaven-sent occasion to celebrate the Allied victory in the company of their former enemies, whom, perhaps, they considered the spoils of war. As for the German women, they, too, had no objections to ending the war on a joyous note.

The MPs therefore searched out Major Milano, the errant soldiers' commanding officer. He saw at once when he reached the hotel and observed the party in full swing that restoring order would be a matter of tact, time, and considerably more authority than he could muster on his own. He therefore returned to the villa where his officers were billeted and summoned them to do their duty, and they went reluctantly to work. Their sympathies were entirely with their men, and if they had been quartered in the same hotel, faced with the same temptation, who is to say that they would have resisted? In any event, by degrees and aided by the natural exhaustion that overcomes soldiers of both sexes after such encounters, Milano and his officers succeeded in pushing all present back into their own quarters. By morning some of the men had bad hangovers, but all had delightful memories and every intention of resuming the party at the first opportunity. The authorities had other ideas. At eight in the morning Milano was summoned by the officer commanding the military police and told that his unit would be moved immediately to a German barracks that had been requisitioned at the edge of town. He was also informed that the nonfraternization policy was a strict order coming from Army Headquarters and must be respected. It was unfortunate that the billeting officers had put the men in the way of temptation, but the wayward soldiers must be punished for their infractions. The MP officer would not himself suggest what form that punishment should take. Indeed, he had not the faintest idea. Major Milano, as commanding officer, must assume that responsibility. Milano saluted smartly and left.

That evening, with the unit safely installed—much to their regret—in their new barracks, Milano called the men to formation. He delivered a short, stern lecture on the nonfraternization policy and insisted that it must be obeyed. As for the events of the previous evening, he said he assumed that the men had learned their lesson and the violation would not be repeated. Therefore he would content himself, on this occasion, with issuing a verbal reprimand. Years later he recalled dryly that they looked at him as though he had lost his mind.

One of them, at least, had a sense of humor. A couple of nights later, Milano was in his hotel room having a drink with a few of his officers. The window was open, and they were suddenly interrupted by shouts from the apartment building across the street. A woman was calling "Major Milano, *kommen sie und schlafen mit mir!*" "Jim, please, *kommen sie und schlafen mit mir!*" ("Jim, please come sleep with me!") Soon an audience, mostly Austrian, formed in the street, attracted by the show. But there were also GIs, and some of them entered into the spirit of the thing and yelled "Come on, Major, give her a break!" Milano resisted temptation and did not respond. The woman was probably drunk, anyway. In due course, the MPs arrived and the shouting abruptly stopped. The gallant major took care not to inquire what had happened and the next day watched suspiciously for a smirk on the face of any of his staff. If any of them was guilty, however, he kept both a straight face and the secret.

We have another account of the Americans' arrival from a different perspective. Princess Marie Vassiltchikov, a Russian aristocrat whose family had fled the Bolsheviks in 1918, spent most of the war in Berlin, working for the Foreign Ministry (and associating with the anti-Hitler resistance). Her diaries are one of the best sources about that frightful period. She gives an unforgettable account of a firestorm that engulfed the city after an Allied air raid. In May 1945, after working as a nurse in Vienna, she was washed up by the retreating tide of war in Gmunden, near Salzburg. The first Americans she met tried to seduce her, but then Major John Chrystal of the Counter-Intelligence Corps (CIC), one of Milano's staff, took her under his wing. She had been billeted in a palace nearby, while working in a local hospital. Chrystal needed interpreters and briefly employed the princess (she spoke excellent English, French, and German, as well as Russian), though the rudimentary bureaucracy of those days found that it had no category for Russian refugees from the Bolsheviks. The palace was being used for rest and recreation by American troops, and a constant stream of women came through to provide the recreation. Chrystal protected the princess from any unwelcome attentions and then shepherded her safely through the de-Nazification process. Though she was, indeed, a refugee from the East, she could tell them nothing of the Soviet armies. She was, however, one of the first of a long list to be interrogated by the CIC.

The Americans settled rapidly into their new role as an occupying army. There was a lot of tidying up to do and a lot of easy money to be made: a day or two after he arrived in Salzburg, Milano was presented with a large cardboard box filled with American currency, mostly twenty- and fifty-dollar bills. It had been found by one of Milano's task forces at a Salzburg bank, which was unable to account for its presence there. Milano was temporarily in charge of it until it could be handed over to the Finance Section of the Military Government, which was settling into Innsbruck. He decided to have the loot counted separately by two men, who were to compare their totals at the end of the exercise. Then, when it was handed over, he would get a receipt for the full amount. It came to some $185,000, a very large sum indeed in 1945, and in due course was handed over to the Finance Section. He thought no more about the matter until two years later, when the Criminal Investigation Division came to call: somewhere between Milano's office and the money's final arrival at the finance office, the sum had shrunk to less than $100,000. Milano could offer no clue to what had happened to the missing money—or, rather, to who might have stolen it. He had kept the original receipts, which he produced from his files, thanking his lucky stars for the moment of official pedantry that had led him to count the money before handing it over.

That was the lighter side of the Americans' first days in Austria. Their time was dominated by much more serious matters and conditioned by the situation they found when they arrived.

The Russians got there first. They took Vienna in the closing days of World War II, on April 12, 1945, while Hitler was still railing against his fate in his bunker in Berlin, ordering his last soldiers to fight to the death for the dying Reich. There was a last, frightful six-day battle for the capital of Austria, one of the most beautiful cities in Europe, as the Red Army drove tanks and infantry through the ruins: the city had been severely damaged by earlier air raids. Then the Soviet troops paused to regroup before moving west, into the Alps.

The Americans and British had by then reached the heart of Germany and had halted their drive on Berlin. General Dwight D. Eisenhower had decided to let the Soviets take Hitler's capital while he sent General George Patton's Third U.S. Army south through Czechoslovakia into Austria. He was afraid that Hitler planned to make a last stand in Obersalzburg and Berchtesgaden, high in the Alps. Meanwhile, in northern Italy, the Allies were negotiating with the German Army. Its commander, General von Vietinghoff, surrendered on April 29. The day before, Mussolini had been caught by partisans while trying to escape into Germany. He had been shot, along with his mistress, Clara Petacci, and other Fascist leaders. Their bodies had been strung up by their feet at a gas station in Milan, the partisans carefully tying Petacci's skirt between her legs to preserve the decencies.

Patton drove unresisted through the remnants of the German Army. There was no last Nazi stronghold in the Alps. Hitler shot himself in his bunker on April 30, and the American and British armies rolled through northern Italy and over the Brenner Pass into Austria as Patton swept down from the north. They found the Red Army entrenched west of Vienna, in the zone it had been allotted.

The Allies had agreed at Yalta, early in 1945, that Austria should be revived as an independent country, thus reversing one of Hitler's early victories, the *Anschluss*, Austria's unresisted unification with Germany in 1938. It would be divided temporarily into three zones of occupation, Soviet, American, and British. The same principle was applied to Germany, and in both countries the French were allocated a zone after the Potsdam Conference in the summer of 1945. Vienna was to be shared among the occupying powers. Like Berlin, which was in the Soviet zone in Germany, Vienna was behind Soviet lines, and months passed before the Western Allies were able to establish themselves there. In the meantime, the Americans moved to Salzburg, Linz, and Innsbruck, the surviving cities in western Austria (Innsbruck was later given to the French). Their first tasks were to feed the people, to round up the German troops who were still at large, and to gather together the large numbers of refugees who had flooded into Austria from the East. Then they set about establishing an administration.

Salzburg was damaged but not destroyed. The dome of the cathedral where Mozart had played was gone, but the church had survived. The town was fortunate. Linz, the major city in the American zone, had been severely damaged. Hitler had grown up there, and he had intended to make it the artistic capital of Europe, filling it with museums and monuments to the Nazis, as well as the loot of a continent. In the spring of 1945, there was little left but rubble. Bombs had demolished the buildings, and fires had consumed the wreckage. Roads were impassable and the railways were destroyed, and the people of Linz and tens of thousands of refugees huddled in cellars or tents or under the few fragments of ruins that were still standing.

The arriving Americans might have expected hostility from the Austrians, bitter resentment at the well-fed, well-clothed armed forces that had destroyed their country. But in fact there was very little enmity. The GIs were well received, almost as liberators. The war, particularly the last year as the Soviets had closed in from the east while American and British bombers, based in Italy, had poured fire and death on the cities, had been so frightful, such a long nightmare, that there was nothing but relief when at last it ended.

The country was destitute, ruined, and starving. The enduring image of those few years immediately after the war is *The Third Man*, Carol Reed's film of a Graham Greene tale set in Vienna. The story concerns petty crooks and corrupt Americans who have set up a black market in diluted penicillin, but the theme is the all-pervasive despair and misery and the corruption caused by fear and hunger. It ends, symbolically, in a chase through the sewers. Vienna in 1945 was claustrophobic and squalid.

The intelligence specialists who came with the occupying armies were first of all concerned with capturing senior Nazis and sorting out the German soldiers and the refugees. They found that the Wehrmacht's discipline had survived the debacle. Once the war was officially over, there was no suggestion of continuing the fight, even by the SS. The soldiers wanted to get home as quickly as possible. All the Americans had to do was to round them up, arrest the senior officers, check on the records of the soldiers, and set them free.

All but a handful of the most senior Nazis were easily captured. Hermann Göring, for instance, had been arrested on Hitler's order in the last days of the war for proposing negotiations with the Allies. He was now detained by Patton's troops near Salzburg. Those German soldiers who did not make their own way home were collected in prisoner-of-war camps, where they were held for a while before being released. The refugees (known in those days as displaced persons, or DPs) were also put into camps, some of which lasted much longer. The camps for Polish, Hungarian, Yugoslav, and other Eastern European DPs were filled with people who had no wish to return home to countries that had fallen under the sway of the Soviet Union or its Communist allies. Some of them had served in the Wehrmacht or in national armies raised by the Germans to fight the Soviets, and immediately after the war many of these unfortunate veterans were sent back to Stalin's tender mercies. Others languished in the camps: twelve years after the end of the war, there were still Polish and other DP camps scattered across West Germany and Austria, often in barracks that they shared with the western armies of occupation.

The Americans assumed, when they arrived in Austria, that the Soviets would cooperate with them in administering the country. They supposed that practical matters such as the provision of food and medical supplies, and the restoration of the railways and the power grid, would be undertaken jointly and that the division of Austria into zones of occupation would be a temporary arrangement. It made no sense to partition a small country like Austria, whatever might be done with Germany itself. But from the start the Soviets put up a blank wall of noncooperation. For months they even delayed admitting American, British, and French troops into their zones of Vienna. Behind this barrier, they started a systematic witch-hunt for their enemies, not only Nazis and their collaborators from the East who had escaped into Austria but also anti-Nazi Social Democrats and conservatives who had survived the Nazi terror. The Americans were struck by the bitter hostility the Soviets showed toward the general population. Red Army soldiers in Austria, like their comrades in Germany, did not forget what the Germans had done to Russia and held the whole population responsible. As a matter of political expediency, the Allies had decided that Austria was a liberated country, like Czechoslovakia or Poland, and should be treated differently from Germany. They decided to ignore the enthusiasm with which Austria had welcomed Hitler when he sent in the troops in 1938, although there was not much reason to doubt that a majority of Austrians had supported their incorporation into the Reich. They had participated as enthusiastically as all the other Germans in the Reich's conquests and crimes, and they had followed Hitler to the bitter end. The Austrians had made large contributions to the Nazi regime: there were many Austrians among prominent Nazis, besides Hitler himself, including Eichmann, who had managed the Holocaust, and Ernst Kaltenbrunner, the head of the Gestapo. All the same, the Allies decided that they would overlook these matters, to the ends of simplifying their postwar problems and breaking up Hitler's Reich. The Americans were perfectly ready to accept the consequences of that decision and treat Austrians as liberated victims of the Third Reich. The Soviets were incapable of these nice distinctions.

The Americans who encountered the Soviets on the ground in Central Europe could comprehend, though they might not share, the implacable hatred the Russians felt for the Germans and Austrians. They did not, however, understand Soviet official hostility to the United States and Britain and came first to resent it, then to fear it as a real danger to their security. The higher reaches of the U.S. Army saw no reason to feel threatened by the Soviet Union in 1945, whatever they may have thought three years later. They judged that the USSR had suffered so severely during the war that it would be quite incapable of aggression against the West—quite apart from the military folly of taking on the United States. In hindsight, this judgment was obviously right for the time. It is now clear enough that Josef Stalin never intended a direct military challenge to the West. His tactic, until he died in 1953, was to pick off Western countries, one at a time, with a combination of military bluff and internal subversion. Stalin started the cold war: he did not intend to become involved in a hot one.

The question of which side would win the cold war depended, from the very beginning, on American resolution. If the Americans pulled their last troops out of Germany, the Red Army would roll west to fill the vacuum. The men on the ground were concerned with Stalin's intentions, which they correctly believed were to Communize Central and Western Europe if the occasion presented itself. They understood that his tactics would be governed by the circumstances, and they believed that the best way to deter the Soviets from any attempt to push the Americans back was to be ready to fight them at all times. Stalin would not start a war unless he was certain he could win it.

The diplomatic and political debate over Europe from 1945 to 1948 centered around the question of where the line would be drawn between East and West. The West reluctantly conceded that Poland

and the Balkans (but not Greece) would fall into the Soviet sphere, for the simple reason that the Red Army was in unchallenged occupation there. They did not concede Central Europe or its greatest prize, Germany. What began as a debate over how best to administer Germany and restore its political system soon deteriorated into a naked power struggle. Relations between the two sides deteriorated rapidly because of Russian intransigence and hostility. By 1948, after the Communist coup in Czechoslovakia and at the time of the Berlin Airlift, it had become evident that a strong military response was needed to back up American political determination to stop any other European countries falling to communism. But in 1945, if the Soviets had behaved with more tact and restraint, the Americans would have seen no need to oppose them so vigorously.

In the High Command, the majority view immediately after the war was expressed by Eisenhower, who said on his return to Washington that Russia "was determined to make friends with the United States, to raise its standard of living, and to live up to every agreement made." In the euphoric aftermath of V-E Day, most of the American government agreed with him, though there were at least two notable skeptics. General Patton complained, "We appear to be leaning over backwards to be nice to the descendants of Genghis Khan. We're letting them dictate to us when patently we could and should dictate to them, and do it now in no uncertain terms." Another skeptic was President Harry Truman.

On the ground, in Europe, the Soviet hostility toward the West provoked an immediate reaction. American soldiers may have shown some naïveté in expecting friendship from the Soviets and were quite possibly far too ready to forgive and forget the crimes of their former enemies, but they were also battle-hardened veterans who did not take kindly to Soviet obstructionism. They responded in kind. The pattern was set early, and in Austria the intelligence units of the U.S. Army led the way. Jim Milano and his colleagues had come into Austria with specific tasks in mind, starting with rounding up the Nazis and then concentrating on counterintelligence activities, but they very soon took up other objectives. Their observations of the real situation, as opposed to the theoretical one they had planned for so arduously in Caserta, led them within a few weeks of their arrival to turn their attention to the potential threat from the Soviet Union. The Soviet army of occupation in Austria was still on full battle alert, facing the Western Allies with granite hostility and obdurate noncooperation. General Mark Clark and his chief of intelligence needed to know, at once, what the Red Army was doing and what it was capable of doing. Army Intelligence was ordered to report on its former ally, and its first, ominous reports were sent back to Washington within weeks of the Americans' arrival in

Austria. That initial assessment of the potential Soviet threat had a dramatic effect in the Pentagon. Whatever the Joint Chiefs of Staff and General George Marshall may have thought of Stalin and his troops, the hard-eyed colonels and generals in Intelligence immediately saw the value of the reports they were receiving, and demanded more. The cold war had not begun. President Truman had not yet left Washington to attend the Potsdam summit with Stalin and Winston Churchill, and the euphoria of victory was still strong in both America and Britain. But Jim Milano and his colleagues were sending back reports of quite different attitudes and behavior among the Soviet occupying forces in Austria. So were their colleagues in Germany, and the Pentagon sensed the coming of a new and differently dangerous era. Its first, overriding duty was the safety of its troops in Europe, and it was becoming apparent, or at least possible, that their safety was threatened by the Soviet Union.

The occupation of Austria had been carefully planned in advance, but the situation that developed immediately after the end of the war was quite different from what the experts had so confidently expected. New objectives were set almost immediately, and that meant a fundamental reappraisal of the whole structure of the occupation. Instead of holding down a sullen and resentful enemy population in cooperation with their gallant Soviet allies, the Americans found themselves sustaining an enthusiastically supportive community and confronting their former ally as a potential enemy.

The long German resistance, even after defeat was certain, had given the Americans plenty of time to get ready: the first systematic preparations had been made in Italy early in 1943. The American intelligence operations in Austria had developed naturally out of wartime organizations in Italy. It was then assumed that the Allied forces that would enter Austria first would be the U.S. Fifth and British Eighth Armies, which were fighting their way up the Italian peninsula. As the war in Italy had drawn to a close, they had organized as the Fifteenth Army Group, under U.S. General Mark Clark, whose headquarters was at Lake Garda in northern Italy.

During the war, the intelligence services had consisted of a number of separate agencies. The best known and best remembered was the Office of Strategic Services (OSS), the forerunner of the CIA. A second organization was the Signals Intelligence Service (SIS), which, with its British counterpart, played an enormous role in the war. Its mission was to listen to enemy broadcasts and decipher their codes. The British success, based on the work of Polish intelligence officers, in deciphering the most secret German codes ("Top-Secret Ultra"), and the American success in deciphering Japanese naval codes had contributed hugely to the victory. The two greatest enemy surprises of the war, Pearl Harbor and the 1944 Ardennes offensive (which developed into the Battle of the Bulge) had been achieved because, in the former case, the Japanese fleet sailing to Hawaii had preserved absolute radio silence, while, in the latter, Field Marshal Gerd von Rundstedt had refused to allow any radio communications with Wehrmacht headquarters.

Third, and far less glamorous than the other two, the Counter-Intelligence Corps (CIC) was concerned with the security of American forces in the field. The CIC's mission, first in North Africa and then in Italy, was identifying all organizations or groups of people among the civilian populations who might be hostile to U.S. forces. That chiefly concerned Fascist groups, but very early on it was extended to Communist organizations, including partisan groups that were fighting against the Fascists and the German Army. The CIC was also concerned with treason, sedition, subversion among Allied forces, and protecting those forces against espionage and sabotage. There were a number of CIC units, each operating with a different Army formation. Milano's unit, the 430th CIC, served with the Fifth Army.

Next, there was the Military Intelligence Service (MIS), which was concerned directly with the activities of enemy forces. This was classic military intelligence, which interrogated prisoners to discover the enemy order of battle and measure its strength and intentions. MIS was in charge of photoreconnaissance, which during the war developed into one of the major sources of intelligence on enemy movements, and it also ran the prisoner-of-war camps. The unit operating in Italy, that moved to Austria, was the 7769th MIS.

There were also specialized agencies devoted to mail censorship. One of them concerned itself with prisoners' mail, both letters received by prisoners and those they sent home. Many a military secret was revealed by an unsuspecting Italian prisoner. Another censorship bureau dealt with civilians' correspondence. The mails, obviously, were not functioning normally and there was no communication across the front lines, but the mails were progressively restored in occupied territory as it expanded northward, and Allied censors searched for information, particularly in the correspondence of people whom they knew had been important, or well-informed, members of the Fascist regime or its armed forces. A third group dealt with the mail of American servicemen, who were quite capable of betraying military secrets through carelessness or ignorance.

The SIS unit in Italy was sent back to the United States on the ground that the war was over and there was no further need to monitor the airwaves. When that policy was reversed, the Army Security

Agency in Germany took up the task. Army Headquarters in Austria had no control over its operations, which is why Jim Milano started his own signal intelligence unit (see Chapter 15). Later, the National Security Agency (NSA) was set up to direct worldwide telecommunications intelligence gathering. In due course, the NSA became the most secret, most expensive, and most important of all U.S. intelligence agencies.

When the staff planning the occupation of Austria examined future needs, they decided to streamline this large wartime system of intelligence and counterintelligence. The censorship organizations were merged and put under the MIS. Its task was not merely to censor mail; it had the authority to tap any telephone in the American zone, and it watched over telegraph traffic as well. This enlarged MIS operation operated parallel to the CIC, and both were put under the supervision of the intelligence staff in U.S. Army Headquarters in Austria, together with the Civil Censorship Detachment. Major Jim Milano, who commanded the 7769th MIS, was also in charge of the Operations Branch of the Intelligence Directorate and was thus at the heart of all Army Intelligence operations in Austria. To begin with, only the MIS and censorship units answered to him; later, at the urging of Colonel James Critchfield of the G-2 staff, Milano's Operations Branch was given control of the CIC in Austria. Milano thus became de facto operations head of all Army Intelligence. Critchfield was subsequently employed by the CIA as liaison officer with the revived German intelligence agency in Germany (see Chapter 14). Milano's headquarters, along with the rest of U.S. headquarters, were provisionally set in Salzburg because the Russians were delaying the American entry into Vienna. Later, when the commanding general and his staff moved to the capital, it was decided that Milano should remain in Salzburg because it was much more secure than Vienna, but that there should be an intelligence station in the capital that answered to him. To start with, he had a headquarters staff of fourteen, six administrative and eight special agents. The MIS battalion that moved to Salzburg had about fifty enlisted men.

The business of counterintelligence, mail censorship, and interrogating POWs and DPs had always been coordinated with the gathering of "positive intelligence," information on enemy forces. This collaboration was continued into the occupation of Austria, under the direction of Milano's Operations Branch and was extended to eavesdropping on Soviet radio communications and recruiting agents and deserters. It also investigated the intelligence resources already available in Austria, meaning former German intelligence officers, as well as spies and specialists of other nationalities who offered their services.

To begin with, however, the main need was for local personnel to man the censorship office and to perform various other tasks. Within two weeks of its arrival in Salzburg, the Civil Censorship Detachment had recruited about two hundred Austrians to read and censor mail, listen to telephone communications, and watch telegrams. The censors monitored communications within the American zone and with the Soviet zone. The other Austrians hired in the first days were secretaries, cleaners, and drivers. The Americans noted with pleasure that when they advertised for such help, the response was immediate and enthusiastic. People wanted to work for them and showed no resentment at their new status as employees of their conquerors.

The CIC divided its operations into Counter-Intelligence, which tried to protect American military operations against Soviet subversion, Positive Intelligence, which gathered intelligence on the Soviets, Technical Intelligence, which concerned itself with Soviet scientific progress (this became enormously important as the cold war developed), and Political Intelligence, which concerned itself with politics in Austria. The Operations Branch gathered together all information provided by the other sections and itself ran the most sensitive cases, such as double agents, deserters, and eventually the Rat Line.

Milano and his team reported to the senior intelligence officer at Army Headquarters, first in Salzburg, later in Vienna. That officer was known as the G-2, or Assistant Chief of Staff, Intelligence. Other branches of the staff were G-1, Personnel; G-3, Operations; G-4, Logistics; and G-5, Military Government. The G-2 was the contact with the Pentagon and passed on to the Operations Branch in Salzburg a steady stream of requests for information, known as Essential Elements of Information (EEIs). This was the heart of Milano's operation. The EEIs he received were demands for information on the Soviet order of battle, armaments, training, and all aspects of the Red Army's organization and procedures. The Pentagon also wanted precise and detailed information on Austrian politics, particularly the local Communist Party. Furthermore, Austria was the best listening post available for news of Soviet activities and intentions in Eastern Europe, especially Hungary and Czechoslovakia.

All this had been in the organizational chart and the overall plan laid down at Caserta during the war. But when the Americans found themselves face to face with the Red Army, the whole balance of the operation changed. Positive intelligence became the most important part of their work; instead of chasing Nazis, they had to ferret out information on the Red Army. Their overriding task very quickly became evaluating the Soviet order of battle—just as studying the

German order of battle had been their prime objective a few months earlier. This sudden shift of perspective led to promotion and success for those young officers who saw what was needed and seized the opportunity to provide it, even if they did not yet know precisely that they were the first warriors in the new, cold war.

5

The Rat Line

On the wall in Jim Milano's conference room hung a Flap Meter, lovingly constructed by one of his subordinates out of white cardboard and brightly colored with crayons from a child's coloring box. The words FLAP METER ran across the top, and in the center, fastened by a brass tack, was an arrow that could be swiveled around to all the points of the compass. The rim was marked and colored in degrees of panic: NORMAL was light green; CALM was light blue; STORMY was a mixture of blue and pink; FLAP was red; FRANTIC was scarlet; DISASTER was purple. The arrow would be swung around by anyone who came into the room to warn his colleagues of troubles to come. It was seldom set to CALM, never to NORMAL. Life at Intelligence headquarters was exciting, and the Flap Meter usually fluctuated between STORMY and DISASTER.

One morning in the summer of 1947, two years after the Operations Branch began its secret operations against the Soviet armies, the Flap Meter was set to STORMY and the question of the moment was what to do with the defectors who had been crossing the borders in a steady stream, or who had been culled from the DPs in the camps. As each arrived, alone or in groups of two or three, he was installed in a safe house, usually in a small town or a village in western Austria, with an intelligence officer to mind him and reliable Austrian civilians to provide for his needs. Then he was interrogated. It was a process that could last for weeks. Milano never had enough Russian-speaking officers, let alone ones fluent in Ukrainian, Lithuanian, or any other of the myriad languages of Eastern Europe and the Soviet Union. The interrogators would take the deserter through his life history, particularly his military experience, to establish that he was, in fact, a genuine deserter. They were always on the lookout for KGB agents in disguise, men who would present themselves in the West as refugees from communism and would learn every detail they could of American intelligence proceedings, the identities of American officers, the places they used for their business. The KGB would be particularly anxious to learn what happened to deserters when the interrogation was over, and this was a secret Milano was determined to hide—though so far he did not know the answer himself.

After a defector's first interrogation, he was grilled in detail on his knowledge of the military units he had belonged to or had knowledge of. Reports on these preliminary findings were then prepared and sent off to the Pentagon, where intelligence specialists pored over them—and invariably came up with lists of additional questions or further clarifications the deserter might provide. The second interrogation, based on the Pentagon questionnaires, would last longer than the first and might produce further leads, and the answers might produce further questions from Washington. The first question put to a deserter always concerned the Soviet order of battle. What had his unit been, how did it fit into the larger military organization, what was its logistical and administrative support system? Next, the interrogators would question the defector on his unit's armaments. What was its equipment, in every last detail? What was its capability, its maintenance facilities, its supply structure? How were its fire control centers managed? After that, he would be questioned about industrial sites, in Eastern Europe and in the Soviet Union itself, that produced armaments or serviced weapons systems. Political questions, which were often the concern of the CIC in Austria, were seldom raised by the Pentagon.

Sooner or later every man was pumped dry, every piece of useful information he could provide was finally extracted from him. Then the problem was what to do with him.

Milano and his four most senior colleagues gathered under the Flap Meter to consider the question. Captain Paul Lyon, who was chief of operations for Headquarters, 430th CIC, was in charge of the defectors. He opened the session with a succinct account of the position.

"It's like this. We have seventeen men squirreled away in half a dozen safe houses. They have all been debriefed, interrogated, reexamined, everything you can think of. What they know, we know; what they don't know, we'll never find out from them. Obviously. They aren't doing us any good, they all want to get out and away—and I'd love to get rid of them. If we don't, sooner or later something's going to snap and we'll face serious trouble. One of them will break out, or someone will stumble across them. It's inevitable. What they all want is to go to the land of milk and honey, the U.S.A. That's where they want to go."

That point, at least, was decided on the spot. Milano laid down the law:

"We've got to be firm. No U.S. visas for Soviet refugees, from here at least. They'd have to be processed through the State Department and the INS and God knows what, and I don't want any of those guys poking around our operation. We get results because we work outside channels. Once we start filling in forms for all these guys, the State Department will have us under their thumbs and we'll never get anything done. Sorry about that—they'll have to make do with somewhere else."

"But not Austria," Lyon interjected. "I've been looking into the law here, and immigrants have a terrible time getting admitted. If you want to be Austrian, you need to show your grandparents, God knows, all your ancestors, were *echt* Austrian. It's all absurd, really, there are people running around everywhere with Hungarian or Czech names, but they've clamped down on immigrants. Anyway, the point is we'd have to provide these characters with names, papers, life histories—and the *Polizei* would never swallow it. They'd know at once these were Soviet deserters—and they don't want anything like that. They just want the Sovs to pack up and go home, and while they're here and the country's still occupied, they're not going to do anything to bitch up relations with the Russians. Not to mention the KGB, which is out hunting for all of them by name, and the PKÖ [Austrian Communist Party], which will be only too willing to help them. They wouldn't stand a chance here, even if they could speak the language like a native, which they don't."

"Yeah," Milano added. "We'd be spending all our time answering questions and telling lies about them if we ever tried to blend them into the scenery here. They have to leave.

"What's more, we want them out of Europe. All their problems in Austria would be the same anywhere else. We need to ship them out and away, as far as possible.

"I've been looking at likely spots. Canada, Australia, and most of South America are recruiting immigrants from Europe. The Australians want to fill up all those empty spaces before the Japs come calling again. But I don't think we can send our friends there. They'd be exposed. The immigration people would soon find they're not simple peasants or whatever and they'd be off squealing to the State Department that the U.S., meaning us, was smuggling Soviet deserters, undesirables of all kinds, heaven knows what, into clean and shiny Australia. Or Canada. And we couldn't bribe them, either. That leaves the Latins."

Then Captain Lyon made his pitch. As usual, he was much more formal than the others. He called Milano "Major" and observed all the military niceties—which never prevented him being the smoothest operator in the unit.

"Major, do you remember Hank Bono, who was in 420th CIC in Italy? He opted out of the Army, but he's still in intelligence as a civilian, based in Trieste. He's an old buddy, and we've visited together: Trieste is a dump, and he's always coming up here to get away from it. He's got a friend called the Reverend Doctor Krunoslav Draganović. We call him the Good Father. He's a Croatian Fascist and a useful fellow to know. He's got some sort of Catholic seminary in Rome, training up Croatians for the priesthood, and runs a visa racket on the side.

"The deal is, various South American countries have allocated a bunch of visas to the Vatican for deserving Catholics, and Draganović hands them out. He's completely corrupt and will sell them for fifteen hundred cash, no questions asked. That's dollars. The only problem is, he's probably also selling visas to Nazis, SS men, Ustashes, and all the other lowlifes in Europe. Particularly Ustashes."

No one in that meeting needed to be told about the Ustashes. After the Germans had occupied Yugoslavia in 1941, the country had been broken up and Croatia had become an independent Fascist state run by an ultranationalist party called the Ustashe. Wartime Croatia had been Hitler's most faithful ally and had enthusiastically followed Germany's example in murdering its enemies, killing up to half a million people because they were Jews, Serbs, or Muslims.

"That certainly seems promising," said Milano. "I don't like the sound of the Good Father, but getting the visas is the stickiest problem, and if he's the guy who's got them, then we have to deal with him, like it or not. What are the terms?"

"Strictly cash. Hank says he'll either provide all the travel documents or leave that to us and just turn over the visas. All he needs is a certificate that they're good and true Catholics, of blameless character and morals. Craftsmen, artisans, good solid workmen. No nasty soldiers allowed, and definitely no Russians. He doesn't give a damn, of course. He'll accept any piece of paper we give him, provided we also give him fifteen hundred green ones. It's the same price for a full service—documents, life history, certificates, the lot— or just the visa. He says he needs the money for some worthy charity but won't say what and won't give any receipts. 'Take it or leave it' is the Good Father's motto. I would guess he uses the money to get some more lowlifes out of Europe. There are a lot of wanted men hiding out all over the place, and the Good Father is the man to see."

"One thing's for sure," said Milano. "We're having none of that. Anyone we help is to be a bona fide defector from the Soviets. No Nazis, no SS, no SD, no nothing like that, no war profiteers or war criminals. I don't like the idea that we may be subsidizing this Draganović's other operations. I don't like the idea of subsidizing his lousy 'charities,' but at least we can limit our dealings to strictly our own business."

"So we're going to buy these visas at fifteen hundred dollars a pop and ship our old buddies off to South America? Sun, sand, and sin? It'll be a change from Land Salzburg."

"It will, indeed. But we'll have to check it out. First thing, Paul, go down to Trieste and bring Hank up to speed. Get him to visit the Good Father and set the ball rolling, find out all the details, make sure it's going to work. Buy a couple of visas to start with. Tell him we'll usually provide all the documentation, but we may need him to do it sometimes, so try and set up both systems.

"Then we'll have to start preparing the visitors. It could take months. What's meant by this craftsman business? Do the Latins want genuine plumbers or whatever, or is it just a ploy?"

Lyon admitted that he was not certain. "The Good Father said they should all be craftsmen, and I think he meant it. I'll check it out in Rome. One of our contacts could find out easily enough. There must be plenty of genuine refugees going through, and I could find out what's involved. But anyway, some sort of practical experience would be the best cover. If these guys are to be kept under wraps, they'd better be trained in some sort of trade. Carpenter, painter, plumber, whatever."

"Okay," said Milano, "here's a first thing to do. Let's ask each of these seventeen men if they're good at anything. There must be some real craftsmen among them. Those that aren't up to anything will have to learn. Check what sort of training we could set up for them. See if you can find an Austrian tradesman for each of them, a sort of apprentice system, to teach them the rudiments of a trade. They're not going to be skilled mechanics or carpenters in a few weeks, but give them a crash course so they can learn enough to pass muster in Latin America.

"Why don't you try the guys who do the maintenance work in the safe houses? Ask if they could take on an apprentice for a couple of months or more. We'd pay them something and pay the guys' wages. Let them learn a bit. Then when they get to Rio or wherever, they'll stand a chance of finding some sort of job. We don't want them destitute and coming begging to the embassy for help.

"Better check out the people who take them on. Get the CIC to run a background. One visitor per Austrian tradesman—that means a lot of checking before we've got the thing up and running."

"So what about documentation?" Dominic Del Greco had kept his peace so far, but this would be his department. "What do they need to get onto a ship and go rolling down to Rio?"

"You'd better pull in the photo and document lab of the 430th. They can do most of the work, if you show them. You're going to need all the black arts you keep boasting about, getting believable passes. We need to get hold of blank forms from headquarters in Vienna without telling them what we want them for. Come to think of it, get a regular kosher travel permit and use it as a model to make a bunch of new ones. Vienna's ridiculously fussy about handing out passports, we don't want to get them involved. We'll make our own. They'll want stateless temporary travel documents. The Displaced Persons Bureau at the Allied Commission hands them out, so you ought to be able to get hold of one.

"Then we'll need ID cards of some sort, transit passes to get them through Italy, other bits and pieces to make it all look authentic. And not a complete set of shiny new papers. Get them some greasy old papers that won't look suspicious."

Lyon considered the matter. "We ought to get some standard Austrian and Italian passports, too. Some of these people would look better with proper travel documents. Can you handle used passports, doctor them with new photos and so on?"

"Sure," Del Greco replied. "A snap. We've done it already. All we need is to decide what the guy's name is, take his picture, and off we go."

"Then we'll need standard GI passes, too," said Milano. "It might be easiest to pass them through to the ship as GIs. We'd better lay in a stock of uniforms for them. In fact, Paul, why don't you set up a wardrobe where they can be kitted out? They'll need mufti, too. Let's start accumulating clothing for them. They'll all need basic stuff when they sail for Rio, and we ought to be able to supply it. Nothing fancy, just what a respectable refugee would take with him."

Jack Whitmore chimed in. He was a warrant officer but always wore civilian clothes. This was not a unit that concerned itself with rank. "We could do with a good supply of trade goods. More whiskey, more cigarettes, nylons, stuff like that. There's nothing like a couple of cartons of Lucky Strikes and a bottle of bourbon to get things done. We're going to have to square a lot of Austrian and Italian officials all down the line, and we'll need the stuff to do it. In fact, we'll have to square a lot of Americans and Brits, too. I've always found they're just as fond of smokes and booze as the Austrians."

"That's another thing. [Milano again.] Money. This is going to cost a packet, just starting with fifteen hundred bucks for each visa. I can draw twenty-five thousand at a time from the chief of staff in Vienna, but that won't last long. Some of these characters will need more than smokes and booze. There's the Italian Border Police, the Austrian Border Police, Italian Intelligence. We'll need a finance officer to keep the books. There's John Zeller, he should do. He can be in charge of changing greenbacks into marks or lire or whatever. He'll need all the proper passes to go visiting Switzerland. That's where he'll get the best rate."

The group was by now in full flood, but even so, Milano was not proposing to enter the black market. The official rate of currency exchange at army posts in Austria was absurdly low. The black market rate was far higher, up to double the official rate—and the gray market, available among money changers in Switzerland, though not so advantageous, was still far better than the official rate. They might get a markup of as much as 20 percent or 30 percent by taking a little trouble. Captain Zeller would need a civilian passport to get to Zurich, and other documents, too. It seemed to them all entirely appropriate. They were breaking the law in every other direction, why not evade American and Austrian currency controls while they were at it and save the Pentagon money at the same time?

One last decision was needed. "What's our code name for this operation?" Milano asked. "Any suggestions?"

Whitmore had the answer. "We had a perfect name for the first consignments of defectors when we ran them through Soviet lines to Salzburg, before they were dressed up as GIs. The Rat Line. Sounds near enough appropriate, and it won't give anything away."

The suggestion was approved by acclamation, and the "Rat Line" was thus formally constituted. The Flap Meter stayed at STORMY: it was going to be a difficult, dangerous operation.

That was the first of a series of meetings at which Milano developed the ground rules and procedures for disposing of defectors from the Soviet bloc. Smuggling them out to South America would require a lot of work and a lot of money. He insisted on keeping close control of the operation at every stage: his staff came to report to him every few days, there were regular meetings with the case officers who were handling the defectors, and a close watch was kept on the defectors' training as artisans or tradesmen. Every week or so, someone from Milano's headquarters would visit each of the Austrians who were training the apprentices to smooth over difficulties, to act as interpreter whenever there was a failure to communicate, and to make sure that the defectors were fulfilling their part of the bargain. They had to work at learning their new trades, and the Americans expected the Austrians to be firm taskmasters.

Paul Lyon and one or two others had to travel between Austria and the embarkation ports in Italy regularly, to make sure that every official along the way was cooperative. Hank Bono had to see Draganović frequently, in Rome or in Trieste, where the Good Father kept an office. Draganović kept in touch with his friends and colleagues in Croatia, mostly covert Fascists, and Trieste was the ideal listening post. The Americans always paid cash for the visas, at the same time handing over documents for each "visitor" that had been prepared in Del Greco's offices, giving a credible but wholly fictitious life history for each of them. They were always described as Czechs, Slovaks, Hungarians, or Poles—all good Catholics, all refugees from communism, all skilled tradesmen, all of unblemished character. Draganović accepted the money and the papers without any quibbling or questioning. Del Greco had done a good job, and the papers appeared authentic, certainly genuine enough to pass muster at the Vatican Office for Refugees, of which Draganović was a senior official. The Vatican imprimatur, added to Del Greco's elegant forgeries, would satisfy immigration officers all over South America. In all the years of the operation, none of the Americans' "visitors" was ever rejected because his papers were not in order.

Milano ruled that they would leave as short a paper trail as possible. There would be no archives, no memoranda detailing their procedures, no lists of names and destinations. The operation was top secret, but, just in case they were ever raided by an unsympathetic superior, let alone by the KGB, they wanted to be sure that the identities and whereabouts of the defectors would not be discovered. These were men who would be shot if ever they fell into the hands of the Soviets. They had taken great risks to escape and had put their faith in the Americans. Milano was determined that, whatever happened, that faith would not be betrayed.

Furthermore, the visitors were allowed to learn as little as possible about the operation. They were kept apart until the last moment, except those who had defected together. None of them ever knew that there were other men in the same situation elsewhere in Austria until they met on a ship heading for South America. Even then, the Americans preferred to send them separately or in pairs. A larger group was too conspicuous. When they first came under American protection, their interrogations were always conducted in safe houses, not in any central office. They never learned the names of the officers who interrogated them or the case officers who watched over them. Since few of them spoke German, their exchanges with the Austrian workers in the safe houses, and with the employers who grappled with mutual incomprehension to teach them the rudiments of their new trades, were kept to a minimum. If they were caught by the KGB, there was very little they would be able to reveal about American procedures. Even so, the mere fact that American Intelligence was recruiting deserters from the Red Army, debriefing them, and sending them to new lives in South America was an important secret, the most deeply clandestine of all Milano's operations, and he insisted that all his staff behave accordingly. The key group of five men, who met regularly beneath the Flap Meter in his office, were under strict orders to discuss the operation with nobody. Other officers would know part of the pattern. There were transport officers, a case officer for each of the defectors, forgers, and quartermasters (whose job was to procure all the surprising variety of goods the operation needed), but none of them was permitted to discuss what he was doing with anyone else. Slogans from the war ("Be like Dad—keep Mum," "Remember: walls have ears," and "Careless talk costs lives") remained very much in fashion in Salzburg. In the event, the only leak that ever occurred, the disaster in Chile, was quickly stanched, and the very existence of the Rat Line was buried for the next thirty years.

Father Krunoslav Draganović had been a well-known scholar and Catholic bureaucrat in prewar Yugoslavia. He had edited the general register of the Catholic Church in the kingdom and had been director of oriental studies at the University of Sarajevo and secretary to the Catholic archbishop there. He was a fervent Croatian nationalist and had joined the Fascist government that was set up with Hitler's approval on April 10, 1941, when the Germans occupied Yugoslavia. The head of that government had been Ante Pavelić, one of the greatest of all European war criminals: the Ustashe regime's crimes had rivaled those of the SS. A third of Croatia's population had been made up of Serbs, members of the Serbian Orthodox Church, and in 1941 Pavelić's minister of education, Mile Budak, had proclaimed that the government's policy should be to kill a third of them, expel another third, and forcibly convert the remainder to Catholicism. "Thus," Dr. Budak had said, "our new Croatia will get rid of all the Serbs in our midst in order to become one hundred percent Catholic within ten years." Ante Pavelić had carried the matter further, proclaiming, "A good Ustashe is one who can use his knife to cut a child from the womb of its mother."

Pavelić and Budak were as good as their word. Ustashe gangs rounded up Serbs and slaughtered them wholesale. They practiced ethnic cleansing by massacre. There exist films of whole Serb villages lined up on the hillside behind their priest. Their Croat tormentors demand that they convert to Catholicism on the spot. They refuse—and the Croat machine guns open up. Tens of thousands of Serbs besieged the Catholic churches of Croatia, demanding to be converted, to save their lives. At first the Church welcomed them, but then the hierarchy began to protest both the massacres and the forced conversions. Their protests were never very effective, however, and were ignored by Pavelić.

Individual priests were among the most extreme offenders, notably including Franciscans. One member of the Order of Saint Francis commanded the Jasenovac concentration camp for six months. It was a Croatian Auschwitz where tens of thousands of people were murdered, including most of the Jews of Yugoslavia. These half-century-old horrors have been used by the Serbs of modern Yugoslavia to justify the genocide they practiced in the 1990s against Moslems and Croats alike.

Draganović was an avid supporter of the Pavelić regime. He became an official adviser to the government in 1941 and moved to Rome two years later as an unofficial ambassador. He was an effective diplomat. Pope Pius XII never explicitly condemned the Ustashe regime in Zagreb, and this may have been Draganović's work. Certainly he was well connected in the Vatican. While there is no doubt of his loyalty to the Kingdom of Croatia during the war and the fact that he continued to help his former comrades after it, he also succeeded in making his peace with Tito at some point in the 1950s. That suggests, at the very least, that he had sold his soul to more than one devil.

He became the secretary of the Confraternity of San Girolamo in Rome, a Croatian seminary that prepared young men for the priesthood. It was also a convenient cover for refugees escaping from Tito's Yugoslavia. There is not much doubt that Draganović first set up his rat line to get former Ustashe war criminals out of Europe. A secret American report prepared in 1947, the year Milano first hired him, stated that Draganović had already smuggled 115 Croat war criminals to Argentina, and there were another 20 hiding behind the walls of San Girolamo. Pavelić himself may have been among them. At any event, he escaped to Argentina, where he lived out his days undisturbed. The Croatian minister of the interior and head of police, Andreyia Artuković, Croatia's Himmler, got away to California, where for many years he was protected by American anti-Communists. Even as late as the 1980s, they defended Artuković against Yugoslav demands that he be extradited for war crimes. Finally he was sent back to Zagreb, where he was tried and convicted of directing the murder of half a million people. He died in prison.

Draganović's base was in Rome, but he also had an office in Trieste, which was then under British and American protection. The town was contested between Yugoslavia and Italy, and, until its fate was settled many years later, the Allies kept the peace. Up to 200,000 Croatian refugees had fled Yugoslavia at the end of the war, and the Allies were doing their best to send them back. The refugees were desperate to escape that fate and appealed to the Vatican for help. No doubt most of them were ordinary people who had been caught up in the whirlwind and deposited in Italy. Besides the Croats, there were people of scores of nationalities. Some had been conscripted into Hitler's armies in Ukraine, Slovakia, or the Baltics and had managed to avoid being deported back to the East by the Western Allies, at least for the moment. Others had escaped over the mountains from Yugoslavia or Central Europe, fleeing before the Red

Army as it drove into Europe or slipping over the borders before they were locked tight.

The Americans never doubted that among the flotsam of war were many criminals, men who had served in the SS or in similar organizations, who were desperate to escape before their crimes caught up with them. When Draganović was brought into the American intelligence system, Milano and his colleagues closed their eyes to the deplorable fact that he was helping war criminals to escape justice because he alone could supply a safe, efficient method of sending their Soviet defectors off to a new life. The American intelligence agencies in Austria were not in the business of catching Yugoslav war criminals. Their job was gathering current intelligence on the Soviet armies, not exacting retribution for past crimes. None of them was ever really comfortable with this rather specious justification for dealing with a man as guilty as Draganović. Milano himself took care never to meet him, leaving that disagreeable necessity to Paul Lyon. The pain of the dilemma continued over the years, especially when they learned that Klaus Barbie, a much lesser figure than Pavelić or Eichmann but an undoubted war criminal, had been sent down the Rat Line from Germany with the connivance of their former colleagues.

In one of the only contemporary reports on the Rat Line that has survived, a memorandum by Paul Lyon written in 1950, the difficulties of using Draganović, and the need for keeping his involvement from the U.S. government are set out clearly.

> *Draganovich is known and recorded as a Fascist, war criminal, etc, and his contacts with South American diplomats of a similar class are not generally approved by US State Department officials, plus the fact that in the light of security, it is better that we may be able to state, if forced, that the turning over of a DP to a welfare Organization falls in line with our democratic way of thinking and that we are not engaged in illegal disposition of war criminals, defectees and the like. . . .*
>
> *Inasmuch as he, although reliable from a security standpoint, is unscrupulous in his dealings concerning money, as he does a considerable amount of charity work for which he received no compensation, it is not entirely impossible that he will delay one shipment for one organization to benefit another organization who pays higher prices.*

The full text of the memo is given in the appendix.

In the late autumn of 1947, some weeks after the first staff meeting on the possibilities of setting up a rat line, Paul Lyon went to Trieste for his first official meeting with the Good Father. They met in San Gabriele, which was Draganović's base in the city. He had a room set aside for him in the church rectory which he used as an office. Draganović received Lyon with open arms. The purpose of the visit had been explained to him earlier by Hank Bono, and he was quite prepared to deal. The two men settled into armchairs in the Good Father's room in the rectory to discuss business over a bottle of Lacrimae Christi from Naples. The encounter was helped by a present of Scotch whisky that Lyon had thoughtfully provided. Draganović confessed that he was particularly fond of Scotch, preferring Chivas Regal, Johnny Walker Black, or Pinch. The Rat Line Committee thereafter made sure that everytime one of its officers went to see him in Trieste or Rome, he would take a bottle or two along.

Draganović told Lyon that he had six visas for Peru that he was willing to sell. The price was $9,000 for the packet. This was an exploratory visit, so Lyon had brought only $3,000 with him, enough for two visas. He said he would buy the remainder on a second trip if the first proved satisfactory. The only condition Draganović set was Lyon's assurance that the two refugees were good, hardworking Catholics and loyal sons of the Church. Lyon put on his most sincere expression and assured Draganović that the visas were intended for good, serious Catholics. Indeed, both of them had been altar boys in their youth and still attended Mass regularly. Later, Lyon admitted to Milano that he was glad that Draganović had accepted his word for it. He did not, on that occasion, have to provide any certificate of good conduct. He felt slightly squeamish at lying to a priest, even one as corrupt as Draganović, even if the priest knew perfectly well that the story was fiction. Putting the lie on paper would have been even more embarrassing for Lyon, although he had come with a pocket full of forged papers to justify it. A little hypocrisy goes a long way, and Draganović expansively insisted that Captain Lyon's word was good enough for him.

Then he produced the visas, simple documents in Spanish and English, issued by the Peruvian Foreign Ministry, with the spaces for names blank. Lyon studied them carefully, pocketed them, and promised the priest that the names, together with the necessary biographical details, would be sent to him in due course, to be passed on to the Peruvian government. Then he laid a sealed envelope on the priest's desk. It contained $3,000 in greenbacks.

When he returned to Salzburg, the visas were examined and found to be authentic. Lyon therefore returned to Trieste for the other four, bearing $6,000 and a bottle of whisky for the Good Father. This was the first of many such transactions over the next four years. Del Greco always prepared phony baptismal certificates, just in case they were needed, to accompany the phony passports and other necessary travel documents. Draganović never asked to see them, nor did he ever count the money in the Americans' presence. He always delivered the blank visas without any further questions. It was a satisfactory, businesslike arrangement.

6

Running the Rat Line

Lyon returned to Salzburg, the visas in his pocket, to discover that preparations were well advanced for the first shipment of "visitors." Captain James Alongi, the unit's administrative and supply officer, had made the most useful contribution to the operation. A few weeks earlier, driving along the autobahn toward Munich, he had passed a huge depot of army vehicles parked in a field. These were the jeeps, trucks, and half-tracks of the Third Army, Patton's army, which had liberated western Czechoslovakia and western Austria. The army had recently been sent home, and had left its vehicles, heavy weapons, and much other equipment behind. It was a typical enough scene: all over Western Europe there were huge dumps of American matériel, and it would be years before they were all disposed of.

Alongi had struck up a conversation with a private first class at the gate and learned that no one had any clear idea how many vehicles were in the motor park. He had also discovered that the soldier was lonely, bored, and open to suggestion. Alongi explained to the sentry that the Army in its wisdom kept his unit short of everything, particularly jeeps. They were as scarce as hens' teeth in Austria—yet here were thousands of them rusting in a field in Bavaria just across the border.

"What would I need for you to go for a walk while some of my men came in and drove a few of these jeeps back up the road to Austria? I can guarantee they'd be used on official business, and it doesn't look to me like you'd miss a few of them."

Later, recounting the story to his friends, Alongi expressed his astonishment at the speed with which his offer was accepted.

"I can't go for long," the soldier told him, "but one bottle of good American whiskey a minute would do. You can't take more than five jeeps, or my sergeant would notice."

Alongi replied by offering six bottles of whiskey for six jeeps and throwing in six cartons of cigarettes as a bonus. The soldier, without blinking an eye, said he would settle for ten cartons: his German girlfriend and her mother were always nagging him for cigarettes.

A week or so later, Alongi returned to the depot in a three-ton truck with six of his colleagues, including Jim Milano. The friendly soldier had arranged to swap guard duty with another man who had the night shift, so Milano's party arrived after dark. They brought the six quarts of whiskey and the ten cartons of cigarettes for the guard, and jerry cans of gasoline and oil for the jeeps. They knew their job. They quickly selected half a dozen jeeps in mint condition, put gas into their tanks and within half an hour were speeding down the autobahn toward Salzburg. As far as they ever learned, the soldier never suffered any ill effects as a result of the theft.

The next day Del Greco's mechanics filed off the serial numbers on each jeep and punched in new ones specially made up for the occasion. Then Del Greco was set to work to concoct documentation for these new vehicles. He discovered that a certain ordnance officer had recently been demobbed and had returned to the States. He found an example of that unsuspecting officer's signature, manufactured the appropriate forms and forged the signature, and had three of the jeeps with their new numbers allocated to a signal unit that had recently left Austria for good. The new documentation was then inserted into the appropriate files in the ordnance depot office by a sympathetic secretary. Del Greco had many qualities: among them was his ability to charm, bribe, or seduce secretaries. Subsequently, if any supplies officer should ever come nosing around the intelligence unit's parking lot, which was shared with other military establishments, and started inquiring about the mysterious surplus jeeps, they would deny all knowledge of them or claim that they had been inherited from the departed signal unit.

Jeeps were useful. They were the workhorses of the American army of occupation as they had been of the Army in wartime. They were needed this time, first of all, to carry the visitors down to their ports of embarkation in Italy. They were off-the-books, untraceable vehicles, and if anything went wrong the unit could deny it had any connection with them or their passengers. Furthermore, Milano might need them for trade purposes. Booze, cigarettes, and nylons were useful, but the senior echelons of the Italian military, police, and intelligence forces cost more than that. A jeep was the most desirable bribe of all, and now Milano had six of them. Two were already allocated: one to the head of the Italian Border Police in Genoa, Major Mario Anselmo; the other to Major Alfredo Capatelli, an inspector in the same unit in Naples. These were two of the key figures whose help, or at least acquiescence, was essential to operating the Rat Line. The head of the Italian Border Police and Customs Service, General Giovanni Barsanti, was too senior to be bought off with a jeep. Instead, the Americans used their most precious advantage, the fact that their zone in Austria included Salzburg. They found the general tickets for the Salzburg Festival.

Other supplies were acquired with equal panache. At the time, the liquor allowance was one quart of whiskey per month for officers and six bottles of beer a month for each enlisted man. This was not nearly enough to satisfy the thirsts of Milano and his staff, let alone provide the needs of their widening circle of agents and contacts— and the people they needed to bribe. The Operations Branch resolved the problem, with the help of "Lefty" Spinosa, a retired bootlegger from Brooklyn.

Spinosa was a native of Benevento, in the mountains above Naples, who had emigrated to New York just before World War I. At the conclusion of that conflict, in which Italy had been an ally of the British and Americans, Spinosa had been working as a laborer in Brooklyn when the U.S. Congress passed the Eighteenth Amendment to the Constitution, prohibiting the manufacture and sale of alcohol. Many Americans had found Prohibition an intolerable infraction of their liberties, and, in the best tradition of the free enterprise system, a large industry had grown up to circumvent it. Lefty Spinosa had joined Angelo Palmeria, head of one of the New York families engaged in the business. He ran a chain of speakeasies and liquor stores in Brooklyn, and Lefty was soon in charge of importing supplies from Canada. It was a highly profitable operation, and Spinosa was able to send his take back to Benevento—until he was caught. The Coast Guard intercepted him as he steered a small tug loaded with booze into a secluded dock in Sheepshead Bay.

The Palmerias' lawyer visited him in jail and set out his options succinctly. He could deny everything and stand his chance at a trial. It was not likely that he would escape, and he would face twenty years in Attica. Or he could talk to the FBI, which was most anxious to find out who that large quantity of bootleg liquor had been destined for. Spinosa could reveal all the details of the Palmerias' operations to the feds, who would undoubtedly agree to release him from prison soon afterward. Unfortunately, he would be dead by then: the family had excellent contacts inside the prison system. Lastly, he could take the rap, but offer up a few, minor sacrifices to the government. Angelo Palmeria was ready to give up two of his less profitable speakeasies and a brothel, Widow Llewelyn's club, in order to protect his other investments. If Lefty would confess that these operations were his and his alone, he would get a light sentence and then be deported back to Italy. The Palmerias would guarantee that he would return home a rich man.

Six months later Lefty Spinosa was back in Benevento with ample resources to set himself up in business. He was by then an expert in the liquor trade and therefore bought himself a distillery near his hometown and a palazzo to live in. He immediately joined the Fascist Party, proclaiming his eternal admiration for Il Duce, Mussolini, and settled down to the life of a prosperous, respected businessman. When the U.S. Army liberated the town in 1943, Spinosa welcomed them with open arms. The unfortunate circumstances that had led to his forced departure from New York were forgiven: Prohibition had been repealed, and besides, the GIs in wartime were in even greater need of booze than their fathers had been twenty years before.

Among his visitors was a nephew who had grown up in Philadelphia and was now in Army Intelligence—and who introduced Lefty to Dominic Del Greco. The Benevento distillery produced a good quality of gin and had limitless supplies of the best Italian wines. Furthermore, Spinosa had some excellent connections elsewhere in the peninsula, including another distillery, near Trieste, that produced a passable brandy. In no time at all, Del Greco had established a regular supply run between Salzburg and Benevento and Trieste. Every few months he would make a "spiritual trip" to stock up on supplies, taking a truck with him to carry them.

Cigarettes came from the Army PX in Italy. They were rationed, one carton a week, but Milano had discovered a mode of exchange that enabled him to buy as many cartons as he wanted. He paid cash for everything but also offered Nazi memorabilia. SS daggers, Nazi battle flags, medals, helmets, and other souvenirs of the German war machine were relatively easily obtained in Austria but were in short supply in Italy. The PX at Livorno was run by the supply staff, men who had made essential but unadventurous contributions to the war and occupation and were only too glad to be offered the opportunity to stock up on interesting items to take home with them as substitutes for more glorious memories. There was soon a regular exchange of souvenirs for cigarettes, and everyone was happy.

The arrangement served Milano well on one occasion: he was abruptly summoned by the general commanding the American garrison in Salzburg, who demanded indignantly how Milano kept himself supplied with good-quality cigars, which were quite unobtainable in Austria. The general had seen Milano walking to work past his office window every day, cheerfully puffing on an expensive cigar.

Milano had shown greater foresight than the general: before coming to Austria he had made a deal in the PX in Livorno. Adding a German Luger pistol and a Nazi battle flag to the price had allowed him to buy twenty-five boxes of cigars. He did not tell the general how he had managed the transaction, merely saying that it happened that he had a spare box of fifty Webster fancy-tail cigars that he would offer him, as a token of respect. The general was far too tactful to ask for details—and instructed his aide de camp to make sure that Major Milano was on the A list for all parties in future.

When Lyon produced the first six visas acquired from the Good Father, the Rat Line committee had already laid in stocks of trade goods, uniforms, and clothing, as well as the stolen jeeps. Del Greco had prepared forged papers for all the seventeen defectors who were to be smuggled out of Europe, and they had been trained, at least approximately, in their new trades. The unit's finance officer had made several trips to Switzerland to change dollars into local currency at favorable rates. Setting up the Rat Line had taken several months, dozens of meetings, much careful planning, and some imaginative and creative improvisation. Now it was time to put the plans into action.

The Rat Line group, after long discussion and much thought, finally chose six of their clients to send on the first transport to Peru with the Good Father's visas. Like all the defectors, they had been given code names. Their own names were struck from the record and are now altogether forgotten. That was part of the plan: their future security and success depended absolutely on starting afresh, leaving nothing behind.

First was Abraham, an artillery captain who had deserted from the Red Army. He was a thirty-five-year-old Ukrainian, older than most of the defectors, and unmarried, a science and mathematics teacher from Odessa. His parents had perished in the great famine that Stalin had inflicted on Ukraine, and he told his interrogators that he had never believed in communism. At the end of the war Abraham had been serving in an artillery regiment on the Hungarian-Austrian border. He had seized his opportunity and deserted in May 1945, at the moment of greatest confusion in Europe. He had made his way to Graz, claiming to be a refugee, and had later moved on to western Austria to get as far away from the Soviet army of occupation as possible. There he had been interrogated by Army Intelligence, which quickly identified him as a deserter.

Moe was twenty-four. He was from Moscow and had served as a lieutenant in the Signal Corps. He had fought the Germans across the breadth of European Russia and the Balkans, taking part in the savage fighting for Budapest and Vienna. In June 1945, his unit had been informed that it would be sent home. He later told his interrogators that he had spent many sleepless nights wondering what to do: he had lived the full horrors of Stalinism in Moscow: the deplorable living conditions, the constant terror of the KGB, the purges. Rather than return to a future that was certain to be bleak

and difficult, he had chosen to desert. It is a measure of the terrible
conditions in Moscow in the 1930s that Russian soldiers should have
preferred the risk of attempting desertion in the devastation of
Central Europe to returning home. Moe had managed to escape
undetected, crossing the Danube at Linz and turning himself in to
the American army. He had been taken into protective custody by
the CIC.

Alex was Polish, from Byelorussia, in the western Soviet Union.
He had been an infantryman in the Red Army when Hitler and
Stalin were allies and had partitioned Poland, in 1939. In March
1940, he had witnessed the massacre of part of the Polish officer
corps in the Katyn Forest near Smolensk. A large part of the Polish
army, escaping from the Germans after its defeat in 1939, had been
interned in the Soviet Union. The officers had been separated out,
and 4,000 of them had been killed at Katyn by the NKVD (the Soviet
secret police, which later became the KGB). Another 18,000 had
been murdered elsewhere. It was a crime that the Soviet Union
admitted only in 1990, after decades of strenuous denial. Alex, who
had been on guard duty at the camp when the NKVD came to take
the prisoners into the forest to shoot them, had been appalled at the
event, no doubt partly because he was Polish himself. When the
Germans had invaded the Soviet Union in June 1941, in Operation
Barbarossa, Alex's unit had been one of those overwhelmed by the
Wehrmacht and he had been taken prisoner. He had been fortunate
enough to survive the horrors of the German prisoner-of-war camps:
most Russian POWs had been starved to death, worked to death, or
murdered. When he had been liberated in Czechoslovakia in 1945,
he had decided that he would stay in the West, and he had escaped
from his liberators, making his way south over the border into the
American zone of Austria.

Two others, code-named O'Toole and Fergus, had also been captured by the Germans early in the war. Unlike Alex, they had served
in the Vlasov army, Soviet troops recruited by the Germans to fight
against Stalin. They were Ukrainians, devout Catholics, and easily
persuaded that their patriotic duty was to ally themselves with the
Germans against Russian tyranny. They may have become disillu-
sioned like Andrei Vlasov, the Russian general and war hero who
had been captured by the Germans before Moscow, in 1941, and had
been persuaded to form an anti-Communist legion out of Soviet prisoners. Vlasov and his men had soon learned the bitter lesson that
Hitler would never trust them and that the Germans considered the
Ukrainians little better than Jews or vermin. They had hardly been
allowed into battle, and never as a unified army under Russian or
Ukrainian command. At the end of the war, Vlasov and most of his
soldiers had been sent back to Russia, where most of them had been

shot. O'Toole and Fergus had succeeded in deserting and had reached the CIC in western Austria. They had had less immediately useful information to offer than the others: even Alex had been able to give a firsthand account of the Katyn massacre. But their intelligence on the Vlasov army had been useful enough to earn them tickets to Peru.

The sixth and last of the first contingent was another artillery officer, Thurmond. He had ended the war a captain posted to a village in northern Austria on the road from Bratislava to Vienna. His decision to desert had been a matter not of principle, like the others, but of circumstance. He had been billeted in a farmhouse, where he had met the widow of a German officer and fallen in love with her. It was just like the classic French film of escaped prisoners in World War I, *La Grande Illusion.* The farmhouse was in the Soviet zone of Austria, and the widow and her Russian lover had decided to escape together to the Americans. Thurmond had been taken in by the CIC and interrogated at great length. He could provide precisely the sort of intelligence that most interested the Pentagon, concerning the state of readiness and equipment of an elite unit of the Red Army. However, his romance had not lasted. Thurmond left for Peru alone, and his lady found a place to live in the American zone.

While the support group was preparing the six for their journey, arrangements were also being made to smooth their path through Austria and Italy. Their ship was to sail from Genoa, in northwest Italy, and after crossing the border from Austria they would have to traverse the whole width of Italy to get there. The Italian authorities had to be prepared, to ensure the six safe passage. What is more, they would have to go through the British zone of Austria between Salzburg and the Italian frontier, so the British had to be squared, too.

This first task was entrusted to Dominic Del Greco, who had developed close relations with the Austrian representatives of British military intelligence (MI6) and counterintelligence (MI5). He was sent down to Klagenfurt, where the British had their headquarters in Austria, to enlist the aid of Captain Archibald Morehouse, head of the MI5 mission, and Butch Groves, who described himself simply as a British intelligence officer, though Milano believed that he was an MI6 case officer. Del Greco told his two colleagues what was in the wind and asked their assistance. This was all perfectly natural: if the State Department was the sworn enemy of American intelligence operations abroad, the British were their natural allies. Morehouse agreed to see the convoy across the border from the British zone into Italy himself, resolving any difficulties they might encounter with the Austrian Border Police. As a token of esteem, Del Greco took each man a carton of cigarettes and—much more valuable—a few pairs of nylons, which they would find most valuable in dealings with Austrian, or even British, ladies.

The Italians cost more. Paul Lyon was sent forth to make contact with the Italian authorities, with the head of the Border Police and Customs Service, General Barsanti, in Rome and the head of the Genoa office, Major Anselmo. He offered a perfect impression of total candor, telling them that the Americans wanted to send some of their clients out of Europe through Italy and would appreciate any help the Italians could give. It was not necessary to say who these clients were, where they came from, or why the USFA (U.S. Forces in Austria) G-2 was so particularly interested in them. It was made most clear to the Italians that discretion was part of the service they were being asked to provide and that the Americans would show their gratitude. In this case, the price was one of Milano's new jeeps for Anselmo and tickets to the Salzburg Festival for Barsanti. In exchange, the general would make sure that Italian intelligence and counterintelligence services, as well as the border police, would help whenever necessary and keep the regular police out of the way. Major Anselmo in Genoa was asked to provide services beyond the call of duty. He would be closely involved in getting the six visitors through customs, currency control, and port police and onto the ship for Peru. What is more, Lyon wanted him to be on hand when the convoy crossed the Alps: the British MI5 officer, Archie Morehouse, would see them through the Austrian lines, under the eyes of the British occupation authorities; Anselmo would ensure that they passed through Italian immigration without incident. In exchange, the Americans would give him a jeep. He would earn it.

Barsanti did more than simply give his blessing to the operation. He introduced Paul Lyon to his representative in Naples, Major Capatelli. The Rat Line was certain to need his services later. It was a matter of principle that the visitors should not all be sent down the same route, and Naples was the main port in Italy, after Genoa. Barsanti was most accommodating, and Lyon crowned the budding friendship by inviting him to Salzburg the following August, for the festival. It was due to reopen for the first time since 1938, and the general and his wife, who had attended the festival before the war, were delighted to have the chance to return. They would be guests of the CIC, put up in a comfortable hotel for a week and provided with tickets for every show they wanted to attend. In the event, the general and his wife came for two consecutive years, in the second bringing with them another Italian official, a senior officer in the National Police. It proved an excellent investment for the Americans.

Lyon had one last task to complete before returning to Salzburg. He stopped in Udine, in the Carnatic Alps northeast of Venice, to visit a hotel run by another of the group's friends. The six visitors and their American escorts were to stay there for the night after crossing the frontier, and Lyon confirmed the bookings. He sealed the deal with a bottle of Scotch. Boris, the manager, was an old friend of American Intelligence. He was an Italian from the South Tyrol, tall, blond, and very Germanic-looking. How he had escaped being drafted during the war by either the German or the Italian army was a great mystery to the Americans. He ran a fine hotel that they always patronized when passing through Udine, whether or not they had any "visitors" with them.

The last detail was to book six passages to Lima aboard a freighter sailing from Genoa. The tickets were bought in the names that had been chosen for the visitors and that had been inserted into their displaced person passports, ostensibly issued by the American High Commission in Vienna but in fact forged by Dominic Del Greco and his staff in Salzburg. The same names were now on the visas provided by the Good Father, as well as on all the other documents the six would take with them into their new lives.

Milano believed that the less his superiors knew of his doings, the better. However, spending large sums of money on sending defectors to South America was a major project, and he did brief two men in Vienna. One was Colonel C. P. Bixell, director of Army Intelligence in Austria; the other was Major General Thomas Hickey, chief of staff to GOC U.S. Forces in Austria. Milano took the *Mozart*, the night train that ran between Salzburg and the American zone in Vienna, passing through the Soviet zone on the way. He had breakfast in the Regina Hotel in Vienna, the principal officers' mess for Headquarters, USFA, and then presented himself in Bixell's office.

He explained the purpose of the Rat Line and outlined some of the methods he and his colleagues had devised to set it up. It was not necessary to go into all the details. The colonel did not need, or want, to know about forged passports or stolen jeeps. He warmly approved Milano's initiative and took him in to see the general. Hickey had authorized all of Milano's activities and had seen the intelligence he produced and forwarded to the Pentagon. He was Milano's strongest supporter, but he needed to know even less of the detail than Bixell did. He contented himself with listening to a general outline of what was proposed for the six defectors and for others who would follow. He was delighted to hear that Milano had found a way of getting rid of the defectors: were they to surface in Austria, there would undoubtedly be a bitter dispute and a major international incident between the U.S. and Soviet armies of occupation. Much better that they simply disappear. The general agreed at once to sign a further voucher for $25,000 that Milano could draw from the paymaster of U.S. forces in Salzburg. He congratulated the two men on solving the problem, wished them well, and sent them on their way.

When all the arrangements had been made, Abraham, Moe, Fergus, O'Toole, Alex, and Thurmond were gathered together for the first time at a CIC safe house in Hallein, outside Salzburg. They were not given their tickets and visas: that would be done at the last moment, when they had reached Genoa. For the trip there, they were to be dressed as American soldiers, in regular GI uniforms, with all the appropriate papers. Years later, Milano remembered with amusement these Soviet defectors' delight with their temporary American uniforms.

They left early the following afternoon, in a convoy of three jeeps, two to a jeep, driven by Paul Lyon, Jack Whitmore, and Charlie Crawford (another master sergeant in civilian clothes). It was a five-hour drive to the border, including a trip through a rail tunnel under the Alps. The jeeps had to be put onto rail cars to get through. The convoy arrived safely at the border, where Archie Morehouse was waiting to shepherd them across. Major Anselmo performed the same service on the Italian side. He returned directly to Genoa but left an assistant with the American party to make smooth their path across Italy. The first part of the journey had been accomplished without a hitch. The six visitors were safely out of Austria and into Italy and were taken down to the hotel at Udine for the night.

Udine is high in the Alps, near the junction between Austria, Italy, and Yugoslavia. Lyon had chosen the hotel because it was remote and peaceful. Boris was expecting them: Lyon had prepared the ground well. He expected no difficulty—but he was mistaken. The following morning, while the six refugees and their three escorts, all in American uniforms, along with Major Anselmo's representative, were having breakfast in the hotel restaurant, two American tourists appeared and came over to chat, expecting to tell the young soldiers how proud they were of the U.S. Army and perhaps to discover where they were from in the States. The uncomprehending Russians and Ukrainians, who spoke no English, fortunately held their peace while Lyon got rid of his unwelcome compatriots by telling them that the six were all under arrest and were being taken to the army stockade in Livorno, and therefore unfortunately could not pass the time of day with them.

It was a long drive from Udine to Genoa and took two days. Fortified by their American uniforms and papers and helped by the presence of an Italian intelligence officer, the little convoy sped across Italy safely and reached the safe house prepared for them outside Genoa on the evening of the second day. The six refugees then changed out of their American uniforms—with some regret—and put on the nondescript civilian clothing that had been prepared for them and brought down in their suitcases. Lyon gave them their new passports and tickets, and they assumed their new identities.

The following evening, after dark, Major Anselmo came to pick them up. This time they drove in unmarked Italian cars down to the port of Genoa, where they were hustled aboard their freighter. The port authorities stamped their passports, asking no questions and expressing no interest in the transaction. Major Anselmo had seen to every last detail. The ship sailed early the following morning.

The six arrived safely in Peru and began their new lives, leaving no trace of their passage behind them. The Rat Line support group made sure that there was no memory of their real names, no means that anyone could use to pursue them. Somewhere in Peru, or perhaps in Argentina or Chile, in Brazil or Bolivia, Moe and Abraham, O'Toole and Fergus, and all the others who followed them started out again as plumbers or carpenters. They may still be alive, married and with Latin American children and grandchildren, old men speaking Spanish or Portuguese with Russian accents, men who served Stalin and then deserted him, who saw all the horrors of the Second World War on the eastern front and then defected to the Americans. They spent a few months in the hands of American intelligence officers in Austria, who fed them, clothed them, and protected them, who asked them endless detailed questions about their previous careers, questions whose significance was usually quite beyond their ken. And then they were packed into jeeps and shipped uncomprehending across Europe to freighters in Italian ports, where the police conspicuously ignored them, waving them through with hardly a glance at their carefully forged papers. Now that they are old, there is no longer any need for secrecy. Communism and the Soviet Union have collapsed together, and it is at least possible that some of them have returned to their homelands, to look for relatives and revisit the scenes of their youth. We can only speculate how they would be received.

7

Mauthausen and the Underground Railroad

The shadows were still heavy over Austria when the Americans arrived in May 1945. Two days after they had installed themselves in Salzburg, Milano and Del Greco were eating dinner in their hotel when two of their lieutenants came up to them in a state of great distress. They were both red-eyed from weeping. They had just come back from Mauthausen concentration camp and were still shaking from the horrors they had seen. One of them, John Gassaway, a Jewish refugee from Austria who had enlisted in the U.S. Army, had seen the place where his parents had been murdered.

Mauthausen was near Linz, Hitler's hometown, but on the north bank of the Danube. It was a work camp, not an extermination camp like Birkenau or Treblinka. This meant that prisoners were not gassed as soon as they arrived but were worked to death in the limestone quarries. In the last three months of the war, over 30,000 people had been murdered there or had died of overwork, disease, or starvation. It was the last major camp liberated by the U.S. Army, on May 4, 1945. In those desperate, final days, though Hitler was besieged in Berlin, and even after he was dead, when Berlin had fallen and German armies were surrendering piecemeal around Europe, the SS guards had tried to evacuate the survivors in Mauthausen and its satellite camps and march them deeper into the Reich. There were 110,000 altogether, and in one of the satellite camps, Ebensee, 30,000 prisoners had been ordered into a tunnel that had been packed with explosives. They were intended to be one last holocaust of the "Final Solution." But they refused to go, and, after a long hesitation, the guards decided not to slaughter them on the spot.

When the Americans reached Mauthausen, they found ten thousand bodies in one vast communal grave. There were other bodies piled everywhere, and thousands of dying people. The soldiers, with misguided generosity, handed out chocolate and army rations to the skeletal inmates, many of whom then died of the shock of eating their fill. Hundreds of people died every day of disease or, in the first few days, of overeating, despite the best efforts of the American doctors and medics. The Americans remained for only a few days and then handed the camp over to the Soviets because the camp was in their zone. First Lieutenant Gassaway and his friend First Lieutenant Martin Wolf had driven up to the camp gates and had been admitted and shown around by the Soviet troops who had just arrived and were guarding the place. The Russians were as shocked and angered as the Americans. They had helped the two young men search through the camp records, which had not been destroyed, and had found the dates when Gassaway's parents had been brought there and when they had died. The Russians showed them lampshades made out of human skin and evidence of bestial medical experiments conducted on the inmates. About a quarter of the survivors were Jews. The rest were gypsies, Russian prisoners of war, Spanish Republicans who had escaped from Spain after Franco's victory and had been deported to Mauthausen from France, and political opponents of the Nazis or Fascists from all over Europe. There were even POWs from the Western allies, including a very distinguished British naval officer, Lieutenant Commander Patrick O'Leary, GC, DSO, who has left a graphic account of the abominations he observed.*

The two young men talked obsessively and emotionally, far into the night, of what they had seen and what it meant. Gassaway was distraught, not only that his parents were dead but that they had died so horribly. He had seen the dead and the dying and was in agony that his parents had perished in that manner. At the same time, news reports were coming in from Dachau, Belsen, and a dozen lesser camps in western Germany, and the Soviets were showing Auschwitz and Majdanek in the east. In those pretelevision days, it took weeks before the full enormity of the crimes committed by the Germans became known and understood, before the news accounts were published and the newsreels were distributed. This was the first direct report that Milano had heard.

---

*The Way Back: The Story of Lieutenant Commander Pat O'Leary GC DSO RN by Vincent Brome

The mass murder of the Jews had begun in June 1941 with the invasion of the Soviet Union. The formal decision to kill all the Jews of Europe by gas had been made on January 20, 1942, at the Wannsee Conference in Berlin. It was an operation conducted in the deepest secrecy, but the killings were on so vast a scale, involving so many tens of thousands of people, that the news had inevitably leaked out. The first rumors of atrocities had reached the West in 1942, and detailed, specific reports from Auschwitz had come a year later. Some had been supplied by Oskar Schindler, through contacts with resistance movements in Hungary. The news had been greeted with incredulity by many who heard it, although the British and American governments had issued a detailed report and denunciation and had announced that those responsible would be tried for their crimes after the war. Milano had heard of the extermination of the Jews in 1943, but he had refused to believe. His unit had reached Naples during the advance up Italy, and one evening, in the mess hall, a colleague, First Lieutenant Leon Marcus, had told a group of intelligence officers that he had heard from his relatives in America that stories of terrible things were coming out of occupied Europe. Jews escaping from Poland claimed that the Germans were systematically gassing all the Jews of Europe in death camps. The little group of American intelligence officers, sitting in their mess in liberated Naples, listening to Marcus's thirdhand account of unimaginable horrors, could not bring themselves to believe. Many of them were Jews: the intelligence services included many Jews, particularly recent immigrants who spoke German and other languages. They had no trouble believing that their coreligionists and relatives were being mistreated and that many had been murdered, but the notion of a considered policy of extermination was impossible to accept. Their war was in Italy, where relations between the U.S. Army and Italian civilians, though former enemies, were always excellent. They might have been less skeptical if they had fought the German Army in Eastern Europe and seen the atrocities for themselves, as the advancing Russians did.

The reports continued to trickle in as the Allies advanced on Berlin, but they were never thoroughly substantiated until the camps themselves were liberated at the end of the war. Milano noticed that stories of the murder of Jews never appeared in the army paper, *The Stars and Stripes*, nor in *The Morgantown Post*, his home paper from West Virginia, which used to arrive in bundles of a dozen or more. It was a local paper, but it carried syndicated columns from the major newspapers and chains, as well as agency reports. He thought that surely if it were true, and known, that the Germans were murdering the Jews, it would be reported in the papers. Now, after the war, the nightmare stories were proved true—and short of the truth.

When the two distraught young officers told what they had seen at Mauthausen, Milano and Del Greco decided they had to see the place for themselves. It was a long drive from Salzburg, and they left early the next morning. They took cigarettes and chocolate for the Soviet border guards, but they were not needed. They drove across the Danube bridge into the Soviet zone and then into Mauthausen without query.

It was all true, the stories they had heard, and worse than they could ever have imagined. This is a problem that all survivors, and those who saw the camps, have faced ever since. They are not doubted, except by fools, charlatans, and anti-Semites who seek to justify Hitler by denying his crimes. But the survivors and witnesses have usually found it impossible to convey the enormity of what they saw. The camps were huge: there was room in Mauthausen for more than a hundred thousand prisoners. Auschwitz was far bigger. That dimension may be understood, but the stench of death, fortunately, is something that cannot be re-created. The filth cannot be imagined, nor can the effect of tens of thousands of corpses. When the camps were liberated, the dead had to be shoveled into mass graves by bulldozers, whose drivers wore masks to preserve themselves from the smells and the dangers of typhus. The survivors, so emaciated that every bone could be seen through their skin, were too sick and exhausted to show much emotion. They sat or lay on the ground or in their bunks, in their own filth, and waited to die or for relief to be brought to them. Milano and Del Greco saw all this and tried to imagine what the camp had been like ten days earlier, at the moment of its liberation. The Americans, first, and then the Russians, helped by Jewish relief organizations, had worked feverishly to save as many of the survivors as they could, but Mauthausen was still a charnel house. After an hour, Milano and Del Greco could bear it no more and returned to Salzburg. It was the worst thing they had ever seen, and they regretted that they had gone, for surely they would dream of the horrors for months to come. They were young men, though they had been through years of war, and they could not conceive how human beings could do such things. Fifty years later, they still cannot understand.

The experience of seeing the camps permanently affected Milano, as it did everyone else who shared it. It influenced his actions for years afterward. As an intelligence officer, he had much to do with the refugee question, because refugees were among the best sources of information on the East. There were Jewish survivors of the Holocaust scattered in camps across the breadth of Europe. Despite their best efforts, the Nazis had not finished the "Final Solution." There were four camps of Jewish DPs in the American zone of Austria and many others in the rest of the country. These were only a fraction of the refugees in Austria, who included large numbers from every country in Eastern Europe and people from all over the Soviet Union. As late as May 1947, there were still more than 181,000 DPs in the American zone, including 21,250 Jews. There were, however, two peculiarities of the Jews, apart from their uniquely horrible recent history. Unlike the other refugees, the Jews had the help of Jewish organizations based in the United States, which followed immediately behind the advancing Allied lines to rescue them immediately and alleviated their conditions rapidly in the months after the war. The other unusual feature was the presence among them of Zionists intent on getting as many of them as possible to Palestine. These groups also used the Jewish network in Europe, based on the relief organizations and the people in the camps, to smuggle arms to Palestine for use in the struggle against the British and, after Israel's independence, against the Arabs who attacked it.

Britain had conquered Palestine from the Turks in 1918, and after the First World War had taken it as a mandate from the League of Nations. Under the terms of the mandate, approved by the League, Britain was to implement the Balfour Declaration, which promised to set up a "national home for the Jewish people" in Palestine without making clear just what was meant by that phrase. The Jews thought it meant allowing unrestricted immigration into Palestine, but when the native inhabitants objected, particularly when Hitler's rise to power in 1933 impelled the first rush of refugees from Germany, the British decided that immigration should be severely limited. They could not foresee that closing the door to the Jews meant condemning them to death. In a government white paper issued in 1939, they ruled that Palestine would not be partitioned but would be given its independence ten years later as a unified state. During that period, Jewish immigration would be limited to a total of 125,000. The white paper's limits were kept in force throughout the war, and those Jews who managed to reach Haifa, and were caught, were interned in Cyprus or on Mauritius, in the Indian Ocean. They at least survived. Many perished on the way, partly because they had no legal destination. One notorious case was a cattle boat, the *Struma*, which escaped Romania loaded with refugees at the end of 1941. It was interned by the Turks in the Bosporus because the British refused its passengers visas to Palestine, and it sank there in February 1942. Seven hundred sixty-seven of its passengers drowned.

The Jews, both in Palestine and abroad, were bitterly opposed to the white paper policy and did everything in their power to circumvent it. British officials in Palestine were less than enthusiastic about enforcement, and as a result about 200,000 illegal immigrants reached Palestine between 1944 and Israel's independence in 1948.

The British thus, deservedly, got the worst of both worlds: they were blamed by the Jews for impeding immigration to Palestine while excoriated by the Arabs for permitting it.

The Jewish Agency, which administered Jewish affairs in Palestine and which in due course became the government of Israel, took a close interest in the activities of the "underground railroad" that developed soon after the war, smuggling Jews out of Europe and into Palestine. There were many routes, the most important running through the ports of the Mediterranean and its affluents. The one that concerned the American intelligence operation in Austria ran through that country and across the Alps to Trieste, at the head of the Adriatic. Refugees would sail from Trieste to Salonika, at the head of the Aegean, where they would be put onto small ships for the run to Palestine.

Trieste lies to the east of Venice, on the Istrian Peninsula. It had been part of the Austro-Hungarian Empire and had been annexed by Italy after World War I. The peninsula itself, and Fiume, on its eastern side, had also been annexed, and, when Italy went down to defeat in 1945, Yugoslavia, under Tito, claimed the whole of Istria, including the two cities. The British had promised Trieste and Istria to Yugoslavia during the war but by the end of it were having second thoughts. Tito seized the place as the Germans retreated. He was allowed to keep Fiume (which was renamed Rijeka) and most of Istria, but the British evicted him from Trieste and occupied it themselves. They then invited the Americans to join them (years later it was awarded to Italy). The British and Americans administered Trieste as a free port, and it was therefore the preferred entrepôt for shipments of arms to Palestine—and to other places, too. Those sending arms to the Haganah, the Jewish army in Palestine, naturally arranged to make their shipments through the American section of Trieste. They soon discovered that the United States was observing their activities but doing nothing to interfere.

This permissive attitude was not government policy but was the unexpressed view of so many Americans that the Jews could safely rely on it. Jim Milano, an Italian-American Catholic from West Virginia, was a good example of the sympathies the underground railroad encountered. On one occasion, the Military Government in Austria, which monitored rail traffic through the American zone, checked a trainload of steel products being sent from Czechoslovakia to North Africa by way of Trieste. Czechoslovakia was still a democratic country at the time, and there was nothing unusual about the shipment—except that the steel products, on inspection, turned out to be arms and ammunition manufactured by the Škoda works. It was legitimate to suppose that the destination on the manifest was as deceptive as the list of contents and that the arms were destined for the Haganah. The military authorities informed the CIC, which informed its superiors. The report was ignored. Neither headquarters nor the Pentagon wished to know anything about it. The U.S. military deliberately turned a blind eye to the shipment of arms to Palestine even though the weapons might be used against the British, who were fighting a Jewish terrorist campaign there.

This was an important incident, because it meant that further shipments would also be permitted, and no doubt the Jewish Agency took advantage of the opening. The Škoda works were one of the major centers of the European armament industry and had been a major addition to Hitler's power when he annexed Czechoslovakia in 1938 and 1939. The main light machine gun of the British army in World War II and for years afterward was the Bren, whose name is an acronym for Brno-Enfield. It was designed at the Škoda works at Brno in association with the British Royal Ordnance Factory at Enfield. Now the Haganah was getting a supply.

Milano did nothing to interfere, beyond informing headquarters in Vienna and the Pentagon. After what he had seen at Mauthausen, he was wholly on the Jews' side. He was equally discreet when one of his assistants, Ed Gestaldo, came to see him with some surprising information. Gestaldo was in charge of the MIS, which interrogated prisoners of war and directed security in internment camps. His staff, like all intelligence operations at the time, included many Jews who had the necessary languages. Gestaldo had agents in all the refugee camps, two of them in one of the Jewish camps near Linz, called Wegssheid. What Gestaldo had to report was that the two were spending their evenings translating U.S. military field manuals into Yiddish and Hebrew. These manuals taught the use of small arms and military tactics and would be of great use to the Haganah. What is more, it appeared that the two officers were also training young Jews in the camps in the use of small arms and conducting close-order drill. Obviously their pupils expected to reach Palestine soon and to put their new skills to immediate use.

Milano was astonished at the news. He told Gestaldo that he knew of no provision in the code of military law that would prohibit soldiers translating manuals. The documents were not secret. Nor was he aware of any rules against training DPs in military tactics. He had no intention of informing himself more closely but decided, first, that he would pass on the information verbally to his immediate superior, Colonel Bixell, next time he reported to him and, second, that Gestaldo should tell his two zealous subordinates that their conduct was inappropriate. He added, however, "I wouldn't waste any time checking that they are taking your advice seriously." In other words, the blind eye would remain turned in their direction unless an explicit order came down the line from headquarters.

It never did. Milano made his report to his superiors, who noted it and offered no comment, let alone a prohibition. Gestaldo made his pro forma order to the two to stop their extracurricular activities and then took steps not to discover whether he had been obeyed. It is to be presumed that the two young lieutenants continued translating manuals and training soldiers, though they were more discreet than before.

The U.S. intelligence staff in Austria kept a close watch on the Jewish organizations, both officially and unofficially. In their official capacity, the Americans were concerned that the Soviets might infiltrate spies into the West via the refugee camps. All refugees were carefully screened, and the Americans relied on the Brycha to filter out suspicious people. This was the Jewish relief organization set up in 1939 to get as many Jews out of occupied Europe as possible. After the war, it provided relief to the Jewish survivors in the camps and played a large role in the underground railroad to Palestine. Its chief contribution was money; the actual smuggling was organized out of Palestine itself. Unofficially, Milano and his colleagues were most interested in the underground railroad. With great care and much discretion, Milano was sending a few dozen Soviet deserters down his Rat Line to South America every year, while the Brycha was sending whole trainloads and shiploads of people, including trained fighters, to Palestine under the noses of the British. He was interested in how it was done, and in 1947, at the same time as the incident of the translation of U.S. manuals occurred, an opportunity arose to check the underground railroad most efficiently. Ed Gestaldo found an American volunteer to go down the railroad himself, all the way to Palestine, to observe and to report.

The candidate was Major Samuel Morivitz, who had served in the U.S. Army in France and was now back in Europe on a second tour of duty. During the war, he had served as a POW interrogator because of his proficiency with languages. He had become commander of an MIS detachment and had become fascinated with the Jewish underground in Europe. He volunteered to go down the railroad himself, as a refugee, and to report back once he had safely reached Palestine.

Milano was doubtful at first: there was no call for information on the underground railroad from headquarters in Vienna, let alone the Pentagon. Intelligence was directed at the Soviet Union and its satellites, not Palestine. Gestaldo countered that all information was useful and that the Jewish organizations were an important part of the secret life of the country. Milano finally agreed that Morivitz should be allowed to try his luck. He would be on his own during most of the time, but he was given the address of the CIC office in Trieste so that he could check in when he reached that city.

A few months later, Milano received a phone call from General Hickey, chief of staff to the U.S. Command in Vienna. The call was over the open telephone line, which passed through the Soviet zone and was tapped continuously. Hickey gave a cryptic order that Milano was to proceed to Vienna immediately and be in his office there the next day. There would be someone to see him, and he need not report to the general afterward. This was all a little unusual, but as a good soldier Milano packed his bag and took the next train to the capital. As usual, he checked into the Regina Hotel and, after breakfast the next day, went to the office he kept in army headquarters.

Punctually at half past eight, there was a knock on his door. The man who came in was dressed in sports clothes and a camel's-hair jacket, not at all the sort of attire usually worn by civilian personnel attached to army headquarters. He was friendly, cheerful, and wholly relaxed, but he was clearly a military man. He introduced himself as a recently retired colonel in the U.S. Army, a graduate of West Point, and he announced that he had resigned his commission in order to go to Palestine, to offer his services to the Jewish army there. The British had announced, in February 1947, that they would withdraw from Palestine in fifteen months, and it was obvious that there would be immediate war between the new state of Israel and the Arabs.

"General Hickey is an old friend," he said, "and he suggested that I should talk to you. I appreciate your position and don't expect you to give me any top classified information, but I'd be grateful for anything you could tell me concerning Jewish organizations and operations in Austria and Palestine."

The colonel came with the explicit recommendation of Milano's boss, so he briefed him for an hour on everything he knew about Jewish activities in Austria and the underground railroad to Palestine. He told him of the smuggled arms from Czechoslovakia that were being shipped through Austria to Trieste and Salonika, the clandestine training provided by some American officers for Jewish recruits in the camps who were destined for the Haganah, and the steady movement of refugees from the camps and across the borders to the ports where they could take ship for Palestine. The colonel listened intently, asked many questions, and, when Milano had finished, thanked him effusively.

"I've given up my career in the U.S. Army in order to help the Jews establish their own state in Palestine, and what you have told me will be a great help. Israel's survival will depend on the number and quality of people coming in and the arms and munitions they can get. Now I have a much better understanding of what I can expect when I get there. I very much appreciate what you have done to help in the past. I hope the Operations Branch will do nothing in the future to interfere with Jewish efforts to help our people in Palestine."

Milano assured him that the policy of the blind eye would be continued unless orders came from Washington. Then the colonel left. Much later, Milano heard that he had enlisted with the Haganah, which became the State of Israel's army at the moment of independence, on May 15, 1948. He played a leading role in the War of Independence, which lasted until 1949, and was killed in action shortly before it ended.

He was not the only military officer who went from Austria to Palestine. Milano lost one of his defectors from the Soviet Union that way. He was a Russian Jew, code-named Norman, a captain in the Red Army and an expert in the Soviet Ordnance Corps. He was a particularly valuable recruit because he could provide precise and detailed information on Soviet munitions and supplies. The Pentagon had been so pleased with the initial reports of his interrogation that it had sent over two experts from Washington to question him further. His information had filled in many gaps in the American knowledge of Soviet military strengths—and weaknesses. When the interrogations were finished, Norman was scheduled for the next Rat Line shipment. He was prepared, with three others, for a new life in Uruguay—and then disappeared.

Milano convened a meeting of the Rat Line support group to discover what had become of the missing man. A general alert had gone out, for fear that he had been kidnapped by the KGB. That was the constant terror of all the deserters, and also of the CIC and the Rat Line group. Paul Lyon was put in charge of the investigation, and after two weeks' inquiries was able to report that there was no evidence of a Soviet infiltration into the Rat Line operation. On the other hand, he strongly suspected that Norman had joined the Haganah underground railroad and was already on his way to Palestine.

Norman had told his interrogators that he had encountered a great deal of anti-Semitism in Russia as a young man, both in civilian life and in the army. He was proud to be Jewish and was not deceived by the Soviet boasts that anti-Semitism was a bourgeois disorder that had been abolished by the October Revolution. Hitler had called the Jews subhuman. Stalin called them "rootless cosmopolitans," and although there were no gas chambers for Jews in the USSR, they were treated far worse than the other persecuted citizens of that vast tyranny. So Norman had seized his moment, when he was posted to a Soviet unit in Austria, to slip over the border into the American zone and turn himself in to the U.S. Army. The CIC had welcomed him with open arms, and he had immediately been spirited away to a safe house in Badgastein. He had been kept there for a month for debriefing and preparation for his trip down the Rat Line, and the agents in charge of his case had found him a job in a local garage to try out his abilities as a mechanic. He had done very well.

Badgastein was the site of one of the main Jewish DP camps, and Norman had soon met the refugees. Lyon believed that Norman had been found by Haganah agents, who had discovered that he was an arms expert and had offered him asylum in Palestine and an opportunity to put his specialized knowledge to work for the Jews. All the signs were that he had accepted and had been sent down the underground railroad. The liaison officers with the Brycha were asked to inquire if anything was known of Norman, and, although that discreet Jewish organization firmly denied knowing anything about him, it also told the Americans that it was quite sure that no harm had befallen him and that they should stop worrying. Lyon took this as proof that Norman had joined the Haganah. The Brycha would never admit it, as a matter of principle, but it knew perfectly well how much it owed to American tact in allowing it to operate the underground railroad in the American zone, almost openly. The least it could do was to drop an unmistakable hint that Norman was in safe hands.

Some weeks later, Milano heard from Major Sam Morivitz, who had succeeded in infiltrating the underground railroad in Austria and had traveled to Palestine and back. It was a remarkable story, and Milano went to Vienna to hear it in person.

"The trip went brilliantly from beginning to end," Morivitz told him. "There was never any doubt that there had been a great deal of careful and precise planning. The whole machine ran like clockwork: they've been doing it for months, and they've got it down to an art.

"To start with, I got myself some old clothes in town, but I had a cobbler build a secret compartment into the heel of one of my boots. I hid my Army ID and some dollars in it. Then I turned myself into the DP camp at Badgastein. I told the authorities there that I came from Lesko, in southern Poland. It's near the Czech border. That's where my mother comes from, so if anyone questioned me, I could put up a good case for myself. Anyway, I told the camp authorities that I'd been drafted into a work camp in Germany and managed to survive. After the war, I'd worked my way south to Austria. The camps are full of people from all over the place, so the story was perfectly believable.

"Besides, I said I had worked for an American concern in Linz, and I gave them the name. It was a government job, of course, and I'd briefed the officer in charge in case anyone came asking about me. But no one ever did.

"Anyway, in Badgastein, I soon fell in with the Zionists. They were only too happy to send me to Palestine. In fact, I was on my way within a week of getting there. Eight of us were packed into a small truck and driven along all sorts of back roads into the British zone. There was an Austrian policeman at the crossing point, and it must have been a regular thing: he had a couple of words with our driver and waved us straight through.

"The truck took us down to the Italian frontier. It was evening by then, and we slipped around the British sentries—and then turned around and came straight back. We'd been told to let ourselves be caught and tell the British that we had come across from Italy, and were trying to get back to our homes in Poland. It worked like a dream.

"We made a lot of noise as we came up to the British border post, and a couple of sentries grabbed us and marched us into a guard-house. We told our story, and they believed it. It was astonishing. Some junior officer turned us around and marched us into Italy and told us never to come back. So we didn't. We hiked a couple of miles down the road, and there was another truck waiting for us, which took us to Udine. We were put up in a house there, and the next day another truck took us down to Trieste.

"We got there after dark. The driver sure knew his way: he slipped us straight into the docks without being stopped once and dropped us off at a warehouse. The whole back end had been converted to a dormitory. There were bunks, tables, showers, a kitchen and plenty to eat, everything we needed. There were caretakers to cook for us and to keep the place clean. It was like a well-run, cheap hotel.

"The next night, we walked out the front of the warehouse and straight aboard a freighter that was waiting for us. It had a great deal of deck cargo, and up at the bow there was a bunkhouse hidden away behind the anchor chain locker. It had bunks for thirty-five or forty people. When we sailed, I counted, and there were thirty-eight people altogether, all bound for Palestine.

"Once we were at sea we were allowed on deck, and we had a very enjoyable and uneventful cruise down the Adriatic, around Greece, and then up the Aegean to Salonika. When we got there, everything was ready for us. There was another converted warehouse, where we stayed. There were no restrictions: we could move around the port as much as we liked. They told us that we would be shipped to Palestine in a smaller boat, and would be landed over an open beach, by life raft.

"That's exactly what happened. We were put on a small freighter. It was a lot less comfortable than the one that brought us from Trieste. We had to sleep on deck, but the trip just lasted two days and then we were put ashore in the middle of the night somewhere north of Tel Aviv. I don't know where the British were. We saw neither hide nor hair of them.

"There were a couple of trucks waiting for us, and we were taken into the city. I suppose the other guys went off to join the army or look for jobs. I just dropped out. I went in to the American Consulate and produced my ID. I found a State Department official, told him I'd been on a sensitive intelligence operation and needed to get back to Austria. I gave him Ed's name and address in case he wanted to check up on me. I don't know if he did.

"Anyway, he got me a lift to Famagusta, in Cyprus, on a British plane. I got another lift from there to Foggia, in Italy, and took the train to Vienna. I have to tell you that the Jews have a much better system than the Italian and Austrian railroads.

"It was an eye-opener. It's marvelous just how well organized and well planned the whole system is. There's a huge investment in transportation, ships, trucks, warehouses, and people along the way. I just saw the movement of people. I guess the system for getting supplies to Palestine is just as efficient. All in all, I'm proud of the whole setup, as a Jew. They've done it brilliantly."

Milano had listened intently to the whole story. "I must admit that's a major league rat line you've been through. It makes ours look like a peanut operation. Anyway, you've done really well. Congratulations. I don't think we'll need a written report, but I'll make an oral report to Colonel Bixell. If he wants a written report, I'll get back to you."

The colonel was as interested in the story as Milano himself had been. He was again amazed at the freedom with which his operations chief interpreted his orders—and once again refrained from reining him in. As for Morivitz, he returned to duty.

8

Trouble in Naples

The Special Intelligence Section was manned by a group of young Americans who had fought the war together and who were experienced in all the subtleties of dealing with the army bureaucracy as well as with spies, defectors, and enemy agents. Then they received an addition. Lieutenant Henry Butcher, a spit-and-polish, by-the-rules, Regular Army, West Point man, was foisted on Milano by the American High Command in Austria: the commanding general was an old friend of the lieutenant's father, another West Pointer. Butcher was too young to have served in the war and was astonished and appalled at the lax ways of his new outfit. He always wore his regulation uniform until Milano called him in, in exasperation, and ordered him to wear civilian clothing. He called superior officers "sir," and it pained him greatly to see his new colleagues' irreverence for army rules and regulations. He also pained his new unit, which had very little time for such pedantry. All the same, they set him to work, introducing him to what they considered the real world of postwar Europe, with its desperation, corruption, and deceit. He found it all very difficult.

He was, however, welcomed by at least some of his new colleagues: Milano's secretary, Pat Walden, popped her head around his door just after Butcher arrived and said, "Gee, boss, thanks for ordering a cute one!"

Milano had to lay down the law: "Let's get one thing straight, Pat. The lieutenant's off limits. He's forbidden fruit, and don't you forget it."

Pat was seriously miffed. "Well!" she replied huffily. "Who put a burr under your saddle this morning?"

Butcher had joined the unit a few days before the monthly crap game. This was a cherished ritual that had been developed by the MIS

81

in Italy out of the boredom and frustrations of wartime and had been carried over into peacetime operations in Austria. It was always held in Milano's room, and between ten and twenty people played, with a complete disregard for rank and privilege. The hotel served the food, and Dominic Del Greco provided drink from his copious stores.

Butcher was invited as a matter of course. He was volunteered to serve bar, because Del Greco was going to be late. The head of French Intelligence in Vienna had called and asked him to find a room for a French lieutenant on his staff who had to pass through Salzburg and would arrive that evening. Del Greco, who was perfectly ready to oblige, booked a room in the hotel and went down to the station to collect the visitor.

The crap game began punctually at 7:00 P.M., and Butcher passed the drinks around while observing the general informality of the occasion with ill-concealed disapproval. Then Del Greco arrived, bringing the French officer with him. Her name was Maxine Prudent, and she was very pretty. She said she was just dropping by to thank Major Milano for allowing her to stay in the mess, but everyone there, of course, insisted that she stay. She very sweetly agreed, and the assembled Americans fell over themselves offering her drinks, food, and a place in the game. She decided, however, that she preferred to watch the men rolling the dice and volunteered to help Lieutenant Butcher man the bar.

As the evening wore on, it seemed to some of them that Henry and Maxine were striking it off well. Henry explained the niceties of the game, and Maxine showed intense interest in his every word. All good things come to an end, however, and about midnight it was time for winners and losers to settle their accounts. Milano, ever the thoughtful commanding officer, suggested that Butcher might care to take Madamoiselle Prudent back to her hotel.

He replied that he would be delighted but added, "You understand, Maxine, that I'll have to leave you at the desk. Men are not allowed into women's billets above the ground floor."

Everyone in the room heard him, and everyone was equally astonished. Maxine instantly seized on the situation. "My dear lieutenant," she replied, "if you were in the French Army and were seen coming out of my room in the morning, you would undoubtedly be awarded the Croix de Guerre. Thank you for your kind offer. I think I can find my own way home." She thanked Milano and Del Greco and everyone in the room in a sultry, husky voice and left. Butcher had the wit to be embarrassed at his own ineptitude and got out as best he could, leaving his comrades to marvel at his stupidity.

The next day, Milano called in his secretary. "Pat," he said, "remember what I said about Henry Butcher? That's countermanded. He's fair game—if anyone wants him."

"Now, what on earth made you change your mind?" she asked in astonishment.

Milano just sighed. "Don't ask. It's simply too painful."

Some months after Butcher's arrival, Paul Lyon was nominated to take two Russian defectors to Naples and see them off on a ship for Buenos Aires. He took Butcher with him, and the four men set off in one of the section's illegal jeeps, pulling a small trailer with their belongings. The journey down the length of Italy was uneventful and stimulating. Italy was a marvelous and invigorating change from the rigors of 1940s Austria. It was spring in Italy, and everything seemed hopeful and cheerful, quite unlike the sullen depression of Central Europe.

The two Russians had been given the code names Edgar and Jess and brand-new Slavic names for their bogus refugee passports. They had been interrogated at length by the Special Intelligence Section and had provided valuable information on the Soviet order of battle and the morale, equipment, and intentions of the Soviet armies. Now they were escaping from Europe to a new life in the New World. They were excited, exuberant, and determined to enjoy themselves. Lyon and Butcher were given firm instructions to keep a sharp eye on them.

When they reached Naples, the two Russians and their minders were taken to a hotel near the waterfront. It was a scene quite unlike anything the Russians had encountered in a lifetime of misery in the Soviet Union: at home, they had known nothing but revolution, civil war, famine, purges, and then the horrors of the Great Patriotic War. They had most recently spent six months in the enforced austerity of safe houses and barracks in the hands of the Americans in Austria. Naples was a revelation. There was constant bustle in the streets, men and women walking, running, arguing, and laughing together. There was no war damage, there was plenty to drink and eat, the women were beautiful, and everyone seemed friendly and happy. Naples has always enjoyed the most vibrant street life of any city in Europe, and in the golden days just after the war, as all the tensions and fears of the dreadful years melted away, Neapolitans enjoyed themselves to the full.

The Russians were put in a room overlooking the street. Paul Lyon went off to dinner with his local contact, Inspector Alfredo Capatelli, the local representative of the Italian Border Police. They left Henry Butcher to keep an eye on Edgar and Jess. The three men ate together in the hotel dining room, drinking a few glasses of the local red wine, and then Butcher sent them to their room with firm instructions to stay there. If they wanted to go out, they should ask his permission—and he would go with them. Edgar and Jess sat in their room, looking at the enticing, exciting scene in the street below, while Butcher retired to his room at the back of the building to study a German grammar.

Just across the street was a bar, its large, uncurtained windows showing the homesick, thirsty Russians an alluring view of the interior. They watched with longing as sailors and civilians went in and out. They could see the drinkers standing at the bar or sitting at little tables in the room or on the terrace outside, drinking and laughing. It was too much for the Russians. It was more than human flesh could stand, to see others enjoying the delights of freedom while they were cooped up in a dreary hotel room with genuine American dollars in their pockets. They each had fifty dollars, provided by the Special Intelligence Section, to make a start in their new lives in Latin America. They decided not to disturb Lieutenant Butcher. He was quite happy studying German verbs, and anyway he might not be sympathetic if they asked him to let them wander forth into the Italian evening. Besides, he was only a lieutenant. If Captain Lyon had been there, they might have restrained themselves.

So Edgar and Jess walked quietly down the stairs of the hotel and strolled across the street to the bar. It was called Niccola's, and the *padrone* made them welcome. They were soon installed happily at the counter, enjoying the first taste of freedom they had known in years. Then they had an idea for another joy they had long missed. At the end of the bar was a staircase leading to the upper floor. It was an elegant staircase with a finely carved banister, there was a lush red stair carpet, and at the top was a most suggestive door. The two observed that every so often a client from the bar would go up and would return an hour or so later. They deduced that the stairs and the door were meant to serve a particular purpose. They were veterans of the Red Army, conquerors of the Third Reich, and they marched boldly up the stairs and knocked on the door.

It was opened by a lady in high heels, makeup, and not much else. They spoke no Italian and she certainly spoke no Russian, but communication was not a problem. The madam introduced the two sex-starved Russians to her two favorite girls, Fatima and Tereza, and a deal was soon concluded. They paid five dollars each, in advance, which the madam took from them, wishing them an enjoyable evening. The whores took the two men off to their rooms for an hour's pleasure. After months—or years—of celibacy, they made the most of the opportunity, and the girls gave them their money's worth.

Jess was a cautious man. He rolled his wallet in his trousers, making a bundle of the whole, and left it where he could see it. Edgar was more trusting—and when he got dressed, he discovered that the rest of his allowance was missing. The limits of sign language quickly became apparent: Edgar demanded his money back in violent

Russian, the hooker denied that she was a thief, in voluble and noisy Italian. The madam arrived, and Edgar grabbed her by the throat demanding his money. By now the brothel was in a turmoil. Jess, scrambling into his clothes, checked that his own wallet was intact and came to his comrade's assistance. The barman arrived and was quickly thrown down the stairs by the thoroughly enraged Russians. They had not defeated Hitler, escaped to the Americans, and journeyed to Naples to be robbed by an Italian whore. Soon there was a full-scale riot—and the police arrived. They spoke no Russian, of course, but it was easy to deduce what had happened. This was not the first time a Naples whore had rolled a client, nor the first time the client had protested violently. The difference was that the two men had no papers, spoke no known language, and had managed to inflict a quite unusual amount of damage on the brothel and bar before the police came to break up the fight.

Later that evening, Paul Lyon and Inspector Capatelli returned to the hotel and checked with Lieutenant Butcher. He had spent a useful and educative evening with the German language. Lyon asked him if his charges had given him any trouble, and Butcher blithely replied that he had heard not a peep out of them. They had promised him to ask if they wanted to leave the hotel, and he had heard nothing and therefore assumed that they had gone obediently and quietly to bed. Lyon, who knew more of the ways of the world than the unsuspecting lieutenant, stepped across the hall to check. The room was empty. Henry was appalled. He had lost his protégés, failing the most important job he had yet been given.

Lyon paused just long enough to tell Butcher what he thought of him, and he and Capatelli ran down to look for the missing Russians. The man at the desk told them he had seen them go out two hours earlier and suggested that they might have headed for Niccola's, across the street. When the two Americans arrived with the police inspector, they found a scene of desolation. There had been a fight, beginning upstairs and ending on the floor of the barroom. The *padrone* explained that two foreigners had unjustly accused two of his barmaids of robbing them and had insulted his house, his wife, and the honor of Italy and of Naples. They had been taken away by the police and were doubtless being dealt with as they deserved.

The two errant Russians were soon discovered in the police station, handcuffed and miserable. Inspector Capatelli intervened with the senior officer, asking that the men be released into his custody. But that was impossible. They had caused a riot. They had broken furniture. They had no papers, their nationality was unknown, and altogether they were most suspicious characters. The two girls' papers were in order, they had passed their latest health inspection, the bar was a respectable establishment that would never rob its clients. He could do nothing until his superior officer, Lieutenant Antonio Donadio, arrived the following morning. All the pleadings of the Americans and their Neapolitan ally were unavailing, and the two Russians spent the night in jail. Lyon wished there was some way he could send Butcher to join them.

This was a serious matter. If the affair could not be settled immediately, the Italian authorities would quickly discover that two Russians, speaking not a word of English, were traveling with American papers and visas for Argentina. The whole Rat Line might be exposed. Furthermore, they were due on board their freighter at two the following afternoon: it was to sail at six. Lyon had to call in the chits for every favor he had ever provided the Italians. Inspector Capatelli went to work directly on Lieutenant Donadio, and various Italian generals, police officials, and politicians in Rome were induced to offer their opinions that this had been a mere barroom brawl, that it should not be blown out of proportion, that the Americans were most concerned to hush the matter up, and that, as a loyal ally, Italy should do everything in its power to keep them happy. One of those Lyon contacted was General Barsanti, the border police official who had been provided with tickets to the Salzburg Festival. He called his friend in the national police, the carabiniere who had also been to Salzburg the previous summer, and that was the key to releasing the two Russians. He was Donadio's superior officer and told him that life would be easier and relations with the Americans and Rome headquarters would be much improved if he overlooked the little disturbance at Niccola's. The argument was persuasive. Donadio arrived at the police station first thing in the morning, and the two Russians were released. They were in time to catch their boat, and they departed to begin their new lives in South America. Lyon gave Edgar another fifty dollars and a stern admonition to protect it in future. Then the two Americans returned to Austria. They had a story to tell.

Butcher was called on the mat by Major Milano, who explained that the world does not work according to the West Point honor code and that he should not always believe everything he was told by Soviet defectors—or other dubious characters. He was also told that for the rest of his tour of duty he should keep to his desk and stay out of trouble. He left the office a chastened young man, and Milano's secretary, Pat, took pity on him. She told him that she was meeting two other girls for a drink after work in a local nightspot, Le Bar, and invited him to come along and drown his sorrows. This was a well-connected establishment with all the booze a man could need, and Butcher and the three girls were soon thoroughly plastered. The girls started discussing how to cheer him up and suggested that he should perform some feat of valor, do something no one else had ever done, to demonstrate that he was not afraid of Major Milano or any of these other Operations jerks who were giving him a hard time.

Hans, the barman, suggested that the thing to do was to drive a jeep up to the gates of Schloss Salzburg, the great Renaissance palace on the hill dominating the town. The road ended a good 150 feet below the top, and there was only a narrow, cobbled passage zigzagging up to the gate. No vehicle had ever been up there. Butcher protested that he was an excellent driver, the jeep was a four-wheel-drive marvel of American engineering—and he was a West Point man who could soberly judge the state of the path when they got there.

Hans promised a round of drinks on the house when they returned from the exploit, and Butcher and the girls piled into the jeep and set off up the trail. Butcher, though very drunk, could still drive: when he reached the end of the paved road, he drove straight on, full speed, up the cobbled path to the top. The girls shrieked encouragement as the jeep swayed around the tortuous, narrow path, with nothing below but eternity. They reached the summit successfully and parked beneath the walls of the castle—and were then faced with the impossibility of getting down again. It was far too dangerous to back down, and there was no space to turn. So they abandoned the jeep and returned down the hill on foot. The girls went to the bar to claim their drink from Hans, who was suitably impressed by their exploit. Henry went to bed. He was sober enough to realize that he would be in trouble in the morning.

One of the girls promised that she would call a friend of hers, who was in charge of the motor pool, first thing in the morning. He would get the jeep back. Alas for caution: all Salzburg was in the streets early the next day, staring up at the jeep in front of the castle, as full of admiration at the feat as ever drunken Henry could have wished. In the cold light of day it was a truly remarkable achievement, and no one could imagine how any driver, however skilled, had managed to get the vehicle safely to the top. The military police were summoned, and a sergeant presented himself to Major Milano's office to report that one of his vehicles, of more-than-dubious provenance, had been found. The culprit came in to face the music. His mood was not helped by a terrible hangover.

The jeep was recovered, with much difficulty and in the course of several hours of nerve-racking maneuvering. Lieutenant Butcher was saved from punishment by a stroke of good fortune: his transfer orders arrived that morning. He was to be shipped back to an army base in California. A regular unit would have insisted on court-martialing him, but the Special Intelligence Section had better things to do. Milano and his colleagues decided that there was some good in the man, after all, that would serve the Regular Army well, even if he were not up to the special demands of secret operations. One of them observed that Lieutenant Butcher had been well trained and prepared for the world, like a Thoroughbred racehorse. Unfortunately, he had been put into the starting box facing the wrong way and would have to be turned around before he could serve any useful purpose or get anywhere.

The metaphor appealed to Milano, and he forgave the errant lieutenant. Besides, Butcher was about to leave. The section threw a party to bid him farewell, and late that evening they drank to Butcher's health and wished him well. He rose to his feet, swaying slightly, and addressed the assembly thus:

"If this were a regular unit, I would say how happy I had been working with you, how well you have maintained the noble traditions of the U.S. Army, how I learned so much and will cherish the memory and all that. However, since this isn't a regular army unit, I'll say that I've never seen anything like it. I never dreamed there was such a bunch anywhere. I've never been quite sure what you were all up to, but I'm quite sure you're playing hell with most army traditions. In fact, some of you don't appear to be any sort of soldiers at all, more like Machiavelli and Mata Hari. All in all, it's an experience I'll never forget and I'm simply delighted to get the hell out of here."

Lieutenant Henry Butcher was accident prone. So was Corporal Elmer Peterson, a mechanic in the motor pool. He had been part of the team since North Africa, but his difficulties first came to Milano's attention shortly after they arrived in Austria. The allotment division of the Army Finance Office back in the United States notified Milano that Mrs. Peterson was collecting marriage allowances from no less than seven different members of the U.S. Armed Forces. Each of them believed himself married to her and had signed over the regulation proportion of his monthly wages. It said much for her ingenuity, though not for the military bureaucracy, that she had apparently gotten away with it for several years.

Milano summoned Peterson to break the news. He asked the corporal about his wife, how he had met her, how long they had been married, what their future plans were. Peterson told a story that might have been repeated by many soldiers. Before being posted abroad in 1943, he had been stationed in Fort Benning, Georgia, working as a mechanic. Like other soldiers at the base, he had spent his spare time and his pay at Phoenix City, a place of ill repute across the Chattahoochee River in Alabama. The town had expanded greatly during the war, in tandem with the expansion of Fort Benning, and was at least somewhat protected from the scrutiny of

the military police by being in a different state. The soldiers appreciated its movie theaters, saloons, gambling houses, and whorehouses,
not to mention the scarcity of MPs. The city equally appreciated the
opportunity to help the men spend their pay, and a great number of
people, notably including many young women, had moved to
Phoenix City.

One evening Peterson had been standing in line at a movie theater
there when he had struck up a conversation with a striking-looking
girl standing in front of him. It was a warm night, and she affected
the fashion of the time, which consisted of light clothes and very-
low-cut blouses. She was a well-endowed girl, showing herself off to
full advantage, and Peterson had been appropriately impressed. She
had told him that she was clerk at a local five-and-dime store and
this was her night off. Peterson had bought her a ticket, and they
had sat together during the film and had gone to a cheap café afterward. Romance moves fast in wartime, and Peterson was due to be
posted abroad in the near future. The girl, whose name was Beulah,
was very sympathetic, and one thing had led to another. She had
told him she liked him, she loved him, but she would not sleep with
him unless they got married first: she was from a small country
town, and her mother had told her that she should not give herself to
a man before her wedding.

Peterson had fallen for Beulah's line. She knew a justice of the
peace, she said, who would not object to being awakened at that late
hour. She had taken her infatuated soldier to the man's house and
succeeded in rousing him from his slumbers. He had agreed to
marry them on the spot. The license had cost two dollars, and the
justice charged five dollars to perform the ceremony. He had done it
often before: there were many impulsive soldiers in Fort Benning.
His wife and daughter had stood up as witnesses, in their dressing
gowns. The newlyweds had then moved to a motel, where they had
stayed until it was time for Peterson to report for the transport
abroad. Milano did not inquire how the lovesick bridegroom had
been satisfied with his new wife's boasted virginity. He had already
concluded that the corporal was very stupid. Evidently all had gone
well, because Peterson had taken her to the personnel office at the
base the next day to register her for her marriage allotments.

He had been sent to join the army in North Africa and had served
with the 7769th MIS Battalion as it fought its way up Italy and into
Austria with the other intelligence and regular units. He had written
to Beulah almost every week, and she had replied equally faithful-
ly—and had always cashed the checks the Army Finance Office had
sent her. Milano listened incredulously to the tale and then had to
tell the corporal that the same Finance Office had written to him
about Beulah and that she had been receiving six other checks

besides his. Beulah's allowances had been stopped, and federal prosecutors were preparing to charge her with bigamy and fraud. As for Elmer Peterson, the judge advocate in Vienna would handle his predicament and extricate him from the bogus marriage. Unfortunately, he would probably never recover the money he had allowed Beulah to draw from his army pay over more than two years.

Peterson was astonished and mortified. He said that he had been looking forward to returning home, seeing Beulah again, and meeting her family. He observed sadly that her deceit explained why she had always found excuses for not visiting his mother in Georgia. He also said that he resented being robbed by Beulah: he had never had as much money as he wanted for his Austrian girlfriend. Milano had trouble keeping a straight face as he showed the amorous corporal the door.

A few weeks later, Milano had another problem with Corporal Peterson. This one involved the Soviet Military Mission in Salzburg and the "laundry queens." It was a ticklish matter, because the Soviet Mission, a four-man operation, was the main Soviet presence in the American zone. If it were hampered in its legitimate work, relations with the Soviets would suffer. The Soviet Mission had been established after a request by Marshal Ivan Konev to General Mark Clark: the Russian wanted to send his officers into the camps in the American zone to interview Soviet and other Eastern refugees and to try to persuade them to return home. Western policy was that no displaced person was to be forced to go home against his will. The rule was not applied uniformly: soldiers in the Vlasov army, wartime Soviet deserters, and many anti-Communist Yugoslav refugees were sent back en masse, particularly from Italy. In Austria, at any event, the Americans tried to protect the refugees from being intimidated or misled. When the Soviet Mission visited camps in Austria, they were always accompanied by a Russian-speaking American officer whose job was to ensure that the Soviets did not coerce the camps' inmates. Another purpose of the Soviet Mission, of course, was espionage. This was low-level intelligence gathering, but the Americans wanted to keep an eye on it.

The senior American liaison officer with the Soviet Mission was Major Garry Hartel. He had studied Russian at an army language school in California and had then been posted to England, where he had acquired an English wife. He was a valuable member of Milano's staff: good Russian speakers were at a premium. Part of his duty was to make friends with the Soviet officers he was watching. The Americans did not expect any of them to defect, but keeping track of them was easier if relations were good. Hartel was therefore friends with Lieutenant Ivan Bergoff, one of the four Russians in the mission, and when the lieutenant found Corporal Peterson in bed with his girlfriend, he naturally appealed to Hartel for advice.

The girl was one of the "laundry queens," a group of five young women who had set themselves up near Salzburg airport to provide laundry and other services to the troops. They were not too far from the American barracks to be inaccessible, not too close to be directly under the eyes of senior officers and MPs. It was not quite clear whether the laundry was a cover for their real occupation or whether acquiring generous American boyfriends was merely a perk of the trade. At any event, they worked hard at both occupations. They had earned enough to renovate the house where they lived and worked, each girl had a room to herself where she could receive visitors in complete privacy, and when the current boyfriend returned to the States, there was always another to replace him. The boyfriends were not all Americans. One of them was Lieutenant Bergoff.

The girl in question was named Inga, and she was attractive and charming and had a good sense of timing. Lieutenant Bergoff spent no more than half his time in Salzburg. He was constantly on the move among the many DP camps in the American zone, and during his absences Inga entertained Corporal Peterson of the MIS motor pool. Major Hartel was unable to learn how long this happy arrangement had continued, but when he reported to Milano he was able to describe very precisely when and how it had abruptly come to an end. Bergoff, accompanied by Hartel, had been visiting a DP camp at Sankt Johann in Pongau. He had intended to stay there overnight but had decided to return early and spend the night with Inga. Evidently, he had failed to inform her of his intentions. When he arrived in her room unannounced, using the key she had given him, he found Corporal Peterson, wearing only a bathrobe belonging to Bergoff, drinking his wine, and making himself comfortable. Inga was also undressed.

Bergoff was enraged. For months past he had been plying Inga with vodka, caviar, wine, and other Russian presents, while Peterson had been giving her goods from the PX. They both also paid her well for her laundry—and other—duties. The two men started a shouting match, which soon developed into a scuffle. Peterson was at a disadvantage, being practically naked. Fortunately, the other laundry queens were there, as were some of their own boyfriends, who imposed order. The two lovers were told to leave, and Inga promised to speak to each of them later, separately. Bergoff refused to go until he had seen Peterson dressed, and they both left together. Then he rushed over to see Hartel, to demand that Peterson be suspended immediately or sent out of the country. Otherwise, he could not answer for the consequences.

He then asked Hartel not to mention the incident to his superior officer, Major Yuri Smirnoff. No doubt commanders of Russian units in occupied territory knew that their officers were likely to take advantage of the opportunities offered them, but, like officials everywhere, they preferred to turn a blind eye to such matters. Hartel told him that he was an American officer and could promise nothing. Besides, the episode could hardly remain a secret for long: Bergoff would be well advised to inform Major Smirnoff himself.

Hartel reported the whole incident to Milano the next day. Milano had already interviewed Peterson, who was just as indignant as Lieutenant Bergoff and demanded that the Russian be expelled forthwith. Hartel had then spoken to John Berg, security officer in the 430th CIC Detachment in Salzburg. It turned out that Inga's arrangements were so well known that Peterson's colleagues had started a pool. Everyone had bet five dollars on the date when Inga's two lovers would meet. They were all certain that the international triangle could not last much longer. Some of them, carried away by enthusiasm, had bet on several days. The winner collected $150.

Milano was outraged. He demanded to know why he had not been informed of this lapse of security, especially since it involved one of his own men. Hartel sheepishly told him that the men in the motor pool had concluded that if he had been told, he would have broken up the love triangle immediately and would thus have spoiled their game. They had not even told their senior officer, who was now protesting loudly that he had been excluded from an important sporting event. Milano shouted at his secretary to fetch Berg and to send word to Peterson to report forthwith.

Lieutenant John Berg was an impressive-looking soldier, in the American mold. He was a good six feet two, loose-limbed, strong, and casual. Like almost everyone else in the unit, he was in civilian clothes, which in his case meant an open-necked sport shirt, jacket, and baggy pants. He had come from the depths of the Midwest, De Kalb, Iowa, where he had been deputy sheriff before joining up. He had found the army, particularly the informal unit under Major Milano, very much to his liking and intended to make a career of it. He was in his mid-thirties, a bachelor, who had discovered that Salzburg was filled with young widows in need of care and counseling and a corresponding shortage of eligible young men. He had devoted himself with such success to his counseling business that he had provoked the fury and jealousy of all his colleagues, who demanded to know his secret. How did he manage to meet so many young women in need of his advice and support, and how did he then succeed in keeping them all happy? He refused to explain his techniques, on the grounds that he did not need the competition, and his friends were constrained to make their own arrangements.

Evidently, he was not the sort of man to take the Peterson-Inga-Bergoff triangle too seriously. Milano tried to play the role of a stern commanding officer: "Big John, what's the meaning of not telling me about this affair? It could have seriously screwed up our dealings with the Reds, not to mention our own security. How the hell can I run this unit if my own officers don't tell me what's going on?"

Berg was quite unperturbed. "Jim, you know damn well that if you'd heard about it you'd have shut it down immediately. I don't think it did any harm. It was bound to blow up soon enough, and it generated a lot of harmless fun in my section. We kept a sharp eye on the lovebirds so they couldn't get up to any serious mischief. Anyway, now that Elmer's been caught with his pants down, I think it's time he was rotated back to the States. He's about due to go anyway: we just won't give him an extension. That should satisfy the Russians. They can do whatever they like with Bergoff, that's their business."

Milano was still angry at Berg, but, short of making a federal case out of the affair, this was probably the best solution. Major Hartel agreed. Keeping the Russians quiet was much more important than keeping the incorrigible Corporal Peterson happy, and Berg had indeed kept a sharp eye on the situation. That, after all, was his job as head of counterintelligence, not watching over the morals of the enlisted men.

Peterson was then called in and once more confronted with the consequences of his love affairs. Milano was kind, giving the man a seat and breaking the news gently. "It's about your troubles with Inga and the Russian. I've decided that it would be best for you to return to the States immediately. All the paperwork should be done in a week.

"I'm sorry to do this. You're a good mechanic, but it seems that you can't keep your love life under control."

Peterson protested that it was all the Russian's fault, that he had been perfectly happy with Inga until Bergoff came along, had even been thinking of marrying her now that he was no longer tied to Beulah. "Is there anything I can say to get you guys to change your minds?" he asked hopefully.

Milano replied firmly: "No, Elmer, there isn't. Sorry. You'll be out of here in a week. It's time to say good-bye to Inga, for good."

Peterson took it like a man. He stood up, saluted, and left—making the parting observation that "It's like my daddy always said: you can't make a wheel turn two ways at once." His superiors were left to digest the remark.

The Soviets dealt with Lieutenant Bergoff equally expeditiously. Scarcely was the lovelorn corporal out of the room, than Milano's secretary, Pat, announced a call for Major Hartel: the Soviet liaison commanding officer, Major Smirnoff, was on the phone. Lieutenant Ivan Bergoff was being recalled to the Soviet Union immediately, without explanation. The Americans would be notified of his replacement in due course.

9

The Pursuit of Love

There was a sour joke in Britain during the war among the male half of the population, that there was nothing wrong with the hundreds of thousands of young American soldiers who flooded the place before D-Day—except that they were overpaid, oversexed, and over here. The belief that American troops enjoyed an unfair advantage with the local girls applied even more strongly in occupied Germany and Austria. All of them, including the intelligence operatives in Salzburg and Vienna, seized every occasion that was offered, and Jim Milano often had to cope with the consequences.

On one occasion, true love came to one of Milano's senior officers, Dominic Del Greco. It was all rather unfortunate, as the lady in question, Lotti von Zastro, had been brought to the Operations Branch and entrusted to Milano's care by her fiancé. He was Peter Pavone, a young lieutenant in one of the infantry regiments in the occupation army, who had breezed into Milano's office one summer day with the request that Milano help him ship Lotti and her belongings to New York. He was being sent home ten days later, but it would take another two or three weeks after that for the army bureaucracy to complete the paperwork to allow Lotti to follow him. He needed help in getting Lotti and her luggage safely onto the flight from Vienna, and an acquaintance had recommended that he apply to Milano. He was a recent arrival and did not know anyone in his own unit he could trust. He needed someone reliable, competent, and protective, so he had come to Jim Milano's office.

This was not at all usual, but the Special Intelligence Section was a flexible organization, and Milano accepted the old dictum that all the world loves a lover. He told Pavone to go ahead with his arrangements: he wanted to prepare his Sicilian-born parents for the prospect of an Austrian daughter-in-law. In due course, Pavone

left for New York, and a day or two after that Lotti came to the
Österreicher Hof Hotel to meet Milano. He was having dinner there
with Del Greco. The maître d' came over and whispered that a
young lady was asking for him. It was Lotti, and all eyes in the
restaurant turned toward her as she made her entrance. She was a
strikingly beautiful, generously proportioned blonde with the smile
of an angel and the gait of a tiger. She was memorably dressed in a
Land Salzburg dirndl, the local dress. She sat at the two Americans'
table for half an hour and charmed them completely. She spoke
excellent English and was witty, amusing, and well informed, as well
as being exceedingly decorative.

It turned out that she was the daughter of a successful banker in
Vienna who had managed to keep clear of the Nazi Party during the
1930s and in the war. Lotti had studied acting in Vienna and had
had minor roles in a couple of Nazi propaganda films. She was looking forward to moving to Brooklyn and was most grateful to Major
Milano for helping smooth the way for her. Milano, of course, was
very struck by her. So was Dominic Del Greco. He offered to take
her home at the end of the evening and vanished into the night with
the lady on his arm.

Over the next couple of weeks, Del Greco could be seen escorting
Lotti around town, organizing her affairs, showing her the sights.
Milano did not inquire too closely into this developing friendship
and was suitably grateful when Dominic volunteered to drive Lotti
to Vienna airport on the day of her departure. It was a five-hour
drive, so they had to leave early in the morning. Milano had breakfast with them, gave Lotti a pair of Hummel figurines as a wedding
present, asked her to give his best regards to Lieutenant Pavone, and
saw them on their way. He was having dinner alone in the Österreicher Hof restaurant that evening, thinking of other matters, when
he saw Del Greco and Lotti approaching. They looked rather sheepish, or sly, and Milano was astonished to see them.

"What on earth happened?" he asked. "Did you miss the plane?"

"Not exactly," Del Greco replied. "She didn't go. There was a
change of plan."

With some prodding from Lotti, and with a mixture of embarrassment and bravado, Del Greco explained what had happened. "When
we reached the airport," he said, "we checked Lotti's luggage at Pan
Am, got her ticket stamped, and so on. Then it was time to walk her
to the plane. I kissed her good-bye, and just as she was about to
climb on board she turned and said she would rather stay in Austria
with me. I said, 'Why don't you?' and that was that. We canceled her
flight. It was too late to get her bags back, so we just piled into the
jeep, and here we are."

Milano was astonished. "What about Pavone? He'll be standing at the gate at Idlewild, waiting for Lotti with a bunch of flowers and his mother in tow. What are you going to do about him?"

"We've got a great favor to ask you, Jim," Lotti answered. "The plane is due in New York in about an hour. Could you call the airport and break the news to him? I couldn't bear to speak to him myself."

"And I sure as hell can't," said Del Greco.

It looked as though Milano had no choice. Muttering to himself about the follies of youth—or at least the follies of Dominic Del Greco—he walked over to the Red Cross Club, a servicemen's establishment near the hotel, which maintained a telephone for calls to the United States. It was not so easy to get a line, and Milano had to offer to take the operator to the ballet as a bribe. She told him crossly that she did not like classical music but would settle for a puppet show. Milano agreed and was given the next available slot to the States. In theory, there was a three-minute limit on calls, but the operator was understanding: it took more than that to get the Pan Am operator at Idlewild to page Lieutenant Pavone and bring him to the phone.

There was one advantage, however: Milano could legitimately keep the call brief.

"Lieutenant," he said, "I've got some bad news for you. Lotti's not on the plane."

"Dear God!" cried Pavone. "What's happened to her?"

"I'm afraid she's decided to stay in Austria with another man. She says she's very sorry, she can't excuse it, but she's fallen in love with this guy and won't be going to the United States."

Pavone was stunned. "I've got my parents here to meet her. We'd got everything arranged for the wedding," he wailed. "What am I going to do?"

Milano was firm and brief. "I'm about to be cut off," he said. "I'm sorry, but could you retrieve Lotti's luggage and send it back? This was a last-minute decision of hers."

The operator then mercifully pulled the plug. It had been an unpleasant conversation. Milano did not feel proud of himself, but at least he had done his duty for a friend and colleague. He went back to the hotel, where the two lovers were waiting for him expectantly. They were much more relaxed now that they had told their story— and got someone else to break the news to Lotti's fiancé.

"Did you get him?" Lotti asked. "How did he take it?"

Milano replied, "He seemed stunned. But we were only on the line for a couple of minutes, so there wasn't time for any long explanation. I said you'd be writing to him." Milano glowered at them for a moment, then added, "Now I'm going to bed. This is the last time I play Cupid."

He made his way out of the hotel restaurant, leaving the two alone. There was nothing else for them to do but order a bottle of champagne. Milano had to look forward to an afternoon at a puppet show with the grumpy telephone operator.

On another occasion, Milano was accomplice, or at least passive witness, to an act of mercy performed by one of his colleagues. The incident occurred when there was a change of command in the censorship section. This was a large part of the work of the MIS section in Austria. The Civilian Censorship Detachment supervised all civilian mail going to foreign countries and opened the mail of those on the security list and all the mail going to certain countries. It also had representatives in every telephone exchange in the American zone, tapped the phones of those on the list, and watched all telex communications. The officer in charge, Major Tony Certa, returned to the United States in 1948 to marry his sweetheart in Wilmington, Delaware, and attend the Law School of Delaware University. He was from a devout Catholic family and had turned out to be an exceptionally competent censor.

His successor was an old friend of Milano's, Captain John Scheering, the officer whose piano had been carried by the unit all the way from Morocco to Italy. After the war, he had returned to the cocktail lounge circuit in New York and had quickly discovered that the life suited him not at all. He had therefore applied for a job with Army Intelligence, as a civilian. He arrived shortly before Certa's departure, and the two of them went around the American zone as one said goodbye and the other introduced himself to the various censorship office detachments. It was after one of these trips that Scheering came to Milano with some surprising news and a proposal.

"Jim, I've learned something astonishing. Tony is a twenty-six-year-old virgin. We were up late in a bar last night, and he confessed that he had never had sex in his life. It's astonishing. It's because he was brought up a Catholic of the strictest sort, and now he's going back to Delaware, after four years in Europe, with nothing to show for it. I think we should do something about it."

Milano was startled—both at the report and at his friend's robust determination to correct the situation.

"Don't you think that's none of our business?" he suggested. "He's had every possible opportunity while here. Perhaps he doesn't want to."

"Oh, yes, he does, only he won't admit it. He's rather ashamed and far too embarrassed to do anything about it himself. I've got an idea, and I need your help."

Milano was finally persuaded to play a part, though a small one, in his departing subordinate's education. Certa and Scheering were to visit a telephone exchange in Gmunden the next day, and Milano had already invited himself along for the trip. They were all to have lunch at the local MIS officer's house in the afternoon, and Scheering proposed that Milano take the unsuspecting Certa along to a bar in the local hotel that evening. He would go ahead to make certain arrangements—though at this stage he was not at all sure what they would be.

Everything went according to plan. The inspection went well and was followed by a long, convivial lunch. Scheering vanished early, and in the evening Milano and Certa went looking for him. When the two men arrived in the bar, they found Scheering installed in a corner with two very pretty young women, whom he introduced as Mickey and Stella. Milano asked what Mickey's last name was, and she replied "Mouse." They all got off to a good start, and then Mickey remarked that the bar prices were outrageous and announced that the girls had a bottle of first-rate Cognac in their room. Why not adjourn upstairs for a more comfortable drink?

Milano could take a hint and promptly agreed. The whole party moved to the girls' room, which was equipped with a large bed, several chairs—and, as promised, a bottle of first-rate French brandy.

At about the second drink, Stella announced that she was hot and asked if anyone would object if she removed her clothes. No one did, and in a moment she was completely naked. Milano and Scheering were unmoved. Certa was showing signs of stress. Then Mickey, too, removed her clothes. Certa's eyes were popping out of his head. Scheering suggested that Milano step outside for a moment, and, as the two men left the room, closing the door behind them, they had a glimpse of the two girls pouncing on the astonished, unresisting young man.

"They're on the payroll for two hours," Scheering informed his partner in crime, roaring with laughter. They returned to the bar for the prescribed period and spent the time discussing golf, baseball, and other important matters.

When the two hours were up, they returned to the bedroom, where they found the three wrapped together under a blanket on the bed. Certa gazed at them, wide-eyed.

"What an experience!" he whispered.

It was not only the men who had a predatory attitude toward the Austrians. There was a small but conspicuous contingent of American women, who had been brought over as secretaries to handle sensitive material. Milano's operation always had a number of them, because of the extreme secrecy of his work, and some of them were quite as liberated from the tedious, moralistic constraints of civilian society back home as any twenty-year-old soldier. Milano had two secretaries, Eileen and Pat. Pat Walden was known to her colleagues behind her back as "P.P.," meaning Parallel Patricia. She was thirty or so, divorced, petite, and very attractive. She was a sociable lady and when once during a party was accused of fickleness, she remarked that while she loved steak, she would not want to eat that and nothing else every day of the year. The men, of course, loved her and gossiped about her, and from time to time she would complain to Jim Milano that she was being traduced. All the same, she kept playing the field as long as she was with Intelligence.

On one occasion, protesting to Milano that her nickname was quite unjustified, she offered as proof of her virtue that she had gone out the previous night with a recent recruit to the CIC, Bob Murray, a new agent working for Milano, and that two very pleasant hours spent in his company had led to nothing at all.

Milano scoffed at the story. "Bob's not a good example," he said. "Most of us in Operations think he doesn't like women, or is a switch-hitter."

Pat was puzzled. "What's a switch-hitter?"

"Baseball. Someone who can hit right-handed or left-handed. A switch-hitter can deal with a left-handed or right-handed pitcher."

"What's that got to do with Bob Murray?"

"Perhaps he likes men and women equally. Or doesn't like women at all. Didn't he even make a pass at you? After all, you are known as a friendly girl."

Milano evidently knew his secretary very well. They were old buddies, and they could gossip about these very personal matters without the reticence that officers should normally show.

She did not take offense, and replied, "No, he didn't, and I was rather surprised. Most men move in right away. They all seem to think they're God's gift to women. Not that I mind: I can handle them. But Bob wasn't like that at all."

For Milano, this was more than casual gossip. It would be a serious matter if Bob Murray were indeed homosexual. The rules were strict and were strictly enforced, particularly in Intelligence. Gay men were considered a security risk and were rigorously excluded. Pat Walden's encounter with him might permit Milano to clarify the situation without the messy and unpleasant business of mounting an official inquiry.

"Why don't we do a little experiment?" he said. "Next time you're in Le Bar, snuggle up to him and see how he takes it. You'll be able to tell."

Pat accepted the challenge at once. The term "singles' bar" had not yet been coined, but the institution flourished. Le Bar was a favorite pickup place for Americans in Salzburg, and behind the bar was a huge sign reading "THE INEVITABLE."

"Okay," she said. "I'll be there tonight, and I'll bet he's there too. I'll bring you the bar tab, and you can pay for the drinks."

Milano agreed to the condition, and a couple of days later Pat reappeared and presented a bar bill for a considerable quantity of champagne.

"I was in Le Bar last night, having a drink, when Bob came in. He sat next to me and we talked and we drank and we were getting on just fine. So when no one was looking I put my hand on his leg and gave him a squeeze." She looked all innocently at Milano at this point.

"It was pretty dramatic. He jumped up, spilling his drink. He was furious. 'Don't you ever do that again!' he said. 'I don't appreciate it at all!' He was really steamed and just stormed out of the place. He didn't even say good night."

Pat evidently thought the whole story was a great joke. She had quite forgotten that two days earlier she had been complaining to Milano that she had been unfairly labeled Parallel Pat, one of the more easily available women on base. Milano was grateful. "That settles it," he said. "We think Bob Murray tried to pick up that new lieutenant who's just arrived, Jack Neeley, last night. I think I'll put him on the next flight back to New York. It's a pity, he was a good agent."

This was not what Pat had expected. Perhaps she had not appreciated what her boss was after, that this was not just a matter of teasing a colleague. Milano initialed her bar bill and she left, rather subdued, to pick up the money from Eileen, who looked after the petty cash.

Eileen came in to ask Milano about it. "What's this bar tab Pat produced? What should I charge it to?"

Milano thought for a moment, then replied, "Put it down to Operation Switch-Hitter."

"There's no such thing," she replied, baffled.

"Well, just start a file. You never know when it might come in useful."

Sometimes the private lives of American secretaries had more serious consequences. Not all of them were content with the choice offered at Le Bar and similar establishments. There was a number of young, and not so young, American women in Vienna who were the subject of a sustained campaign of seduction by the KGB. Eastern Europeans, usually Poles or Hungarians, were the Lotharios. They were invariably young and handsome, speaking good English, and describing themselves as students or recent graduates of one of the universities in Vienna. They had nice apartments in the American zone of the city, and they appeared to have plentiful allowances.

Jim Milano was sometimes called in to mediate such affairs. The most sensitive concerned the secretary to Colonel Arnold Potter, deputy chief of staff for operations at American headquarters. The secretary was Susan Fox, from Pocatello, Idaho. She had worked in Washington for her congressman, and after the war she had applied for an overseas job with the Army and had been assigned to head-quarters in Vienna. She was forty-two and had never married. She was rather plain, solitary, and repressed. On one of Milano's trips to Vienna, where he kept an office, he was informed by his counterin-telligence chief there, Park Hancock, that she had apparently fallen for a tall, good-looking, dashing twenty-two-year-old Hungarian named Frank Lazan. The young man had earlier had an affair with the secretary of a minister in the Austrian government, and the CIC strongly suspected that he worked for the KGB.

This was potentially a serious matter. Colonel Potter's office was one of the most sensitive in the American HQ, and there might be a disaster if the KGB succeeded in seducing or blackmailing the colonel's secretary into treason. Milano decided that his superior, Colonel Bixell, should be informed. He was an old friend of Colonel Potter, and the two could decide what to do. They all had offices in the same building, and Milano marched in to Bixell to break the news. The intelligence chief was very concerned and said that he would tell his friend Colonel Potter immediately, and inform Milano of whatever they decided.

Within the hour, the two colonels appeared in Milano's office. They were both appalled at the security risks involved: the chief of operations, among other things, directed planning for the Allied response to a possible Soviet invasion. If Miss Fox ever succumbed to the blandishments her friend was presumably offering, she could do immense damage. On the other hand, there was no proof at all that she might be disloyal, and the two officers hesitated to confront her. So they asked Jim Milano to do it.

He protested vehemently. That was not in his job description. It was a matter for the CIC in Vienna, not at all something that the head of operations in Salzburg should be involved in. All the same, the two colonels insisted. Perhaps they thought the interview would go better with a younger man. Perhaps they were just cowardly.

Susan Fox arrived at Milano's office at 8:30 the following morn-ing. She seemed to him an altogether formidable lady. She said, "I understand you want to see me, Major," and sat down across the desk from him, looking stern and rigid.

There was no point in beating about the bush. "I've been asked by Colonels Bixell and Potter to ask you some questions regarding your relationship with Mr. Lazan."

He got no further. "Don't they have the guts to talk about it directly? What's it got to do with you who I spend my off-duty hours with?"

"Please, Miss Fox, I know it's embarrassing. Believe me, I find this just as difficult as you do. But there are valid security reasons, and that's my only interest. I've no moral ax to grind at all. It's my job to do this. You have access to highly classified materials, and so I have to be interested in your relationship with an East European twenty years younger than yourself. Surely you must understand."

His attempt at the gentle approach was a complete failure. "You people make me sick with your harping on national security! What about all those officers here whose wives haven't arrived or are still back home who have been shacking up with every woman in town? Is it your job to check up on them, or do you just check up on the ladies, and the men can do what they please? What about Colonel Potter, who had an Austrian girlfriend here before his wife arrived? Are you going to check up on him?

"Major, I will not be humiliated by your interfering, twisted, suspicious so-called national security. What's more, I know several congressmen, and if you try anything funny I'll expose the whole damn lot of you, including Colonel Potter." With that she got to her feet and marched out of the room.

Milano reported the interview to his superiors. He had to confess that he had not covered himself with glory. In fact it had been a one-sided rout. On the other hand, Susan Fox's extreme reaction showed that this was a serious affair. A further meeting was held with Colonels Potter and Bixell, and Park Hancock. They concluded that Miss Fox should be sent back to the United States immediately and should cease working for Colonel Potter that afternoon.

Then Colonel Potter asked his colleagues: "But what if she does know something about me and tells my wife?"

There was a long pause. Then Milano said, "Sir, if that happens, there's only one thing to do. Lie to your wife with complete sincerity. You must look and sound sincere, and you might want to practice in front of a mirror."

Everyone laughed, but as they left Milano observed that Colonel Potter was looking extremely thoughtful.

10

The Central Intelligence Agency

During World War II, the chief of American clandestine organizations was the Office of Strategic Services (OSS), which had been set up by President Franklin D. Roosevelt just before the United States entered the war. Its head was the legendary William Donovan, known as "Wild Bill," who set his mark indelibly upon American intelligence gathering. As late as the 1980s, William Casey, director of the Central Intelligence Agency (CIA), who had served under Donovan during the war, was still operating in the Donovan style. He ran the Iran-Contra affair with a complete disregard of the legal niceties and the requirements of congressional approval. Donovan would have approved. The OSS was dissolved immediately after the war, in 1945, because it seemed to people in Washington, notably the State Department, that cowboy spy operations were no longer needed. Besides, they had never liked Donovan, and his great patron, Roosevelt, was dead. A residual operation, the Strategic Services Unit (SSU), was continued. When the CIA was set up in 1947, it absorbed the SSU, which thus served as a transitional link between the wartime exploits of the OSS and the long cold war campaigns of the CIA. The SSU played only a slight role in intelligence affairs during its few years of independent existence. It operated independently of Army Intelligence and reported directly to its own headquarters in Washington, preserving the tradition of competing intelligence agencies that continues to this day. However, Army Intelligence in Austria had various dealings with this transitional organization during the first three years after the war. Milano was constantly in touch with its agents, including the station chief in Salzburg, Bert Lifschultz.

When President Truman set up the Central Intelligence Agency in 1947, its director was given the additional responsibility of coordinating all American intelligence services, and the new agency set to work bringing them all under its control.

The various departments of Army Intelligence gathered intelligence, of course, but that was not always their only, or even main, purpose. The defined role of the Counter-Intelligence Corps (CIC), in Austria as everywhere else, was counterintelligence. Under army regulations, the CIC was directed to "contribute to the operation of the Army Establishment through the detection of treason, sedition, subversive activity and disaffection, and the detection, prevention or neutralization of espionage or sabotage within, or directed against, the Army Establishment." But the 430th CIC in Austria had also been given the job of pursuing positive intelligence. That was a much more glamorous and exciting task than counterintelligence. Washington was constantly making demands for intelligence gathering, and they were passed on to the 430th, whose officers took to the task with zest, in close collaboration with the MIS and Milano's office. In Austria, that meant chiefly local intelligence. They spied on the Soviet forces in their zone and peered across the borders into Hungary and Czechoslovakia as far as they could, to monitor the activities and intentions of the Red Army units there. Their chief contribution to the wider fields of intelligence, the gathering of information on the military, economic, and political situation in the Soviet Union and its satellites, came from their interrogation of defectors. At the same time, the MIS teams discovered a great deal of information by interrogating DPs, who often brought useful knowledge with them from their homes or the places to which the tides of war had taken them. This source of information practically dried up by 1948–49 but was then supplemented by returning prisoners of war, who had often been sent to work in important Soviet installations or factories far to the east, beyond the Urals, where normal American intelligence could never penetrate. They often provided exceedingly useful information. The Army Intelligence operations left to other agencies the task of attempting to penetrate directly into the deepest recesses of Stalin's dominions but at all times maintained close contact with them. The various agencies could help one another, if necessary, if only by making sure that they did not inadvertently interfere with some particular operation.

USFA Headquarters produced a weekly intelligence summary, classified "secret," of course, which contained much of the routine intelligence picked up by the CIC, the MIS, and the three censorship offices. A section of the director of intelligence's staff was devoted to political intelligence and included two analysts whose job was liaison with the Austrian government. Another aspect of intelligence gathering was handled by the Technical Intelligence Group on Milano's staff, headed by Major Samuel Townsley. It concentrated on German equipment, missiles, and field encoding devices and rounded up and interrogated Austrians who had worked in those fields during the war. William Wagner, whose exploits in radio intercepts are described in Chapter 15, ferreted out virtually everyone in Austria who had been involved in signals intelligence for the German Army during the war. The idea was to discover what these agents knew of Soviet practices and abilities in such matters.

Milano was not always on good terms with his American colleagues in Washington. At all times, he tried to stay clear of the State Department. He wanted its stuffy officials to know nothing of his operations—indeed, he would have preferred them to know nothing of his existence. As for the CIA, a certain measure of cooperation was inevitable. The two were operating in the same country, and the CIA chief of station in Vienna had regular meetings with the director of intelligence in the Army Staff. They usually discussed political matters, such as the activities of the Austrian government and the position of the Communist Party in Austria. Some CIA officers kept in close touch with Milano and his office, usually hoping to elicit useful information. Milano was guarded in his answers, except when the general good required full confidence. There were occasional conflicts of interest that had to be ironed out, and it was not difficult: Milano and his colleagues knew many of the CIA men from earlier days. The new CIA officers were often old hands who had served in Army Intelligence during the war. But in general the two institutions regarded each other warily: the Army side thought the CIA rather snobbish and resented being looked down on. Milano and his friends, on the other hand, after their much longer experience in intelligence in postwar Europe, tended to look on the CIA agents as pussycats—the Army men were the real tigers.

On one occasion Milano fell afoul of James Jesus Angleton, the Agency's counterintelligence chief and one of its most celebrated figures. Once again, Milano had been exceeding his authority, this time over a possible double agent. The CIC chief in Vienna told him that the Soviets had approached a U.S. Air Force officer to ask him to spy for the Soviet Union in exchange for money. The officer had immediately reported the matter to the CIC. Milano met the two men and urged them to accept the Soviet offer. The double agent would be supplied with false information to pass on to his Soviet case officer. Milano wanted to see how the KGB handled its agents and also thought it an excellent occasion to feed the KGB with inaccurate technical information that might cause Soviet scientists and technicians great trouble. At the very least, it might lead to a considerable waste of time in Soviet laboratories.

The problem with this enterprising project was that Milano and his colleagues had no experience in running double agents. They had some idea of the basic ground rules, including the principle that the agent must never be given the misinformation directly. He must be allowed to steal it, in a convincing manner, so that he could account for every detail when asked by his Russian case officers. The Air Force officer agreed with Milano's proposal, and a first package of misinformation was prepared. The agent was then allowed to steal it, and he submitted it to his Soviet contact. Milano, thoroughly pleased with himself, prepared a report on the case and sent it off to the Pentagon.

Within a week he got his reply. The Pentagon had passed his report on to the CIA, which was furious at his initiative. Angleton himself would be in Geneva shortly, and Milano and the CIC chief in Vienna were to meet him there to be informed of his objections. Milano and Hancock drove to Geneva to make the rendezvous, which was at one of the hotels in the city, and had just sat down to dinner when Angleton appeared.

Milano had met him once before, during the war. They had both been at Caserta, which had for a time been Allied Military Headquarters in Italy and was the center of intelligence work. Angleton had then been working with the OSS, while Milano had been with Army Intelligence. They had met by chance in the bar of the Allied Headquarters, which was then housed in the royal palace, and had talked together for an hour or so. Milano had not been impressed. The man was clearly a highly competent intelligence officer, but Milano had thought him a self-satisfied snob. Now he had reappeared, clothed in all the authority of the Central Intelligence Agency, to reprimand Milano for his temerity.

He declined the offer to dine with the two young men. He said that he had another engagement. Instead, he sat down for twenty minutes and lectured them sternly on the need for Washington to control all double agents, particularly the information sent to the unsuspecting Soviets. Low-level officers, like Milano, could not be allowed to judge for themselves what was appropriate or inappropriate. Such things had to be coordinated in Washington with various agencies. In future, he said, Milano would please leave such matters to the CIA. Then he got up and left.

Milano was suitably chastened. Angleton was right. If the Americans were running double agents, it was at the least necessary that each agent's story should conform with those of other agents, or the KGB would deduce that they were all fake. Running double agents, what the British in World War II called the "double-cross system," was a difficult, complicated task, requiring a whole staff of specialists and a coordinated effort. The CIA then took over the case of the Air Force officer, and Milano heard no more about it.

Jim Milano's man in Vienna was Major Peter Chambers. He was one of those colorful eccentrics who thrive in the stimulating and exciting conditions of wars, open or covert, but are less well suited to the piping times of peace. Chambers was a cavalryman who chewed tobacco, swore ceaselessly, and had no time at all for the protocol and discipline of military headquarters. He came from a wealthy New York family that had made its money in sugar plantations and refineries in Cuba. Pete Chambers had grown up in the exclusive community of the very rich on the north shore of Long Island. It had not been to his taste. He had gone first to the New York Military Academy (not to be confused with West Point) and then to Yale University.

He had abandoned his studies after two years and had set out to see the world without leaving a forwarding address. His family had called in the services of a private detective, who had finally caught up with him driving a dogsled in the Yukon. He had unwillingly returned to New York and had then informed his parents that he had decided to be an opera singer. He had been sent to study music in Paris for the next six years, and, although he had never made a career as a tenor, he had lived happily in that city at his father's expense. He had married an American diplomat's daughter, who had divorced him after two years. When his father had died in 1938 and his will had been opened, it had been found to contain nothing for Pete except a note that it was time for him to start working for a living. The allowance had abruptly come to an end, and Chambers had returned to the United States to join the U.S. cavalry as a private. His family connections had won him admission to the Cavalry Officer Candidate School at Fort Riley, Kansas, whence he had graduated a second lieutenant at the age of thirty-two. He had been one of the oldest lieutenants in the U.S. Army, but his timing had been excellent. The war had come, and he had served with distinction as an intelligence officer, ending as a major. He had been on General Mark Clark's intelligence staff in Italy and had arrived in Vienna with the general in the summer of 1945.

He was a tall, commanding figure with bushy eyebrows, a crew cut, riding boots, and breeches—and he carried a riding crop at all times. He looked the caricature of the cavalry officer, the sort of man who would have ridden with Ney at Waterloo or with the Light Brigade at Balaclava. In reality, he was a subtle, inventive intelligence officer, particularly skilled at managing and manipulating his agents. He was a brilliant linguist and completely at home in the netherworld of Viennese intrigue and suspicion. However, he was quite unsuited to the politics and posturing of Army Headquarters.

The trouble was that, as an intelligence officer, he was constrained by the regulation chain of command to report to Lieutenant Colonel Joseph McCray, who was executive officer to Colonel Charles Bixell, who, in turn, was chief of staff to the G-2, General Thomas Hickey. This was the usual, tidy, hierarchical arrangement of all large organizations, including the Army, but unfortunately McCray and Chambers were oil and water. McCray was the pure West Point man, all spit and polish, and believed that every rule and regulation was sacred and should be followed at all times. He knew nothing of the gray, confusing world of intelligence operations and found constant cause for complaint at Chambers's unorthodox procedures. Chambers, on the other hand, was always on the brink of being court-martialed for insubordination: he could see no reason why he should have to report to anyone so indifferent to intelligence questions as Colonel McCray. Their conflict paralyzed the Vienna intelligence operations until Bixell cut the knot by transferring Chambers's operations from his own direct command to Milano's in Salzburg. Milano would supervise him and then report the fruits of his endeavors to Bixell—without disturbing him, or his executive officer, with the messy details of espionage, deceit, and the entrapment of unwary Soviet soldiers.

The only problem Milano met with Chambers was anti-Semitism: he once expressed horror at the prospect of working with a senior agent in Vienna, Karl Brewer, a Viennese Jew who had escaped to the United States at the time of the *Anschluss* and had returned as an intelligence officer seven years later. (Henry Kissinger had followed the same path from Fürth, in western Germany.) Milano had to assert himself very firmly to bring Chambers into line.

Over the years, Chambers ran a series of networks in Vienna. The first, and most enjoyable, was a riding stable that he christened Operation Horsefeathers and that was put into jeopardy by the Rover Boys (see Chapter 16). Chambers was a cavalryman, and, when the dust settled after the war and he found himself in Vienna, he went looking for horses to ride. He discovered a stable run by a former Austrian cavalryman, near the Prater, the big amusement park in east Vienna in the Soviet zone. The stable had five horses, and the owner, a retired major, hired them out to Soviet officers and the occasional American. He also had a couple of French customers.

Chambers started patronizing the stables and would ride around Vienna with the major. He soon discovered that the business was barely surviving and that its owner would be most willing to accept a subsidy in exchange for performing special services. Within a year the riding stables had become a prosperous operation with several employees and many horses. They attracted many more Russian officers, though Major Chambers himself discreetly stopped riding there regularly. As the Rover Boys episode demonstrated, the Soviets were suspicious but were never able to prove anything, and the fact that Soviet officers were still allowed to ride there suggested that the major had succeeded in covering his tracks. Operation Horsefeathers was one of the most productive American intelligence schemes, producing a steady stream of defectors. Since most of them were officers, the information they provided was particularly valuable.

Chambers's second network was the simplest. He had a girlfriend, Sonya, whose mother and aunt worked as cleaning women at the Soviet Army Headquarters in Vienna. They proved only too willing to collaborate with the Americans, for a fee. Indeed, they recruited two other cleaning women, and the four collected all the wastepaper in the Soviet wastebaskets and turned them over to Sonya. Chambers and a team of interpreters then spent a few hours every morning going through the papers. Perhaps the Russians had never heard of shredders, or perhaps they trusted the anonymous Austrian women who cleaned their offices every night with true Teutonic zeal, leaving them spotless and tidy, however much Slavic disorder had been created there. In any event, it was a major breach of Soviet security. Chambers called it Operation Paperchase and claimed many an intelligence coup. The Russians locked their important papers in safes, out of the reach of Sonya's friends and relatives, and in any case Chambers had no wish to endanger them by asking them to steal papers. The rubbish was treasure enough. Soviet officers would draft reports and memoranda, letters and notes, they would annotate and correct them, have them retyped in clean copies to put into the safes—and then tear up the drafts and drop them in the wastebaskets. American Intelligence learned many a secret from this Soviet improvidence.

Chambers's third operation was known as Claptrap. It was the least orthodox, and probably the most effective, of all intelligence operations in Austria. Its very name was anathema to the likes of Colonel McCray: everyone in the army used the term "clap" to designate venereal diseases, but to use it in official documents, even top secret ones, was a vulgarism that offended McCray's every sensibility. That, of course, was a further example of Chambers's deliberate insubordination or determination to needle his superiors. The code name was precise and expressive, as well as being a vulgar joke. It was a scheme for entrapping Soviet soldiers who had the misfortune to become infected by the Austrian ladies and persuading them to betray the Red Army's secrets in exchange for a cure for their afflictions.

Chambers had discovered a young Bulgarian doctor who had
studied medicine in Vienna during the war and had wisely decided
to stay in Austria at the end of hostilities rather than return home.
He had opened a clinic for venereal diseases in Wiener Neustadt,
south of the capital, in the Soviet zone. He had a constant stream of
Soviet officers and soldiers among his patients, but he had to act discreetly: catching a venereal disease was a court-martial offense in
the Red Army. He could not advertise his services. The existence of
the clinic and the fact that it could offer help to suffering soldiers
was a secret spread by word of mouth in the Red Army. What the
Russian soldiers did not know was the source of the Bulgarian doctor's success: Major Chambers had access to a supply of penicillin in
the U.S. military hospital in Vienna and passed it on to the doctor.
The drug was the most effective way of treating gonorrhea, syphilis,
and less dangerous diseases, and the patients at the clinic were suitably grateful. The doctor and his drugs saved them not only an
unpleasant disease but the probability of being summarily shipped
back to the Soviet Union.

Chambers had given the doctor a camera, with which he managed to photograph documents that his patients had with them and
left in waiting rooms while they were being treated. Much more
important, once he had won the confidence of his patients by
promising to cure them, he was able to learn many important details
of their units and their activities. The doctor spoke excellent Russian
and met Chambers once a week to discuss what line of questioning
he might most usefully follow. Chambers, of course, made sure that
the doctor understood the need for tact. His questioning had to be
casual, elliptical, indirect. Chambers was at his best in suggesting a
line of unthreatening questions that would lead young, worried
Soviet soldiers to unburden themselves.

Best of all, some of the doctor's patients, particularly those who
were due to be sent home, could be persuaded to defect. A number
of defectors recruited in this way later found their way down the Rat
Line to South America. One of the most important was a major who
had been cured of gonorrhea and who himself raised the possibility
of defecting. The Bulgarian doctor passed on the suggestion to
Chambers, who treated the matter with great care: it was possible
that the major was a double agent, sent by the KGB to follow the
trail of defectors. If he were a Soviet agent and were accepted by the
operations staff, he would not only expose the doctor and Operation
Claptrap but would then find out all about American debriefing procedures in the Salzburg area, as well as the Rat Line.

Chambers's solution to the problem was to send one of his
Austrian agents to investigate the major. He found him billeted with
an elderly Austrian lady, a woman in her sixties who was not merely

anti-Communist but a secret royalist. She remained nostalgic for the golden days of the Hapsburgs. She spoke highly of the major, saying that he was an honest, interesting man who was taking lessons in German. Chambers promptly recruited her to keep an eye on the major and, after several weeks, concluded that he was perfectly genuine. The Bulgarian doctor was then told that he could tell the major that, if he were ready to desert to the West, arrangements would be made to get him to safety and then out of the country to start a new life in South America.

The climax of that operation came when the major presented himself to his new American contact, as arranged—and brought his Austrian housekeeper with him. He told the astonished Chambers that he was worried about her security if he left her behind in the heart of the Soviet zone. Milano had to make hasty inquiries among American military families in Salzburg to find one who needed a housekeeper. It was not difficult: the Russian recommended her highly.

In 1949, the Bulgarian doctor told Chambers that he wanted to leave. He had a thriving practice at Wiener Neustadt and had directed a steady stream of Soviet defectors to Pete Chambers, but now he was getting nervous. He assumed that sooner or later the KGB would make the connection between the defectors and their medical history and come looking for him. Besides, he had acquired an Austrian wife, they had a one-year-old child, and he had to consider their safety. Chambers came to Milano, therefore, and asked if he could arrange a passage out of Austria for the doctor and his family on the Rat Line.

The doctor's request did not surprise Milano or his colleagues. Indeed it had been obvious for several months that Operation Claptrap would have to be closed down one day, perhaps suddenly. In the event, the doctor preferred an orderly retreat, before the KGB came visiting, and Chambers had come to arrange it.

Milano was sympathetic and determined—on one condition. "Not on the Rat Line," he said. "That's for special cases—and anyway, it's very expensive. The three of them would cost us $4,500 just for the visas, and while he certainly deserves a bonus, he'd probably prefer it cash on the barrelhead.

"Besides, there will be no trouble getting him a regular refugee visa. He's a genuine Bulgarian and his papers are all in order, so we don't have to make up a name and identity for him. There are openings for skilled doctors all over the world. I'm sure we can get him admitted somewhere on a regular visa, if we can get him out of Wiener Neustadt safely. Why don't you ask Park Hancock to see to it? All he needs is to load them into a car and bring them over one afternoon. Then bring them on to Salzburg."

Then Chambers made an additional request: "The good lady has all her family treasures. Silver, porcelain, linen, stuff like that. She wants to take them all with her and asks if you can arrange it."

"Absolutely not. No excess baggage. We never promised to ship household goods around the world for anybody. She'll have to pack whatever she wants into the car, and that's it. She must leave the rest behind.

"I'll get Dominic to set to work getting the doctor a refugee visa. I don't suppose there will be much trouble."

Indeed, things worked out well. Del Greco had no difficulty in finding a South American country, in this case Colombia, to take a highly qualified doctor and his family. The three were picked up discreetly from Wiener Neustadt by one of Park Hancock's agents and driven first to Vienna and then to Salzburg—the wife grumbling the while about having to leave so many of her possessions behind. The doctor, however, was pleased at his bonus. He had earned it. He had recruited some of the most productive of all Soviet defectors and agents, and Milano was relieved that he had been extracted from the Soviet zone with so little trouble. No doubt he prospered in Colombia.

11

Operation Backfire

In February 1948, Milano's office was warned that the Communists in Czechoslovakia were planning a coup against the government. The warning came from the French intelligence service, but through an unorthodox route, and—perhaps for that reason—it was ignored. The source was the exuberant and exotic Pete Chambers, who heard the news from a friend he had made in his Bohemian days in Paris before the war, when he was studying music in the hope of becoming an opera star. In Paris, he had acquired an American wife and many friends, one of them a lieutenant in the French army.

His time in Paris had been a crucial period in his life, quite apart from his brief marriage, and he cherished the memories. In the interval between his departure from France in 1938 and the German occupation in June 1940, he had continued to correspond with his French friend and with his ex-wife. When Paris was at last liberated four years later, in August 1944, Chambers had been with the U.S. Army in Italy. He had seized the first opportunity that offered to return to France to find out what had happened to them. His ex-wife had survived, with difficulty. Chambers had been able to help her in recovering her apartment. She had been turned out of it by supporters of the Vichy collaborationist regime, and, like many people all over liberated Europe, she needed some muscle to get it back. In France, that meant either the Resistance or the Americans: the legal procedure for evicting unwanted tenants would have taken years. Chambers solved the problem for her by arriving at the place with two or three large, well-armed GIs. The *collabos* left without arguing.

Chambers's friend, who was a lieutenant in the French Army, had escaped to North Africa when the Germans had occupied France and had joined the Free French, General Charles de Gaulle's resistance movement. He had returned home in triumph with the general when the French Army had been given the honor of driving the Germans out of the capital. Chambers and he had a happy reunion. They were struck by a coincidence: both had become intelligence officers, Chambers in the U.S. Army, his friend in the Deuxième Bureau of the French Army. After the war, when Chambers was stationed in Vienna, his friend came to visit him almost every month. The two officers were most discreet, but Chambers deduced immediately that the Frenchman was concerned with an intelligence network that his service was running in Czechoslovakia.

In theory, that country was still democratic. There was a coalition government in which the Communists were the dominant partners, but they did not rule uncontested, as their comrades in Poland and Hungary did. They were relentlessly pushing their strength in every corner of the administration, particularly the police and the armed forces. The French, like other Western governments, were in constant contact with the democratic ministers, who could see the noose tightening around their necks and were increasingly desperate at their situation. The French intelligence network concerned itself with the Communists and their partners, the Social Democrats. Thus Chambers paid particular attention when his friend, who was in Vienna on one of his regular visits, told him that the Communists, on orders from Stalin, intended to eliminate the democrats from the Czechoslovak government within two weeks.

The plan was very simple. The Communist minister of the interior, Václav Nosek, intended to dismiss the last senior police officers who were not Communists. The Party would then control all the levers of power in Prague. The armed forces were already neutralized: the minister of defense was the fellow-traveling General Ludvík Svoboda, who lived to betray his country to the Russians a second time, in 1968. If the democrats resisted, they would be crushed. If they did not resist, they would be crushed all the more easily. The Party had planned everything most carefully, directed by Valerian Zorin, a special adviser Stalin had sent to Prague to help them. The French officer had already passed the information back to Paris. He suggested that Chambers should alert Washington.

The next morning, Chambers went to see Milano, who was in Vienna on one of his regular visits. Milano told him to report at once to the director of intelligence at Army Headquarters and to prepare a report to be sent back to the Pentagon. The director listened to Chambers's explanation of the situation and his evaluation of his source. He examined the draft report, ordered a few minor changes, and sent it off to Washington immediately. He then told Chambers to pay a visit to the CIA office in Vienna and repeat his story there. Chambers went to see the head of station and gave a careful report of everything he had been told. The station chief listened politely and asked him several questions about the reliability of his source. Chambers assumed that he would pass the information on to his own headquarters, but he never learned if this had been done.

Meanwhile, Milano called his old friend Butch Groves, who was a senior British intelligence officer, and arranged to have a drink with him at the Sacher Hotel that evening. Groves's official position was that of a civilian working for British Army Intelligence in Graz and Vienna, in an unspecified capacity. Milano was convinced that he was, in fact, a senior officer with MI6. The two men had known each other since they had met in Italy during the war and used to see each other regularly in Austria. Groves's office was in Graz, where the British forces were based, but he often went to the capital, as did Milano himself. Groves was in his mid-thirties, which seemed a great age to Milano at the time, and the younger man respected his abilities and experience in intelligence matters and often consulted him about the techniques of espionage and intelligence.

This time, they talked about Czechoslovakia. Groves knew something about Chambers and was not impressed. He had heard about Operation Horsefeathers. He may also have heard of some of Chambers's other operations, such as Operation Claptrap. Although these two affairs had been highly successful, Groves did not trust Chambers. He told Milano he thought him "odd at best, kooky at worst." When Milano told him about the reported coup being planned in Prague, he thanked him for the tip but questioned Milano closely about Chambers's reliability and his source. The British were notoriously dismissive of the French, and a French report passed on by a kooky American was not likely to be taken very seriously. Milano assured Groves that he had every confidence in Chambers and that he believed him when he vouched for his French friend. He had been one of two French officers who had parachuted to General von Vietinghoff's headquarters when the Germans in Italy had surrendered shortly before the end of the war. Milano did his best but left the meeting with the impression that he had failed to convince Groves of the seriousness of the warning. All the same, he was sure Groves would pass on the news to London.

There was no follow-up. Neither the CIA, the Pentagon, nor the British came back to ask for any clarification or to demand further information. The warning was apparently ignored—or perhaps the event had already been anticipated by the various governments and an additional report, however persuasive, made no difference. Two weeks later, just as the Frenchman's source had predicted, Václav Nosek dismissed eight non-Communist police chiefs. The cabinet ordered their reinstatement, and the minister ignored the order. The democratic ministers protested vigorously at this act of flagrant illegality—and, in a moment of collective folly, resigned from the government. The president was Eduard Beneš, a democrat who had allied himself with Stalin during the war, partly because he had been betrayed by the British and French at Munich in 1938. He had not been able to stand up to Neville Chamberlain, Edouard Daladier, and Hitler. When the next crisis came just ten years later, he failed once again. He told the democratic ministers that he would not accept their resignation and would instead use the crisis to form a new government, excluding the Communists. But the Communists were ready and mobilized. A general strike was called for February 24, and Prague was flooded with Communist-led workers from the factories. There were huge, violent demonstrations, and the police and army did nothing to protect the democratic parties, their leaders, and their headquarters. Communists occupied the rival parties' buildings and seized newspapers and radio stations. It was a classic coup, and Beneš, after several days of vacillation, capitulated. He accepted the resignations and replaced the departing democrats with Communists and fellow travelers. The Communists had won and they soon imposed Stalinist totalitarianism upon the country.

It is not at all clear that even if the warning had been taken seriously, the result would have been any different. What could the Americans, the British, and the French have done? The Communists were the strongest party in Czechoslovakia, and the democratic parties lacked the will to confront them—and any force they could rely on. Although there were no Soviet troops in Czechoslovakia, the army was under Communist control, or at least neutralized by its commanders. All the same, the examples of Greece, France, and Italy show that determined democratic parties—in France the Socialists and in Greece and Italy the Christian Democrats—could face down the Communists if they had the courage—and the backing of the United States. Perhaps if the democrats in Czechoslovakia had been warned in advance and assured of unconditional American and Allied support, they would have shown more resolve. In the event, they did not resist seriously, and a long nightmare began that did not end until 1989.

Milano always got on well with the French in Austria. His contact was a French officer, Captain Muti Gillette, who was on the intelligence staff of the French headquarters in Vienna. Gillette was a close friend of Karl Brewer, one of Milano's agents in Vienna, and the three men spent one sentimental Christmas Eve together in the city. Another useful contact was the secretary of the French commanding general. She was an Austrian girl from Innsbruck who had a boyfriend in Salzburg, and every time she went to visit him or passed through Salzburg on her way to visit her family, Milano's staff always arranged for her to stay at the Österreicher Hof, the best hotel in town, at their expense. She proved a most useful and cooperative contact in French headquarters.

That was not the only indirect approach Milano used to maintain contact with Allied authorities. Shortly after he and his colleagues set themselves up in Salzburg, the Italian government opened a mission there. Its chief function was to help the repatriation of the thousands of Italians who had been left stranded in Austria at the end of the war or who passed through the country from Central Europe. Late in the war, after the Allies occupied southern Italy and Mussolini set up a Fascist republic in the North that was wholly dependent on the Germans, thousands of Italians were sent to Germany to work for the Todt organization. That was the institution that built munitions factories and fortifications all across Europe—including the Atlantic Wall. Milano and his assistant, Dominic Del Greco, both being Italian Americans, helped the Italians set up their office. They supplied gasoline, C rations, cigarettes, and other necessities, on the self-interested calculation that the head of the office, Giorgio Smokvina, an Italian despite his name, might be useful later. Indeed, after a year in Salzburg, he became the first Italian consul there and was most helpful over the years in supplying Italian visas to the clients of the Rat Line.

Of all Allied organizations, the American intelligence services in Austria collaborated most closely with the British. Those two services kept up the closest possible relations during the war and afterward, until a series of British traitors absconded to Moscow. At one point, the most important of those secret spies, Kim Philby, was head of British intelligence in Washington and the closest confidant of James Jesus Angleton, the CIA's head of counterintelligence. These subterranean struggles of moles and defectors never troubled the CIC in Austria, at least not in Jim Milano's day. He never had any doubt of the loyalty of his British colleagues, and, so far as is known, that confidence was justified. The Americans in Salzburg kept their most private operations, including the Rat Line, to themselves. Even so, if there had been a British mole in Austria, he might easily have discovered enough to ensure a nasty reception for escaping Soviet defectors in South America.

Milano himself had a particularly close relationship with the British, starting with his earliest days in intelligence in North Africa. He had been adjutant to the 7769th MIS battalion when it had gone ashore at Fedala, Morocco, in November 1942 as part of Operation Torch, the Allied attack on French North Africa. A British officer, Lieutenant Colonel Charles Norman Cavendish Boyle, had been seconded from British Intelligence to take command in January, to direct the unit's training program. Boyle was the very model of a British colonel: tall, thin, with white hair and a mustache. He could have been played by Alec Guinness. He was a regular officer who had gone straight from Sandhurst to the trenches in 1914. He had been wounded twice in World War I and had served in India between the wars. In 1939, despite all the strings he could pull and all the pleas he could offer, he had been judged too old and medically unfit to command an infantry battalion and had been given an intelligence posting instead. In due course, he had been sent to train a fledgling American intelligence unit, composed of men who had all the qualifications but none of the training they needed. It is a great tribute to him that he succeeded so well, and particularly that his American subordinates remember him with much affection.

One incident showed the man's style. Eight Americans had gone on a boar hunt in the hills around their base and returned empty-handed. On the way, they passed a Moroccan chicken farm and helped themselves to a number of birds. It was a common enough military tactic, a means of supplementing the depressing diet served in the battalion mess hall. However, the Moroccans did not take kindly to being robbed and protested to Colonel Boyle. He summoned the battalion in formation and announced that he would not tolerate such nonsense in the future. Then he walked along the ranks and glared each man in the eye, one after the other, mustache bristling, demanding of each of them: "Do you understand me?" In every case, the intimidated GI replied, "Yes, sir." After that, he had no trouble from his command.

He turned the unit over to his American second-in-command at the end of 1943 and returned to the British army. Milano met him again a year later, when Boyle was a lecturer at an intelligence course organized by the British army at Castellammare di Stabia, near Sorrento, on the Bay of Naples. The course was designed to prepare Allied intelligence officers for their duties in the occupation of Austria: Milano's unit had already been designated for that task. The course dealt with such matters as war criminals and what to do with them, the Nazi Party, paramilitary organizations in Austria, displaced persons, and the history, geography, and politics of the country. It was a well-organized, well-run course, and the instructors, including Boyle, were on top of their subjects. Clearly, a lot of work had gone into preparations for the occupation, well before the end of the war. Half the students attending the course were British and half American, and the friendships that were formed at Castellammare proved invaluable in later years, when the graduates had to work together.

Milano moved to Caserta the following month, where detailed planning for the occupation was being done by the Armed Forces Headquarters intelligence staff. His own task was to select the location where each of the U.S. intelligence operations would be based and decide on its strength. Those decisions depended upon a clear definition of their mission. At Caserta, too, he worked closely with the British officers who were getting ready to administer their zone in Austria and to carry out all the multifarious intelligence tasks that would be required. The planning group for the U.S. and British occupation of Austria was headed by a British officer, Colonel Peter Lovegrove, and Milano worked closely with him.

The day after the war in Italy ended, there was a final session of the Allied Austrian planning staff in Caserta, under the supervision of Colonel Lovegrove. The last details were settled, and Milano then prepared himself for the drive over the Brenner Pass into Austria. As the meeting broke up, Boyle turned to Milano and told him that he could expect some recognition from the British government for all his work in Italy. He did not elaborate, and Milano was too astonished to ask just what he meant.

Charles Boyle became one of the senior British intelligence officers in Austria, dealing with censorship of mail and telephone and telegraphic communications. Milano met him regularly, as he did the other senior British officers in Graz, where the British had their Austrian headquarters. He met Boyle every month in Vienna, where they were both on the Quadripartite Censorship Committee, together with French and Russian officers. The committee may not have done much business, but it was one of the institutions where Western and Soviet officials could meet without too much hostility. Milano usually found that he agreed with the British most of the time, with the French some of the time, and with the Russians never.

In some cases, the British and American intelligence communities continued to work as a single organization. In 1948, the American CIC and the British Field Security Service established a joint interrogation center in Trieste. It had two American and two British officers, and it dealt with the constant flow of refugees that passed through the city. Milano and his staff were in constant touch with that center.

Boyle was Milano's contact on matters of censorship, Butch Groves on positive intelligence, and Archie Morehouse on counterintelligence. Apart from the usual business meetings, he used to meet the three separately or together, often for dinner, and discuss hypothetical intelligence operations. More often than not, these were real operations that they all preferred to treat as mythical. The book of rules, after all, strictly forbade any mention of American operations, even to the closest allies, without specific authority from on high. Milano found the three British officers extremely useful: their own experience and judgment, and the fact that they were not directly involved in any particular operation, gave their opinions and advice great weight.

It was, no doubt, a two-way street, and the British certainly derived great benefit from their contacts with the Americans. They had paid in advance: about two months after the end of the war, Milano received a letter from the British Embassy in Washington, informing him that he had been awarded the Order of the British Empire. The Order, divided into various ranks, is the chief means by which the British government recognizes outstanding service by ordinary British citizens—and a few foreigners. He has been James Milano, OBE, ever since.

On June 24, 1948, the Soviet High Command in Germany abruptly closed all Western ground access to Berlin. All trains were stopped at the border, the three roads leading across East Germany to Berlin were closed "for repair," and so were the canals. Only air traffic continued: Stalin never imagined that the Western Allies could supply a huge city entirely by air. It was the first, and perhaps the most serious, of the great crises of the cold war. Czechoslovakia had fallen to communism in February, and the Communist parties of Italy and France were planning to follow their Czech comrades' example. The last non-Communist parties in Eastern Europe had been suppressed, though Tito, in Yugoslavia, had defied Stalin: he was expelled from the Cominform on June 28, four days after the Berlin Blockade began. Another turning point in history occurred at the same time: the British informed Washington that they could no longer be responsible for the security of Greece and Turkey. The civil war in Greece was reaching its climax, and the government could defeat the Communists only with Western help, which would now have to be provided by the United States. It was a moment that tested American resolve to the full. President Truman, who was facing a difficult election campaign that fall, had to meet the Soviet challenge head on or risk losing all Europe to the Communists.

These great events were immediately felt in Austria. The American command in Vienna hastily moved to Salzburg, in case the Russians decided to isolate the capital of Austria as they had Berlin. The Western powers, led by the United States, were starting an airlift to keep that city alive, and, if the same operation were needed in Austria, it was obviously essential that the operational commanders of the American forces there and all their support staff should be located in the American zone, not isolated and at the Soviets' mercy in Vienna under siege. The commanding general, General Geoffrey Keyes, his chief of staff, General Thomas Hickey, and a select few remained in Vienna: they could always be flown out in an afternoon. The political staff, those concerned with monitoring Austrian political developments, and the members of the various quadripartite commissions that administered Austria also remained. But the bulk of the headquarters staff moved to Salzburg. In the event, Stalin left

Vienna alone, concentrating his efforts on Berlin. But in the summer and autumn of 1948, tensions were rising to fever pitch, and the pressures on the intelligence services to provide the most up-to-date information were at a peak.

The telephone lines from Milano's offices in Salzburg to army headquarters in Vienna ran through the Soviet zone, and it was quite certain that every call was monitored by the KGB. Urgent messages, therefore, had to be sent in code by telegraph, a lengthy, laborious process in those days—or a more creative approach could be used. On a warm day in October, 1948, Milano called General Hickey's aide-de-camp, Captain William Williams, on the open line with the following message:

"Bill, I am alerting you to a situation. The message will not be repeated. The message is 'Horace Greeley/Amelia Earhart.'" Then he hung up.

He thus announced one of the most dramatic public episodes of the intelligence battles of the early cold war. It was dubbed Operation Backfire by the intelligence agencies. Colonel Williams had no difficulty in understanding Milano's message, which must have remained unintelligible to the listening Soviet agents. Greeley was the man who advised "Go west, young man, go west" and Amelia Earhart was the famous pilot who had crashed in the Pacific. Williams informed the chief of staff immediately that a Soviet plane had fled the East and landed at an American base in Austria. The news was sent at once to U.S. Air Force Headquarters in Weisbaden, Germany, and to the Pentagon, and all three headquarters scrambled to prepare themselves. The new arrival was a Tu-21 medium bomber with a crew of three. It had flown eight hundred miles from western Russia, evading the Soviet air force and ground stations, and had landed at Horshing Air Force Base, a former Luftwaffe facility near Wels in western Austria. The pilot, copilot, and gunner had immediately been taken into custody by the local CIC, and the plane had hastily been towed into a hangar, out of sight of inquisitive agents.

The defection could not be kept secret. It would have to be announced, and then the Soviet Union would demand the return of the plane and its crew. But Milano's impromptu code gave his colleagues a head start of a day or two to prepare themselves for the inevitable confrontation. This was the second air defection that year. In the spring, a fighter pilot had flown his MiG to a Western base in Turkey. The Soviet government then announced that the sentence for desertion with an aircraft was twenty-five years in the gulag. If the pilot did not return, his family would pay the penalty.

Milano and his staff had no need to make long-term preparations, with safe houses in the mountains and secret interrogations for the defectors, let alone to send them down the Rat Line to South America. These men were quite different from the deserters who were seduced by Milano's agents or who made their surreptitious way across the lines to an American post in Austria and had to be hidden and protected until they could be smuggled to safety. The air-crew's arrival would be formally announced, with much fanfare, and they would be treated as heroes. Unlike the others, they would be allowed to settle in the United States and to make new lives for themselves under their own names, or at any rate with only minimal concealment. This was at the height of the Berlin Airlift and was a major news story and a propaganda coup; it was to be played out for all it was worth. Furthermore, from an intelligence point of view, the three men were all of the greatest interest. They could report on the state of morale of the Soviet air force and describe conditions in bases and among units far from the front lines in Central Europe. It was not often that Army Intelligence found a direct window into the heart of Soviet forces, and the defectors could give concrete evidence as to whether or not the Soviets were preparing an onslaught against the West.

The crew were first kept in a safe house in Linz. They were guarded around the clock and left to themselves while the American commands in Vienna and Germany prepared themselves and awaited orders from Washington. Milano discussed the situation with the head of the CIC station in Linz, Tom Lucid. Milano told him he would stay clear of the area, which would be crawling with KGB agents. He had no wish to be recognized. On the other hand, he needed to be kept constantly informed, on a daily or even hourly basis, of what was happening to the three Russians. Over the next few days Lucid's people reported that the three men were constantly quarreling, drinking heavily, and frightened that they were going to be returned to the Soviet Union. The two pilots had been overheard discussing committing suicide if that happened. When these reports were brought to him, Milano had the men moved to a more congenial house. He had the use of the country estate at Steyr belonging to the founder of the automobile company of that name. It was a big house surrounded by a beautiful park, where the defectors could walk and enjoy themselves until their fate was decided. It was a far better place for them than the claustrophobic atmosphere of a small, heavily guarded house in a suburb of Linz.

A week after their spectacular defection, orders came from Vienna that the three men were to be interviewed by an American-Soviet commission that would convene the next day at the air base where they had landed. The three would be asked whether they wished to remain in the West or return to the Soviet Union. It would be a formal occasion, and they were all told in advance what to expect. They were assured that if they wanted to stay, they would be resettled in the United States, a promise that comforted them greatly. On the day of the meeting, they were taken from their estate in the country to Horshing Air Force Base, accompanied by a CIC escort, including one who spoke fluent Russian. They then had to wait more than two hours while the Americans and Russians on the commission argued over the arrangements: How would the two delegations sit, how would the three men appear, what sort of questions could they be asked?

After prolonged argument, it was decided that the commission should consist of an American colonel, a Russian major, two secretaries, and two interpreters. The Russians sat at a small table on one side of the room, the Americans at another table opposite them. Each member of the air crew was to be put in turn on a chair in front of them. The Russian major wore the uniform of an infantry regiment, but he was much smoother and more sophisticated than the usual Soviet officer. It was quite apparent that he was in the KGB.

When these matters were at last decided, the three airmen were brought in, one at a time, beginning with the copilot. The American colonel assured him that his choice would be respected: if he wanted to return to the Soviet Union, he could leave immediately and freely. If he decided to remain, the American government would settle him in the United States. The Russian then began his interrogation. He asked the man how he had come to fly to Austria. Might it not be that he had been lost, that bad weather conditions or faulty instruments had misled him and that his so-called defection had, in fact, been a trivial mistake? The copilot assured the commission that flying eight hundred miles due west from his air base had been no mistake: he and the pilot had decided to defect and had flown to Austria deliberately.

The Russian major, not the least put off by this, opened a second line of attack. He said that often soldiers and airmen get depressed. They become disturbed by transitory, unimportant difficulties with their comrades and superiors. In this case, the major insisted, if the copilot returned, the incident would be overlooked, and indeed the Soviet Motherland would be grateful and happy to receive her errant son back with open arms. The copilot flatly refused. He repeated that his decision was final and that he wanted to stay in the West. The discussion lasted forty minutes or more, until the American colonel declared that further argument would serve no useful purpose. The man was told that he could leave. He was escorted back through the waiting room, where he had time to whisper to the pilot to watch out for the Russian: "The bastard's definitely from the KGB."

Then it was the turn of the gunner, a sergeant. The American colonel once again laid out the conditions: The gunner could return

or stay. It was his choice. The man announced at once that he wanted to return. He had not been aware of the pilots' decision to defect.
He had been isolated from them in the gun turret and had known
nothing of their destination until the bomber was surrounded by
American troops when it landed. Nothing that had happened to him
since he had involuntarily arrived in Austria inclined him to stay in
the West: he just wanted to go home. The KGB major was all smiles.
The young Russian saluted the Americans smartly and was taken
away by Soviet military police. History does not record what became
of him, but this was Stalin's time and the height of the cold war, and
it is only too probable that he was arrested immediately. Paranoia
reigned, and anyone suspected of contact with the West was auto-
matically condemned. Tens of thousands of Soviet prisoners captured by the Germans during the war had been shipped to Siberia
immediately upon their liberation. The gunner was likely to be suspected of being a potential defector or, even worse, an American
spy. Perhaps he was lucky and was released in one of the general
amnesties that followed the mad dictator's death in 1953. Perhaps
he was shot.

Finally the pilot, Lieutenant Pyotr Pirogov, the leader of the defection, was brought into the room. Once again the American officer
explained his options, and then the KGB major turned on him. He
made no effort to smooth-talk the man, as he had with the copilot.
Presumably he had already concluded that the task was hopeless
and he was making the case for the record. The major demanded to
know how he had dared betray his trust, leading two other men on
such a dangerous adventure. Not only had he deserted the Soviet
Union, Mother Russia, which had nurtured him and trained him,
and whose armed forces had defeated German fascism in the most
terrible struggle in recorded history and were still standing guard
against all the dangers of Western imperialism and aggression; he
had betrayed his friends, his comrades, and his family. The Soviet
Union was stern but just. If he agreed to return, he would be treated
leniently. Pirogov was not impressed. He vigorously defended himself and his friend, the copilot. They had discussed deserting for
months before the occasion offered itself. They had decided to
escape from a country where all freedom was suppressed and the
regime ruled by fear alone. He had no intention of returning. He was
committed to the West and to freedom and gratefully accepted the
American offer to let him remain.

There were more rather heated exchanges between the two
Russians, and then the American colonel formally asked Pirogov if
he were determined to remain in the West. The pilot replied emphat-
ically that he was, and then he, too, was allowed to leave. As he was
getting up, the Russian interrogator remarked pleasantly that if he

should ever change his mind, the Soviet consul would be delighted to help him. Then he escaped, to be greeted with backslaps and cheers by the Americans waiting for him outside and the embraces of his copilot.

The Russians had another request. They wanted their plane back. It was still on the base: one reason the commission had not convened for a week had been to allow American mechanics to examine it closely. It was not a new model—indeed it was the standard Russian bomber used in World War II—but the experts of Air Force Intelligence always had something to learn. They could study the condition of the plane, measure the efficacy of the Soviet air force's maintenance schedules, and check on the standard of navigation equipment to be found on Soviet planes. They had taken the Tu-21 apart most carefully, ostensibly to prepare it for its return, and in the process had learned everything there was to know about it. Then they had put it together again. Its wings had been removed, and it was ready to be loaded into a trailer to be towed back to the nearest Soviet base.

The two pilots were then presented to the international press in a press conference at the air base. They did well for themselves under an intensive grilling from Western and Communist reporters alike. They explained why they had defected and described the long, anguished months of planning and their escape. They recounted their apparently routine departure, their flight across Soviet territory, their terror that they might be detected and shot down, their arrival in Austria. They vehemently denounced the Soviet system and gave many details of its cruelty and injustice.

From a Western propaganda point of view, the press conference was a great success. The defection and the pilots' accounts of conditions in the Soviet Union were broadcast around the world, confirming Western determination to resist Soviet aggression.

The two pilots spent several weeks in the care of the CIC, undergoing the careful debriefings that all Soviets were subjected to. Then they were sent off to their new lives in the United States. Three years later, Pirogov published his memoirs, *Why I Escaped.*

The West did not win every battle. Another incident at that time was a serious setback to the operations staff. A young Ukrainian officer, Nicholas Borosky, paymaster to a Soviet army unit based on the Danube in the Soviet zone, defected with his Austrian girlfriend, Karen Klaus, who had been employed as a secretary in his office. They were young and personable and had soon become friends. She was a devout Catholic and offered him a different set of values from the militant atheism he had learned at home. Finally, she persuaded him to attend an Easter-morning Mass in her local church. The following day, he told her that he wanted to defect and wanted her to go with him. She agreed, even though it would mean leaving her parents to the tender mercies of the Soviet occupation authorities.

Karen hid her suitcase in a barn behind her father's farmhouse, and, late in the evening of the following Saturday, Nicholas came to fetch her. They walked along the bank of the Danube, constantly in fear of meeting a Soviet patrol, but escaped undetected. They found a small boat at a local landing stage and rowed themselves across the river into the American zone. In the morning, when the villages came to life, they took a bus into Salzburg and sought out the American headquarters. The girl noticed that her lover paid their fares out of his suitcase, which appeared to contain a large sum of money. Borosky told her he had taken the money, 20,000 schillings, from his office safe. He did not consider it theft: as far as the Russians were concerned, the real crime was defection. Helping himself to the money was a trivial offense that would allow them to keep themselves for several months after they reached the West. Besides, he intended to tell the Americans immediately.

When they found the American headquarters in Salzburg, they asked for a German-speaking officer and told him their story. He summoned the local CIC representative, who in turn reported to Dominic Del Greco, telling him that the new arrival had apparently stolen a large sum of money from the Soviet forces. Dominic sent an urgent message to Jim Milano, who was out of town, that he should return at once to deal with a sudden emergency. He did not explain further.

When Milano got back to his office, he found that the Soviets had already reported the defection, claiming that Lieutenant Borosky was a thief. The Americans had admitted that they were holding him, and the Soviets had demanded that he be returned immediately. A CIC special agent, John Burkel, took the two fugitives to a safe house outside Salzburg, where he interrogated the young man thoroughly on the whole matter. He also asked for a first report on the condition of Soviet forces in the zone and whatever Borosky could tell him of their morale, equipment, and plans. Then he told the two to make themselves at home: they would be well cared for while their fate was decided.

Burkel knew the commanding general, Geoffrey Keyes, quite well. He was at the time staying in a hunting lodge that had once belonged to the Krupp family, at Bluhenbach, near Salzburg. It had been taken over by the U.S. Army for the use of the commanding general, and Keyes was there for the weekend. Burkel went to see him, to discover if there was any chance of keeping Borosky, debriefing him properly, and sending him to safety down the Rat Line. Keyes refused. This was not a case of a simple political defection. Borosky had stolen money, and the Allied High Command could not condone a theft. Burkel argued that if the man were sent back, the news would immediately be spread far and wide among Soviet troops in Austria and there would be no more defections, drying up an invaluable source of intelligence. The Soviets would obviously present Borosky's return as a great victory, as a sign that the Western powers would in future cooperate in punishing desertions from the Red Army. Keyes remained adamant. He admitted the strength of Burkel's argument but said his hands were tied. The regulations agreed by the four occupying powers left him no choice. This was not a deserter, like the two pilots who had flown to the West, seeking political asylum. The man was a thief and would have to be returned. As for Karen, she could stay.

When Jim Milano returned to Salzburg, he convened a meeting of the Rat Line support group to examine the situation. They concluded that there was no hope of changing General Keyes's mind. Lieutenant Borosky would be returned, and no doubt he would be shot. The Soviets would publicize the case among Soviet troops in Austria, Czechoslovakia, Hungary, and Germany, and there might be no more defections for a long time to come. The next day, Nicholas Borovsky was handed over to the Soviet Military Police at the Urfahr bridge across the Danube. Karen Klaus, devastated by the event, went to live with relatives in Vienna.

12

Tales of the Vienna Woods

For Jim Milano and the rest of the intelligence community, the Soviets were the enemy, and the most dangerous agents were in the KGB. Not only was the Soviet spy agency devoted to ferreting out the secrets of the CIC and the Western military establishment in general, it was also a highly efficient counterintelligence organization constantly on the watch to catch potential defectors and to unmask Milano's operations. The KGB was a dangerous, skilled, and completely ruthless agency, like a combination of the Nazi Gestapo, SS, and Abwehr. It was totally detestable, but sometimes its Western rivals were caught up with it in a sort of professional relationship that was part rivalry, part recognition that agents on both sides had many things in common. John le Carré's books are fiction, but there is a substratum of truth to his premise that George Smiley and Karla are brothers under the skin.

When Jim Milano took the *Mozart* to Vienna in the fall of 1947 to inform his superiors that the first shipment of visitors was about to leave down the Rat Line, he stayed, as he always did, at the Regina Hotel. It was a comfortable establishment of the second rank and had survived the war. Though rather shabby, it could provide the sort of accommodation and food that officers of an undemanding army of occupation might expect.

After dinner that evening, Milano went out for a walk around the Ringstrasse, the boulevard that encircles the center of Vienna. The main buildings of the Austrian government stand on the Ring, as does a series of grand hotels, places far nobler than the Regina, that the four occupying powers had taken for their own in 1945. The

Americans had set up their headquarters in the Bristol, the British in the Sacher, the Soviets, with no sense of irony, in the Imperial, and the French, of course, in the Hôtel de France. Milano walked along the Ring, smoking a cigar and heading in the general direction of the Imperial. The wide sidewalks of the avenue were filled with people out for an evening stroll, like Milano himself, and he passed many Allied and Soviet officers. Among them, walking alone toward Milano that balmy evening, was a Soviet officer, and as they approached each other Milano recognized him as Major Pyotr Poncerev, chief of military intelligence operations for the Soviet Armed Forces in Austria. The major and his assignment had been identified by Allied intelligence, a photograph had been obtained and circulated to senior Western intelligence officers, and Milano had no doubt about the identification.

Neither did Poncerev. As they approached, they looked each other in the eye, smiled, and stopped. "I believe I know you," said Jim Milano. "Good evening, Major Milano," the Soviet officer replied in excellent English.

It may have meant nothing that the two men should have encountered each other that evening. The Ring was a favorite promenade for all Vienna, and the various headquarters were within a mile or two of one another. Officers and men of the four armies met and mingled in the streets of Vienna all the time. All the same, Milano was instantly on the alert. He was about to launch his most ambitious and expensive intelligence operation, the Rat Line, and bumping into the head of Soviet intelligence operations, a senior KGB officer, a man who would go to any lengths to discover details of the operation, might not be a coincidence.

The two men chatted amiably enough, and Milano decided to hear what Major Poncerev had to say for himself. He suggested they adjourn to the bar of the Bristol Hotel, the American headquarters, for a drink. The Russian countered with an invitation to the Imperial. Milano, quite determined to keep out of the lions' den, remarked that the bar at the Bristol served excellent hors d'oeuvres and offered a wide selection of whiskeys. Major Poncerev was instantly persuaded. "I've never tried American whiskey," he said. "That's an excellent idea. Let's go to the Bristol."

Once they were installed in a comfortable stall in the Bristol's vast and splendid barroom, Milano introduced Poncerev to the taste of bourbon. The conversation soon moved from comparative alcohols to personal matters. Milano remarked that he had a file on Poncerev, who evidently had one on him, and suggested that they should fill in each other on the details of their life histories. They were not going to talk about their work, even in the most general way, but they could discuss their careers and perhaps exchange glimpses of each other's motivations.

Milano described his immigrant, Italian family, his youth in West Virginia, his progress through school and university, and the great hiatus in his life that had opened in 1941, when he had been put on active duty (he had been an officer in the reserves before Pearl Harbor). He had merely to say that he had been taken into Military Intelligence once he reached North Africa. He did not explain what that might have involved. Poncerev would know perfectly well the sort of work intelligence officers do in wartime, and, if he did not, Milano was not going to enlighten him. As for his subsequent career, even though Poncerev was clearly well informed, Milano was silent.

Poncerev was equally candid and equally circumspect: he told of his childhood and youth but offered no details at all of his career in the KGB. He had been born in Saint Petersburg during the First World War, when the city had been known as Petrograd. It had been rechristened because its original name had appeared too Germanic. In 1924, it had been renamed again as an imperishable memorial to Lenin. Poncerev barely remembered his parents. His father, a builder, had been killed in an accident in 1918, shortly after the Revolution. His mother had died of tuberculosis a year later, as the horrors of civil war and famine had fallen upon the country. The child had been taken in by a convent orphanage, run by an aristocratic woman who had lived in England but had decided to devote her life to charitable works. She had taught him English, encouraging him to read the works in the school's small English library. By the time he was sixteen, he had been sufficiently qualified to win admission to a technical school. That had been in 1931. Poncerev did not say what had become of the aristocratic nun and her orphanage. No doubt she had been sent to the gulag and the orphanage turned into a school for young Communists. It was, indeed, entirely possible that the conversion had taken place in the 1920s, when the last traces of the ancien régime had been swept away, and the young Poncerev had therefore been one of the first young Russians to be molded into "Soviet Man," according to Lenin's and Stalin's directives. He had impeccable proletarian credentials and his parents were safely dead, so he could not be accused later of hereditary counterrevolutionary leanings.

Poncerev had become an electrician and in due course had been drafted into the army. He had done well and had been sent to officers' training school. This must have been in the mid-thirties, when the senior ranks of the army had been decimated in the great purges. There had been many openings for bright young men to step into dead men's shoes, and one of the growth areas of the Soviet economy, and the army, was the KGB. Poncerev, of course, told Milano none of this. But he was of the age, the class, and the rank to serve Stalin and his sinister henchmen, Genrikh Yagoda, Nikolai Yezhev, and Lavrenti Beria, who needed young men like Poncerev to carry out the great purges and direct the death camps. KGB officers who survived those frightful years had to be utterly ruthless and loyal to Stalin. As for his later career, Poncerev told Milano simply that he had served two years in the infantry during the war and had then been an assistant to the military governor of Moscow, where his command of English had been useful. There had been large delegations of Americans and British in Russia, and the KGB had needed English-speaking officers to keep an eye on them. After the war, he had been posted to the army of occupation in Austria and had come, one warm summer evening, to drink bourbon with Jim Milano in the Bristol bar.

Before they parted, Milano issued a challenge. "You Russians seem to think pretty well of yourselves in this business. So let's see how good you are. I come to Vienna from time to time: next time I'm here, give me a call." It was a challenge with a purpose: Milano was interested to discover how closely the KGB kept a watch on him and particularly how closely they watched the *Mozart*, the daily train between Salzburg and Vienna.

Poncerev was delighted to accept, but he set a price. "I have always wanted to read *Gone with the Wind*. Could you get me a copy?" Milano promised that he would do so and escorted his rival to the door. It had been a most instructive evening. He had learned that the Russian intelligence chief was very smart, very good at his job, and very well informed. His age and career path suggested that he had some dreadful deeds to his credit. He was an altogether formidable opponent.

A few weeks later, Milano returned to Vienna. He took the *Mozart* from Salzburg and dropped his bag at the Regina Hotel for breakfast. He had brought a copy of *Gone with the Wind* with him, just in case his Russian colleague should reappear. He had scarcely given the waiter his order when the maître d' approached him. "You are Major Perry?" he asked, that being Milano's alias. "Sir, you are wanted on the telephone in the lobby."

It was Major Poncerev. "Good morning, Jim," he said, with no trace of triumph in his voice. His service had done its work. Milano was suitably impressed, and congratulated Poncerev on his success. "I've brought your book," he added. "How do you want to pick it up?"

"Why don't you come to my apartment," Poncerev replied. "It's just behind the Imperial, and you could drop in for a drink."

Milano agreed at once. This was a challenge, and he had always met challenges without flinching. It was only when he was back at his table, eating breakfast, that he began to have second thoughts. This was not perhaps the smartest thing he had ever done, to accept an invitation to visit a senior KGB operative in an apartment in the Russian sector of Vienna. He finally decided that he would keep the appointment, but would notify his office where he was going and why, and arrange to have backup, a couple of beefy young men from the Vienna station to keep him company. They could stay in the street and await developments while he was seeing Major Poncerev.

Milano had urgent business with his headquarters in Vienna, and devoted the rest of the day to it. In the afternoon, he told Major Karl Brewer of the CIC Vienna station of his rendezvous with Poncerev, and asked for backup. Karl was not at all happy at the idea. He reminded Milano that the Soviets had been known to kidnap people in Vienna and spirit them out of the country. Milano, with the optimism of youth, assured him that all would be well and set out for Poncerev's apartment, trailed by the two bodyguards.

Poncerev lived in an elegant old apartment building that had survived the war and had been taken over by the Soviet occupation authorities. When Milano rang the bell, the door was opened by a strikingly beautiful Russian female lieutenant in full dress uniform. She welcomed him in perfect English and took him into the living room, explaining that Poncerev had been delayed but would be there shortly. She served Milano vodka and caviar on fresh toast but declined to join him. They had talked about Austria, Vienna, and its cultural offerings for about twenty minutes when Poncerev at last arrived. The lady lieutenant disappeared, leaving the two men together.

Milano congratulated his host on the lady's beauty, but Poncerev refused to be drawn. Milano therefore produced the book and solemnly handed it over. Poncerev expressed his delight and then surprised Milano by offering him a book in exchange, an English-language *History of the Civil War in the USSR, 1917–22*. It was no doubt a polite gesture, though the book would be quite worthless as history: Soviet histories of the Revolution and Civil War, from the late 1920s until the late '80s, were mainly works of fiction. The edition Milano received was devoted largely to eulogizing Stalin and inflating his role in events.

The two adversaries spent half an hour in banalities, and then Milano got up to leave. They agreed that they should meet again, this time in Milano's Vienna apartment for dinner. Milano suggested that the Russian should bring his beautiful lieutenant along to add a little glamour to the occasion. Then he left, noting with approval one of Karl's men in a doorway across the street.

It was a bizarre and puzzling episode. Milano had wondered if Poncerev wanted to sound him out about spying for the KGB or would try to pump him for information. Nothing of the sort had happened. The meeting had been purely social and meaningless. He never saw Poncerev again—or the lovely lieutenant.

But Poncerev did not forget. Perhaps he had been weighing up Milano and had reached some conclusions from the meetings. His job was to infiltrate American Intelligence, or at least the American military establishment in Austria, and he set to work with a will. He suborned cleaning women working in American offices and the homes of American officers (though he never succeeded in infiltrating American headquarters, as Major Chambers's friend Sonya had infiltrated Soviet headquarters). He sent his most prepossessing young men to work seducing American secretaries (see Chapter 9), and he may well have been behind the recruitment of the unfortunate American MPs, the Rover Boys (see Chapter 16).

The next encounter in this shadowy war between the two intelligence services was more straightforward. Milano was notified that a maid at the Regina Hotel, where he usually stayed in Vienna, had been summarily fired. She had been passing on details of his movements to a Soviet agent. There was not much information she could impart, besides the comings and goings of Milano and his colleagues, but it was a breach of security all the same. It explained how Poncerev had been able to call Milano immediately after his arrival in Vienna and claim his reward: he had not been spying at the railroad station; he had simply bribed the maid.

She had been caught because she had been observed meeting a suspected Soviet agent in a restaurant near the hotel. When she had been pulled in for interrogation, she had confessed immediately. The Soviets had recruited her to report on Milano's arrivals and departures, on guests he brought to the hotel, and whatever she might overhear of their conversations. The CIC was intrigued, but not surprised, that the KGB should take so much trouble. This is how effective intelligence operations succeed, by paying close attention to the most mundane details.

The most interesting aspect, however, was not the maid's petty espionage, it was the chain of information it had been spun into. The maid reported to a suspected Soviet agent, who in turn reported to one of the most prominent of Soviet citizens in Vienna, Sylvia Kusmich, the *Pravda* correspondent in Austria.

She was a striking woman who wrote not only for *Pravda* but also for various left-wing Austrian papers. She had a clear agenda of discrediting the Americans and promoting Soviet policies. Perhaps she was part of some devious KGB plot to weaken Milano's position and thus to subvert American intelligence operations. He convened a meeting of his Vienna colleagues to discuss the Sylvia problem. He discovered that she was one of the Soviet residents who frequented the famous riding stable. It was rather a long shot, but Milano decided to try what American charm might do to with the beautiful Sylvia. Pete Chambers still went to the riding stables once or twice a month. Now Milano suggested that he make the lady's acquaintance and see where that led him.

Chambers was not enthusiastic. He had just become engaged to an Austrian girl, and, though he had enjoyed a long and varied career as a bachelor, he was now determined to be a faithful lover and husband. Milano, and everyone else, was astonished. This was not the man they had known and envied for so long. Milano insisted. "Just strike up an acquaintance with her," he said. "Pass the time of day, make friends. Use your charm on her." Chambers agreed, most reluctantly, and all that remained was to find a suitable occasion. It came when the mysterious Sylvia turned up at the press conference at which the two defecting Soviet pilots were presented to the world.

Sylvia was there and played the part of a skeptical reporter to perfection. Just before the conference began, Milano noticed Pete Chambers talking to her. Afterward, he asked how the meeting had gone. Chambers said that he had told her he remembered her from the riding stables. They had talked about horses and sport, but she had given no indication that she wanted to pursue the acquaintance. So far as she knew, he was just another American officer, and his famous charm had apparently failed him on this occasion. He told Milano that the chief reaction he had detected was puzzlement: she had wondered why he wanted to talk to her. He decided to leave the matter for a while but to arrange to be riding at the stable the next time she went there.

Chambers did his duty. He pursued her to the riding stables, but she once again turned down his suggestions that they get to know each other better. The Americans had to admit that they had drawn a blank. Not all their intelligence coups were successful, and this, they assumed, was one of their failures. Sylvia remained one of the KGB's most dangerous undercover operatives in Austria. However, it is possible that Chambers's approaches may have served a useful purpose after all. Perhaps someone was watching her, someone who knew or suspected that Chambers was connected to American Military Intelligence. Perhaps her superiors, Beria's paranoid KGB, concluded that she might be tempted to defect. A few months later, she was abruptly recalled by her newspaper and was never heard of again.

As for Pyotr Poncerev, he dropped from sight but continued his work in the shadows. In 1950, three years after his unexplained encounters with Milano, he set a small disinformation operation under way against him. Milano was abruptly summoned to meet the intelligence deputy chief of staff, Colonel Bixell, who sat him down

in his office and tossed a photograph across the desk. Some anonymous friend had sent it to him through the mail. It showed Jim
Milano, in the uniform of the Signal Corps, sitting in a sidewalk café
with three Russian officers. The scene was a familiar one in Vienna,
which rivals Paris in the number and popularity of cafés where people can while away an hour, or a whole day, watching the world go
by and chatting with their friends.

This was clearly what Milano was doing, and the intelligence chief
wanted to know what he was up to fraternizing with the enemy. The
only snag was that Milano had never sat on a sidewalk café with a
Soviet officer, let alone three. The photograph was a fake.

Fortunately, the fake could be proved, even though the photograph had been doctored by a master. The man in the American uniform looked like Major Milano and the uniform was completely
authentic, down to the medal ribbons and the corps insignia on the
man's shoulders. But Jim Milano was not in the Signal Corps. He
was an infantry officer, and on those rare occasions when he wore
uniform, he wore General Staff insignia. Major Poncerev had
slipped. Milano and Bixell were left to speculate why the KGB had
gone to such trouble to frame him. There was no Signal Corps officer in Austria at the time who resembled Milano at all. This was a
wholly concocted photograph, designed to sow suspicion in the
minds of Milano's superiors.

A second photograph turned up two weeks later. Like the first, it
had been posted in Vienna, like an ordinary postcard, but with no
message on the back. This one showed the bogus Major Milano dis-
porting himself in the Prater amusement grounds, in a sport jacket
and slacks, accompanied by a very pretty girl. She was dressed in
the dirndl, the Austrian national costume, and her hair was plaited
into two long braids. The costume, too, must have been part of
Major Poncerev's disinformation campaign or else some subtle
Russian joke. Austrian women in central Vienna did not dress up
like characters from *The Sound of Music* in the normal course of
events, and Milano and Bixell were wholly at a loss.

Milano called Poncerev and joked with him about the fake photographs. He asked when he would meet the beautiful blonde with
the long braids. Poncerev professed complete ignorance, said he had
no idea what Milano was talking about, and ended the conversation.
He declined an invitation to meet the American for another drink,
pleading the press of business.

13

Rivals and Enemies

One of the most enigmatic and important of all the agents who fell into the net of American Intelligence was a mysterious Bulgarian rug merchant who called himself Kauder Kopp. He was discovered a year after the war, living under a false identity in a house he had rented on the Mondsee, near Salzburg. A local policeman, who had been recruited by the CIC on a retainer, reported that a Bulgarian in Mondsee appeared to be quite different from all other refugees. He had arrived shortly before the end of the war and had avoided all contact with the German Army. He appeared to be rich and to have saved a most elegant wardrobe and considerable possessions. The policeman passed his suspicions on to Vernon Hubert, a case officer in the SSU office in Salzburg. Hubert called in the mysterious Bulgarian, and during the second interview he revealed his identity and offered to work for the Americans.

Hubert had already heard of Kauder Kopp, and he was high on the list of wanted men: he had been one of the most important of all German spies during the war. The Americans had first come across his traces when they examined the surviving archives of the Abwehr. They found that Kopp had provided his control in Vienna with a long series of high-quality reports on the Soviet Union from 1938 until the end of the war. U.S. specialists carefully interrogated captured Abwehr agents and officials, and many of them who had seen Kopp's reports said that they believed that he had been the chosen contact of a very highly placed Soviet officer who had betrayed his country to Hitler. Kopp's German control officer had been Colonel Heinz Huffner, who had been the Abwehr chief in Vienna. He was interrogated by the Americans and told them that Kopp had supplied a steady stream of intelligence throughout the war and that his reports had been reliable and exceedingly important. Some of his

reports on Soviet troop strengths and dispositions had served as crucial information in the planning for Operation Barbarossa, the invasion of Russia in June 1941, when the Wehrmacht had inflicted over
a million casualties on the Soviet army in the first month. The
Soviets had been taken completely unprepared.

Huffner said that he and his colleagues had constantly pressed
Kopp to reveal his source, or sources, but he had constantly refused.
He had said that their value could easily be checked and that his
German control could rely upon him. Kopp was Bulgarian, a carpet
salesman whose business contacts spread across Eastern Europe
and the Middle East. He had no business in the Soviet Union itself,
nor could the Abwehr find any evidence in his biography or even in
his own interests that would explain how he had become a super-
agent. The most he had ever told Huffner was that he obtained much
of his information by monitoring shortwave radio transmissions
between Moscow and the Soviet Mission in Sofia. The Abwehr's own
signals traffic monitors, sent there to check on the alleged transmissions, had been able to find no trace of them. Bulgaria had been a
member of the Axis. It had joined Germany in its war on Yugoslavia
and Greece and had annexed parts of those countries, as well as
parts of Romania, but it had never declared war on the Soviet
Union. The Soviets had therefore kept a mission in Sofia throughout
the war. All its radio traffic had been carefully monitored by the
Abwehr and, perhaps, by Kauder Kopp. It seemed most doubtful to
Huffner that Kopp's reports could have been based on any information that Moscow might send to its isolated and beleaguered mission
in Sofia, even if he had been able to intercept transmissions that the
Abwehr missed.

Many years later, there was a report that Kopp's source had, in
fact, been Japanese. The Japanese intelligence service had had a
major outpost in the Balkans, and one of its employees allegedly had
been a Japanese reporter who had supplied information to Kauder
Kopp. In the way of intelligence services, if Kopp's reports confirmed information supplied directly to the Abwehr by the Japanese,
then his reliability would be accepted absolutely. However, this
hypothesis has not been confirmed. The other alternative hypothesis
was that Kopp had been a KGB plant, feeding false information to
the gullible Germans. There were (and continued to be) plenty of
instances of Soviet intelligence disinformation, and it is entirely possible that Kauder Kopp was one of them. It would certainly explain
how a Bulgarian rug merchant had obtained top-level information.
At any event, at the time he appeared, the Germans and Americans
believed him to be genuine and acted accordingly.

Huffner reported to his American interrogators that in March
1945, as the Allied armies were driving across Germany and the Red

Army was approaching Vienna, Kopp had suddenly arrived in his office. He did not reveal how he had escaped from the Balkans. He told Huffner that the German Army was certain to capitulate shortly and asked him what plans the Abwehr had made to protect its agents. He wanted guarantees for himself and for one other person, whom he refused to identify. Huffner was constrained to tell him that there was nothing that could be done for him. The ship was sinking, and Abwehr officers were concerned with saving their own skins, if possible. Their agents would have to fend for themselves. Kopp was unlucky in his control. At about the same time, a German spy in Britain, Tate, who had turned himself in to British Intelligence as soon as he landed in England and worked for them for the rest of the war, sent a last radio message to his control in Hamburg, asking him to take care of a suitcase of personal items he had left there. The message was, of course, approved by British counterintelligence. On May 2, 1945, a few hours before the British occupied Hamburg, Abwehr headquarters sent a last message to Tate, informing him that the suitcase had been confided to his sister and was safe. British Intelligence, which had controlled all German agents in Britain throughout the war and had written and sent all their messages back to Germany, noted sardonically that the Abwehr had been loyal, and deceived, to the last. Its chronicler wrote, "If you wish agents to serve you well you must satisfy their personal wishes and personal interests; in their last message to TATE the Germans gave a shining example of how the good case officer should behave, and gave it too in circumstances which even the most phlegmatic must have admitted to have been a little trying!"* Huffner heard no more of Kauder Kopp after his brief visit to the Vienna office. He simply vanished.

Vernon Hubert, whose family was part of the German immigrant community in South Dakota, spoke fluent German and had spent the war with the OSS in London. He was a very thorough and competent intelligence officer, and as he investigated Kopp's story he became convinced that his new client might become a major intelligence asset. If he had really had a source on the Soviet Army General Staff during the war, the SSU needed to know how he had been recruited and run. Best of all, might he now be ready to spy for the Americans as once he had spied for the Germans, and, if so, how should the SSU set about making contact with him?

Hubert moved Kopp into a safe house in Salzburg and began the prolonged business of interrogating him thoroughly on all his wartime activities. Hubert kept Milano informed of the case and after

---

The Double Cross System in the War of 1939 to 1945 by J. C. Masterman.

a few weeks asked for his help in protecting his new agent. He had become increasingly impressed with Kopp's knowledge and value as an intelligence source and concluded that he might be in danger of kidnapping or worse by the KGB. Hubert assumed that the Soviets had caught a number of former Abwehr agents and perhaps found some of the Abwehr's records in Berlin. Somewhere, most probably, they would find traces of Kauder Kopp and his reports. They would easily deduce that he had agents inside the Soviet Union, perhaps even in high rank in the Red Army—and would go to any lengths to find him and extort the names of his agents from him. Hubert became increasingly worried that Kopp was vulnerable to a KGB attack and finally arranged with Milano and the head of the CIC station in Land Salzburg, John Burkel, that he should move into a building shared with two of Burkel's agents. He was given an apartment immediately below theirs. Hubert had floodlights installed in the building's courtyard that could be switched on from either Kopp's apartment or that of the two CIC men.

These precautions proved their worth barely two weeks later. At about eight one evening, two cars, each with two men in it, drove into the courtyard. Two of the men went inside, while the others stood guard. The first two went up to Kopp's apartment and started hammering on the door, demanding that he open it immediately. They shouted that they were U.S. Military Police. The two CIC agents heard the noise, immediately turned on the floodlights, and rushed down the stairs, their pistols drawn. They found Major Yevgeny Rustakov, head of the Soviet Repatriation Mission in the American zone, dressed in the uniform of an American MP officer. The other man with him was in civilian clothes.

One of the two agents held the Russians at gunpoint while the other phoned for reinforcements. Within minutes, the CIC duty officer and three other CIC agents arrived, including Major Garry Hartel, who was the unit's liaison with the Russians. They were quickly followed by three MPs and an Austrian policeman. They arrested the two Russians who had remained outside the building and ordered the four prisoners back to CIC headquarters. Major Rustakov refused, insisting that the Americans had no jurisdiction over him or his men. The CIC men grabbed him and forcibly handcuffed him. He and his comrades were then taken to CIC headquarters, where John Burkel was waiting for them. He called USFA Headquarters in Vienna and gave a summary account of the incident. He said he would keep the four Russians prisoner until he received instructions from Vienna. They were provided with cots to sleep on and were given a meal. In Vienna, the duty officer alerted the commanding general, General Keyes, and at a meeting the following morning, he decided to expel the entire Soviet Repatriation

Mission. The attempted kidnapping of a displaced person by Soviet officers masquerading as Americans was intolerable. The marshal commanding Soviet troops in Austria was informed of the imminent expulsions, together with the generals commanding British and French forces. The Russian coldly told the American general that he knew nothing of the matter and would investigate.

That afternoon, the four prisoners were driven back to their hotel, where they were permitted to collect their possessions. They were told that any effects they left behind would be packed up and sent after them. They were then allowed to drive in their own vehicles to the bridge over the Danube at Urfahr, in a convoy escorted by American MPs. Lieutenant Colonel Glenn Sawyer, commander of the MP detachment in Linz, accompanied the convoy and delivered the members of the Soviet Repatriation Mission to Soviet officers at the bridge. He asked for a receipt.

Some days later, the Soviet marshal called on General Keyes and informed him that the errant Major Rustakov had acted entirely on his own responsibility and would be punished accordingly. He requested that a new Soviet Repatriation Mission be permitted to return to Salzburg. After consulting the Pentagon, General Keyes agreed. As for Kauder Kopp, he was spirited out of Austria altogether, though not by Jim Milano's Rat Line. He was far too important an agent to be put into danger again, and the SSU took care of him. The CIC heard no more of him, and history does not record if he ever reactivated his secret source inside the Soviet army—if he had one.

The fact that the KGB came hunting for Kauder Kopp, of course, hugely increased his value in American eyes. Other cases were much more difficult to resolve. The Americans never hesitated to use former German agents to spy on their former Soviet allies. The question came up as soon as the first intelligence operations got under way in the summer of 1945. The Soviets were showing ever-increasing signs of hostility, and the Americans, along with the British and French, needed to use every source of information they could find to discover what their new adversaries' intentions were. The men in the field, of course, debated the morality of working with agents who, a mere two or three months earlier, had been serving Hitler. Some of them, no doubt, had been conducting intelligence operations against the Western allies and might have been responsible for American soldiers' being killed or wounded. All of them had been serving one of the most evil regimes in history: Allied personnel in Europe at the time were horrified by the revelations from the concentration camps and were still under the influence of years of wartime hatred for the enemy. The CIC, MIS, and SSU officers had to overcome their natural antipathy for their former enemies so that they could work with them in the new, cold world of East-West rivalry. Fortunately,

American intelligence officers in Austria had to deal chiefly with Germans who had been working against the Soviet Union. They soon came to terms with whatever scruples they felt.

However, there were general, unwritten guidelines they were meant to observe. In no circumstances were they to deal with, first, known or suspected war criminals; second, members of the Gestapo, the German secret police; third, members of the SA (*Sturmabteilung*), who had been the original Brownshirts, or storm troopers, the muscle men of the Nazi Party; or, fourth, members of the SS (*Schutzstaffel*), who had developed later than the SA as the elite military arm of the Party. These rules were laid down from the beginning, but as time went by it sometimes became necessary to bend them. In one case, a man who had been an intelligence officer in the SA offered his services to the CIC station chief in Linz, Tom Lucid. He claimed to have a residual network of informants in Budapest. As we have seen, this was a matter of crucial importance to American Intelligence, because it was the stamping ground of the Soviet 17th Mechanized Guards Division. The question arose whether this proffered intelligence should be used, despite the ban on recruiting former members of the SA.

While the debate was under way, the man was arrested and charged with war crimes by Austrian police. In due course, he was tried and acquitted. The question of using his services was then reconsidered, with the additional burden that, even though he had escaped the courts, a cloud of suspicion still hung over him: he perhaps fell into two of the four prohibited classes, membership in the SA and being a suspected war criminal. He submitted a sample report on Soviet troop deployments, but the CIC liaison officers with British and French Intelligence reported that he had also offered the report to each of them. This was too much for the three Allied services, and the man was told that he would not be employed by any of them.

A problem that occurs constantly in intelligence is judging the reliability of sources. Some of the Americans' new German recruits were reliable, steady, and competent intelligence officers. When they claimed they had contacts in Eastern Europe that could be brought together again as a new anti-Communist network, they were telling the truth. They were, after all, far better placed than the newly arrived Americans to open contact with the underground in Stalin's empire, because those contacts would necessarily consist, first of all, of people they had worked with during the war. But other agents were much less reliable. Their commodity was information, and they offered it for sale to the various American and Allied intelligence organizations. The problem was checking it. How could case officers decide whether a report was true, partly true, or wholly fictitious? How could they determine whether a new agent really had useful contacts in Eastern Europe or was simply concocting his reports from newspapers, books, and his own imagination?

The only solution was to check every report from a new agent most carefully. Milano also checked with his French and British colleagues, partly to enforce the rule that an agent can work for only one master. The former SA man was by no means the only operator who tried selling his wares in more than one market. Whenever one was detected, he was struck from the rolls. On one typical occasion, a German agent sold the same report on a Soviet tank factory to the Americans, the British, and the French. The British checked his report with their French colleagues, found the similarities, and then informed the Americans—who had been sold the same story. They suspected the man's claims of having an intelligence network inside Russia were hugely inflated or perhaps entirely bogus. It seemed much more likely that he had picked up some details of the factory from refugees or returning prisoners of war. These were the MIS's own best sources, so it was entirely possible that freelance German intelligence agents might be drawing water from the same well.

All information coming in was classified according to a standard grid. Sources were listed in order of reliability from A to F, and their reports in order of credibility on a scale of 1 to 6. The various German networks produced information that was usually classified C-3, though sometimes it fell to D-4. Nothing lower than that was considered trustworthy, though the information might be upgraded (from D-4 to D-3, for instance) if some corroboration came in.

One of the most difficult decisions the Operations Branch ever faced occurred at the height of the cold war, in 1949, when it became apparent that one of the German agents whose reports had been accepted as reliable was in fact a double agent. Paul Lyon had a network of six agents in the Soviet zone of Austria. The group was coordinated by one of them, who was Lyon's contact. Then the contact reported that one of his agents had disappeared, simply vanishing without trace. This was sufficiently disturbing to warrant a full-scale review, and the other agents were called on to investigate. After two weeks, two more agents disappeared. The contact investigated the matter himself and concluded that one of his two remaining agents must be a traitor. He told Lyon that he wanted to get out of the Soviet zone as quickly as possible, for fear that he would be next to vanish. By this time, Milano and his staff had analyzed all the reports the network had prepared and had discovered that the suspect's contributions were clearly superior to the reports of all the others. Some of his information included details of a Soviet military formation that would have been very difficult for anyone except an insider to obtain. In other words, the information had been given to him by the KGB in order to impress his American paymasters.

All the evidence pointed to this man as being the one responsible: he had identified the American agents, and the KGB had then eliminated them. Milano and his team then set up a conference with the contact agent and the suspect in the American zone, near the border. They were told that the Americans had a special task for the suspect that they wanted to discuss with him in person. He took the bait and arrived with the chief agent at the meeting place at Steyr. Lyon and one of his American agents who spoke fluent German then set to work interrogating him. After several hours, they were convinced that he was a double agent. They had him locked up by the Austrian police in a jail in a small town nearby.

The interrogations continued for several days. The suspect never confessed, but it became clear that he was playing games with his supposed superiors. They had excellent contacts with the Austrian police throughout the country, including in the Soviet zone, and established that there was no trace of the three missing men and no bodies. Presumably they had been hauled away into the Soviet Union, where they had been shot. The contact man and the sixth surviving agent were called back to the safety of the American zone, and the network was wound up. Milano and his closest associates had long, anguished discussions about whether or not they would be justified in having the man eliminated. In later years, of course, the CIA was much less squeamish, but in those early days intelligence officers were uncertain. On this occasion, finally, they concluded that they would be justified in finding a gunman and having the man shot. They were certain beyond a doubt that he was responsible for at least three deaths, but there was no other obvious way to punish him or to prevent further losses: he had thoroughly infiltrated their own networks.

A week after the interrogations began, Milano was called in the middle of the night by a CIC agent. The suspect had escaped from jail. It was a small, country facility, and two men had broken in, overpowered the jailer, and released their prisoner. Evidently, it had been a KGB operation. The Americans were thus spared making the choice of eliminating the man or setting him free, unpunished.

14

Former Enemies, Future Allies

The most important of all West German espionage networks was the one set up by General Reinhard Gehlen, a former senior officer in the Abwehr, the German military intelligence agency. He had been in charge of all German Army intelligence on the eastern front in the latter part of the war. Just before the final Soviet offensive against Berlin in early 1945, he had moved his office and his files westward: the future Allied zones of occupation were known, and Gehlen had no intention of being caught by the Red Army. On the contrary, he had decided to offer his services to the Americans as soon as the war was over and spent the last weeks of the dying Reich getting ready for his change of allegiance. He had surrendered to the Americans and in due course had been recruited by Army Intelligence. He had been established in offices in Pullach, near Munich, that had been used by Martin Bormann in his capacity of Reichsminister, or head of the Nazi Party.

Gehlen then set about reactivating his networks. Those of his agents who had been less nimble than he and had been left behind Soviet lines in the Soviet zone were the first candidates. East Germany, which later became the German Democratic Republic, was the main Soviet army base in Central Europe and the chief target for Gehlen's operations, just as West Germany was the main target of the GDR's intelligence operations. Some of Gehlen's former Abwehr colleagues were already building up their own secret service in the East that later developed into the Stasi, one of the most efficient of all Communist spy systems. Then there were the surviving Abwehr agents in the Baltic states, Poland, Czechoslovakia, Hungary, the Balkans, and the Soviet Union itself who might be brought back into a reconstituted intelligence network. No doubt many of them were very unsavory people, men and women who had spied for Hitler against their own countries. Perhaps Kauder Kopp's secret source, if genuine, was one of them: Gehlen, as commander of the Abwehr's eastern office, had of course known about Kopp and his source, and if the Americans needed a skilled operative to revive the Kopp network, once the inscrutable Bulgarian had been picked up in Austria, then Gehlen was the obvious man to do it. His other agents were intelligence officers who had worked for the Nazis out of Fascist conviction or detestation of the Russians. Gehlen employed many Latvian, Lithuanian, and Ukrainian Fascists and war criminals in Munich. They best knew the names of their former comrades and friends who had been left behind in what was now the Soviet bloc and might be called to arms again. At any event, Gehlen set about building an intelligence network to serve the Americans against the Soviets who occupied Eastern Europe. He quickly became the most important of American intelligence assets in Central Europe, and the fact that he employed a considerable number of SS, Gestapo, and similar officers was not held against him. When the Federal Republic of Germany was set up and recovered its sovereignty, he transferred his allegiance again, to the new government. The service he had set up, of course, remained closely allied to the CIA.

Milano, as a senior American intelligence officer in Austria, knew all about Gehlen, though he did not deal with him directly. A friend of his, Colonel James Critchfield, was seconded from the Army to work for the CIA in Pullach as head of liaison with the Gehlen organization. Before that, Critchfield had been on the G-2 (Intelligence) staff of Army Headquarters in Vienna, which is how Milano had met him. Critchfield and Milano had worked very well together: it was Critchfield who had recommended to Colonel Bixell, chief of staff in the G-2 section, that Milano be given operational control of the CIC in Austria. When Critchfield had been posted to Pullach, they had stayed in contact.

This was more than a social relationship. While Gehlen's chief preoccupation was with Eastern Europe, particularly the Soviet zone, he also occasionally ran agents through Austria. That meant that he had to clear things with Milano, or sometimes with the British and later with the Austrian authorities. Critchfield had a captain on his staff whose duties were to liaise with Army Intelligence, and once a week this officer would present himself in Milano's office to brief him on Gehlen's operations. These briefings never included the details but covered anything in which the Operations Branch might have an interest. Milano also helped with any problems that arose with the Austrian police or the British. He maintained the closest possible relations with both parties, and if one of Gehlen's runners were picked up by them and found to have inappropriate papers, Milano could usually arrange matters.

Over the months of this association, Milano came to acquire a great respect for the Gehlen organization. They were professionals who had been engaged in European intelligence far longer than any of the Americans or British and might have much to teach. He asked Critchfield if he could arrange for him to visit Gehlen at Pullach, and he made the visit in 1950. He had three topics he wanted to discuss with the Germans: First, he wanted to compare notes with them on some German networks that had offered their services or that Army Intelligence had come across. Milano was particularly interested in the "Stockholm Abwehr" of Karl-Heinz Kramer. Second, he wanted to learn how the Germans had operated some of their best-known agents during the war, such as the celebrated Elyesa Bozna, who worked as valet to the British ambassador in Ankara, Sir Hughe Knatchbull-Hughessen. Bozna had been able to make duplicates of the ambassador's keys and copy the dispatches in his safe and dispatch box. It had been one of the Abwehr's most successful coups. Third, Milano wanted to know how the Abwehr had checked on its agents' reliability. How could it be sure that its own agents had not been caught and turned, and how could it check the bona fides of agents who offered their services? How could it be sure that such people had not been planted by the other side? At the time, he did not know that during the war the British had succeeded in capturing and turning every single agent the Abwehr had sent into Britain and had used their radios to send false information back to Abwehr headquarters. If he had, he might have been less impressed by the Abwehr's skills at counterintelligence.

Milano spent a large part of the day with Dr. Schaaft, Gehlen's chief of operations. He spoke excellent English and briefed Milano extensively on his activities and methods. Then Gehlen appeared, and Milano spent the rest of the afternoon with him. They discussed Gehlen's wartime activities, including his contacts with Hitler and other senior Nazi officers and officials, but dealt chiefly with the Germans who were still working in intelligence, either in the West or, under cover, in East Germany. They discussed counterintelligence operations and the problems of operating in Berlin and communicating with that city. Milano faced much the same problem in Austria, where Vienna, like the German capital, was isolated behind Soviet lines.

The Germans were as suspicious as Milano himself of Karl-Heinz Kramer, who later became known as the Stockholm Abwehr. For several years he had sold reports to the Americans on the Soviet airframe industry. He claimed that he had contacts inside the Soviet Union who had access to that particular and important target. His information appeared accurate, and could sometimes be checked against other sources. Milano was very doubtful of the Kramer network. Gehlen, too, expressed great skepticism. Much later, an analyst in the Pentagon noticed that all Kramer's reports had come from newspapers and aircraft manuals available in Sweden. His "Russian" network turned out to be the catalog of a bookstore in Stockholm.

A more reliable American agent was the archbishop of Salzburg. He was nothing so vulgar as a spy, nor did he attend secret meetings in safe houses or plot with the Americans to send defectors down the Rat Line. Indeed, he never met American officers at all. Instead, he lent his name to clandestine purposes when the need arose. Early in the occupation, the CIC established a trucking firm in the Soviet zone of Austria. It was in every way a respectable and legitimate outfit, moving goods around Austria with all the proper permits, using respectable drivers, its every action apparently open and aboveboard. Best of all, it was listed as the property of the Archbishopric of Salzburg. The accommodating prelate had agreed to the subterfuge when the CIC explained to him the urgent need they had of reliable informants in the Soviet zone and how important it was for them to be able to move around freely. The company was based in Melk, a small town in northeast Austria, and was therefore known as the Melk Trucking Company. The archbishop designated a Franciscan friar, a member of his staff, to sit on the board of the company to look after his interests. The Americans who secretly controlled the company at times had difficulty explaining to the holy friar the rather peculiar actions and financial transactions that were occasionally made necessary by the exigencies of espionage, but in general both sides found it a satisfactory arrangement.

There were occasions when American Intelligence was less successful. The Military Intelligence Service (MIS) was one of the keys to the entire American operation. During the war, MIS units had been attached to every division and regiment to interrogate prisoners and then to run the temporary POW camps. They provided crucial tactical information on enemy formations and capabilities. After the war, three MIS detachments were set up, in Vienna, Linz, and Salzburg, to interrogate POWs in order to find the important Nazis and SS men and to screen refugees and displaced persons from the East. They also screened Austrian prisoners of war returning from the Soviet Union.

The commander of the MIS in Austria, who reported to Jim Milano, was Ed Gestaldo, who had served with Milano in Italy. He had left the army as a major after the war and had been hired as a civilian. Late in 1949, he had the unenviable duty of reporting to Milano, and then to the general officer commanding U.S. forces in Austria, that one of his officers had deserted to the Soviets.

The deserter was Captain Samuel Blazen, who was supply and transportation officer with the MIS group in Vienna. Gestaldo had already reported Blazen to Milano as a possibly disruptive element. He belonged to a poker club and regularly lost much of his pay there. He had appealed for money to his wife in Macon, Georgia, and she had written to Gestaldo about the problem. Blazen had not told her why he needed the money, and though she had sent off all she could raise, $900, he had demanded more. She was worried about him and had appealed to his commanding officer.

Gestaldo found out that Blazen was playing far above his class, losing constantly and seeking consolation in the bottom of a bottle of bourbon. He was a stupid man: his colleagues wondered how he had managed to earn a commission in the first place. He had risen to the rank of captain during the war and had a good war record. But MIS standards were high: most of its members were linguists and intelligence specialists, and they were good poker players. Blazen would have done better in an infantry regiment. His poker partners complained to Gestaldo that Blazen was not paying his debts, an unforgivable sin, and then Gestaldo looked into the state of the supply stores and discovered serious discrepancies. Blazen was in charge of "special" supplies, meaning the unit's stock of whiskey and other booze, and was helping himself. Gestaldo called him in and told him to confess his sins to his wife—and to stop playing poker and hitting the bottle. Blazen admitted his problem and complained that half his pay went to his wife's allotment, leaving little for himself and his Austrian girlfriend. The story might have ended there if Blazen had listened to his superior's advice. But when he had paid off the bulk of his poker debts, he went back to playing for high stakes and was soon deep in the hole again.

Gestaldo was sufficiently concerned to mention the matter to Milano and to tell him that he wanted the man transferred out of his command. Blazen had already run up several hundred dollars more in poker debts. The two friends discussed ways of disposing of the unwanted officer, but they were too late: a few days later, Major Park Hancock of the CIC detachment in Vienna, who ran spy operations in the Soviet zone, reported that two of his agents had seen an American officer at Soviet headquarters in Wiener Neustadt. The man was soon identified as Sam Blazen of the MIS. He had deserted to the Soviets to escape from his debts, his superiors, his wife, and his troubles—taking his Austrian girlfriend with him.

This was a serious matter. There were very few American desertions to the Soviets, and Blazen was an intelligence officer. He dealt only with supply and transport matters, but he could certainly offer the KGB some useful information, if only gossip picked up during the poker sessions. Milano convened a crisis meeting with Gestaldo and Hancock to assess the damage. They concluded that this was more an embarrassment than a disaster. Blazen did not know enough to be dangerous and had had few opportunities to learn any really sensitive information. He knew, of course, what the mission of the MIS was, but that was hardly a secret from the Russians. He knew nothing at all—or at least he should know nothing at all—of other intelligence operations. The three officers consoled themselves with the further reflection that Blazen was very stupid and would probably not recognize good intelligence if he saw it.

The three men went immediately to general headquarters to make a report to the chief of intelligence, General Hickey. His chief of staff, their immediate superior, Colonel Bixell, was out of the country, so they went straight to the general. He saw them immediately: it was clearly urgent when the three senior intelligence officers in Vienna demanded to see him at once. The news was indeed serious, and the general questioned them closely, appalled that one of his officers should have deserted. He was particularly concerned at the intelligence implications of the event: Had Blazen taken anything with him? Did he have any information to sell the Soviets that might compromise American operations?

Milano and his friends were able to reassure the general on those issues. Blazen's defection was an embarrassment, not a disaster. Hickey then asked what they intended to do about it. How did they propose to get Blazen back into American custody? Milano replied that as far as he was concerned the Soviets could keep the man. He was no loss to the United States, and the KGB was most welcome to him. Hickey was not amused and bawled Milano out vigorously, insisting that while Blazen might be a deserter, he remained an officer in the U.S. Army, and every effort should be taken to get him back.

Milano was suitably chastened and replied that he would see how best to recover the missing man. The general then said that there was a procedure to follow, the one used every time a Soviet officer defected. He would go to the marshal commanding Soviet troops in Austria and ask if he had Captain Blazen in his custody. The Americans might be able to gauge the Soviets' intentions by their reply: whenever a Soviet officer defected, Milano made sure that he was spirited out of the American zone immediately (he was usually hidden in a chalet in the British zone), so that the American commanding general could truthfully inform the Russians that the missing man was nowhere in his territory. If the Soviets pulled the same line, it would be clear that they intended to keep Blazen.

The three intelligence officers then retired to Milano's office in the headquarters building to consider the situation. Milano concluded that there was nothing to be done immediately. He thought it would be a mistake to make any effort to contact Blazen. If the Soviets thought their prize was worth anything, he would be taken off to the Soviet Union, or at least to somewhere in the Soviet zone of Austria that was less accessible to Western intelligence. If, on the other hand, the KGB merely sucked him dry and spat him out, he would be left to his own devices at Wiener Neustadt. After a suitable interval, he might then be approached by American agents and persuaded—or perhaps forced—to return. There could be no question of kidnapping him while the Soviets were still interested, but in Milano's opinion, they would soon find that he was not worth his keep and drop him.

Gestaldo disagreed. He thought that, however stupid and worthless Blazen turned out to be, the Soviets would still keep him for propaganda purposes. The three men concluded that all they could do at that early stage was to keep a close watch on Blazen. Hancock's agents were instructed to report on every sighting of the man or his girlfriend. General Keyes made his formal request for information to the Soviet authorities. After the usual period of stonewalling, they replied that an American officer who answered the description had visited Soviet headquarters in Wiener Neustadt but that his present whereabouts were unknown.

Within a week, the agents were reporting that Blazen and the woman were staying at a seedy hotel in Wiener Neustadt and appeared to have no occupation and no plans. They had been seen wandering around the town, apparently unescorted by any Soviet officer. After the first few days spent at Soviet headquarters, Blazen had stopped visiting the place, and it appeared that the Soviets had lost interest in him. Two weeks after that, Blazen's girlfriend presented herself at CIC headquarters in Vienna and asked to speak to the commanding officer, Park Hancock. She told him that Blazen wanted to return. The Soviets, after interrogating him closely and presumably discovering how little use he was to them, had refused to accept him as a deserter and had left him to his own devices in Wiener Neustadt. The two fugitives were virtually destitute, with no hope of finding a job or escaping. They had no alternative to returning: Blazen was ready to face the music.

Hancock sent a coded message to Milano in Salzburg, describing the woman's report. He replied that the whole matter should be handed over to the military police. The intelligence services were to have nothing further to do with the case. Colonel Bixell and General Hickey were informed and approved the decision. Blazen's girlfriend was told to tell him to hand himself over to MP headquarters in Vienna. He arrived there the next day, chastened and miserable, was arrested, and in due course was court-martialed for desertion. He was sentenced to fifteen years' hard labor, to be served at the federal penitentiary in Fort Leavenworth, Kansas.

Years later, in 1954, long after Milano had left Austria and the intelligence services and was back in the Regular Army, he was posted to Fort Leavenworth to attend a Staff College course. The college was next to the prison, and one day, as he was walking to class, he noticed a group of prisoners working a trash truck. One of the team was former captain Sam Blazen, heaving garbage cans into the truck and picking up the litter on the ground. There was a big letter "P" on the back of his jacket.

15

Peering over the Iron Curtain

When the Communist Party of Czechoslovakia staged its coup against the government in February 1948, suppressed the democratic parties, and established a Stalinist state, the Western Allies in Austria found themselves under siege. Soviet troops occupied about a third of the country: their zone of occupation completely surrounded the capital. The southern borders of Austria were flanked by Yugoslavia, which was still a member of the Soviet alliance, and by Communist Hungary. After the coup in Czechoslovakia, the northeastern border was in the hands of the enemy. As a result, the American, British, and French forces in Austria felt themselves exceedingly vulnerable.

There were some mitigating circumstances. For one thing, Austria was a sideshow. The main issue would be decided in Berlin and the Fulda Gap. For another, the Red Army itself did not occupy Czechoslovakia, and the Czech Army was not particularly redoubtable. Then the strategic balance shifted. On June 28, 1948, four days after the beginning of the Berlin Blockade, Stalin expelled Yugoslavia from the Cominform, the international Communist organization. It was a melodramatic event, falling on the thirty-fourth anniversary of the assassination of the Archduke Franz Ferdinand in Sarajevo, the event that had precipitated the First World War. The West, of course, welcomed the breach between Stalin and Tito, and in Austria it meant that the long southern frontier with Slovenia was no longer an immediate danger: the Red Army would not come that way again, as it had in 1945.

The main danger was Hungary. The Soviet 17th Mechanized Guards Division was posted in the Soviet zone of Austria and along the border, west of the Danube and north of the Alps, and there were no physical barriers to stop it if it ever drove across the Austrian plain. It was one of the crack units in the Soviet army and was the most important of all American Intelligence targets. The Order of Battle Section of Army Intelligence had an office devoted to studying every movement of every unit in the division, always on the lookout for any suggestion that it was deploying to attack. One of the big events for the American intelligence community in Austria every year was the Guards' annual maneuvers, when every possible source of information was brought to bear on the target. The Order of Battle Section, at this period, was run by Captain Harold Craven. He would send queries to Milano, documents known as EEIs (Essential Elements of Information). Milano would then pass them on to one of three people: the chief of operations for the CIC in Vienna; the chief of operations for the CIC Headquarters in Salzburg, Paul Lyon (who was also the man who ran the Rat Line); or Milano's chief agent in Vienna, Pete Chambers. The other intelligence organizations, the MIS (interrogators), and the Civil Censorship Detachments were constantly on the lookout for any information on the 17th Guards and passed it on to Milano or directly to Craven. The British, in Graz, had also developed techniques and sources for gathering information on the Guards, and they pooled their findings with the Americans.

The CIC detachment in Vienna also ran Austrian agents to gather information on the Guards and made a small but significant contribution. However, Pete Chambers supplied 75 or 80 percent of the information that was gathered on the unit. This was the ultimate purpose of Operations Horsefeathers and Claptrap and all of Chambers's other maneuvers. His most difficult challenge was to recruit agents to send across the border. This was before the full panoply of barbed-wire barriers, watchtowers, minefields, and ceaseless patrols had made the Iron Curtain all but impenetrable. It was still possible for Chambers's men to slip across at some remote location, stay a few hours or a few days, and then return with whatever snippets of information they had gleaned. It was a dangerous business and became more difficult with every passing month. But it was a vital mission: every clue provided by Chambers's agents was carefully examined as a piece of a vast, ever-changing jigsaw puzzle.

During that perilous spring of 1948, the Soviets and their Hungarian allies were strengthening their control of the border. They set up a series of radio posts along the frontier to communicate with their patrols. Chambers's agents sometimes managed to listen to these broadcasts, which were mostly in cipher, and noted that the radio messages were most frequent and longest whenever there was a change in the guard. They guessed that orders were being given and noted, and they reported that if they could intercept the messages regularly and decipher them, they would discover the Soviets' movements along the border and thus be able to send American agents across safely. Chambers saw this as a challenge and soon found an answer to the problem. He invited Milano to his headquarters in Vienna to hear the proposal.

Chambers wanted to make use of the unusual abilities of William Wagner, the son of a Harvard professor and now a contract employee of the CIC. Wagner had studied mathematics at the University of Virginia and had been drafted into a signal intelligence battalion during the war in Italy. He had been set to work intercepting Italian and German military radio signals and then breaking their codes. Signal intelligence (known to the trade as Sigint), was one of the most important, successful, and secret of all Allied intelligence operations. At its most advanced level, the interception and decoding of top secret German and Japanese communications was one of the key weapons that won the war. The Germans had developed an encryption machine known as Enigma, which they believed gave them unbreakable codes. The machines were used to send messages between the High Command in Berlin and its field commanders, between the naval command and naval units, and between Luftwaffe headquarters and the German air force field units. Enigma machines were also used by Japanese diplomats, reporting from Berlin to Tokyo on whatever the Germans were telling them of their plans and operations. Polish Intelligence obtained one of these machines before Poland was overrun in 1939 and passed it on to the British (who later recovered another Enigma machine from a captured submarine). British specialists then managed to decipher most Enigma messages that their signals units could intercept. They used the first, primitive computers for the task. The product was classified Top Secret Ultra, and its existence was not revealed publicly until thirty years after the end of the war. It provided a vital edge to Allied commanders in many battles, including the sinking of the *Bismarck*. In June 1944, decoded Japanese diplomatic messages confirmed that Hitler believed the Normandy landings were a feint and that he would keep the bulk of his armor ready for a later attack on the Pas de Calais.

The British shared all their intelligence, including the Enigma decodes, with the Americans (but not with the Soviets or the French). The expertise and techniques of decoding, chiefly used at Bletchley Park in Oxfordshire and at Navy Headquarters in Hawaii, were also used in the field to break lesser codes used by German and Italian forces. The U.S. Army established large listening posts behind the lines, advancing them as the front moved forward. Each was accompanied by radio technicians and cryptanalysts. William Wagner was one of those working in that program. As the end of the war approached, he was at U.S. Intelligence Headquarters at Caserta in northern Italy. Army Intelligence was then planning for the occupation of Austria and decided that it would need telephone monitoring equipment. It recruited a few men from Signals, including Wagner. He wanted to go to Austria because his parents had taken him to Salzburg and Vienna in 1936 and he had liked the place and wanted to return. He joined the censorship detachment, and until his discharge he worked in the telephone monitoring office. It was a less demanding task than cryptanalysis, involving selecting phone calls to be monitored and then transcribing significant passages in the overheard conversations.

In due course, his turn came to be demobilized. He left the army as a sergeant but remained in Austria and, like many others, became a contract worker for the CIC. He proposed that he should drop out of the business of intercepting telephone calls and instead analyze the cryptintelligence capabilities of the German Army. The Pentagon approved the idea. It wanted to know everything possible about Wehrmacht Intelligence during the war, particularly how far it had penetrated Allied intelligence operations and deciphered Allied codes. Wagner set to work to discover everything possible about the organization, capabilities, and equipment of German wartime intelligence. In the process, he discovered many out-of-work German agents, who told him everything they could about their wartime activities. This was not pure altruism: they needed work and were only too willing to offer their services to American Intelligence. They were usually strongly anti-Communist and saw no objection at all to working for their former enemies.

Wagner, a mathematician, was fascinated by the theory and practice of cryptanalysis. According to Chambers, he would talk for hours about the great coups of past wars, including the German intercepts of Russian radio communications at the outbreak of World War I, which had led to the first great German victories in East Prussia, and British success in deciphering German naval codes in the same war. Wagner would describe the American triumph in deciphering Japanese codes in the Second World War: on December 7, 1941, the secretary of state, Cordell Hull, had read the Japanese declaration of war before the Japanese ambassador had. It had been transmitted, in code, to the Japanese Embassy in Washington to be delivered to the State Department—and had been intercepted and decoded by the Americans more rapidly than by the embassy staff. The attack on Pearl Harbor, however, had been a surprise because for once the Japanese Navy had maintained absolute radio silence. In 1943, American radio intercepts and cryptanalysts had discovered that Admiral Isoroku Yamamoto, who had directed the Pearl Harbor operation, was on a tour of inspection in the Solomons. The Americans had ambushed and killed him. All this was in the public domain; what the public did not know was how U.S. Naval Intelligence had obtained the Japanese "Purple" codes. If Wagner knew about Top Secret Ultra, he kept his silence.

Chambers had heard all Wagner's stories at length, and, when the problem of the radio transmissions along the Hungarian border came up, he decided that Wagner might be just the man to solve the problem. He put the idea up to Milano, who agreed at once that the radio expert should be brought in. The alternative would be to ask the Army Security Agency (ASA) to set up an interception and decoding program in Vienna. The ASA (which later developed into the National Security Agency, the largest, most sophisticated, most secretive, and most expensive branch of U.S. Intelligence) then based its European operations in Frankfurt, Germany. Milano and Chambers were both certain that they would get no help from there in anything so low-level as intercepting the exchanges of Russian border guards. Even in those early days, the ASA concerned itself only with much more serious issues.

Wagner was delighted to be consulted. He had nothing of the military man about him: he looked much more the typical professor, with unkempt brown hair, horn-rimmed glasses sliding down on his nose, and always the same tweed jacket and green pants. He immediately proposed that he be allowed to recruit some of the retired German intelligence agents he had been interviewing for his own project. They would need the garret of a high building in Vienna, which would give them an unimpeded radio view of the border forty miles away. He said that he could get hold of surplus radio receivers that had been used on B-17 bombers, and with three or four radio operators he could maintain round-the-clock watch over Russian radio traffic. He would need two or three German cryptanalysts and was confident he could break the Russian codes. They would not be the sort of high-level, impenetrable codes used by the High Command for top secret communications. All the local units needed were serviceable low-grade codes. They did not know how good the Western Allies were at code breaking and did not suspect that a few men with antiquated Air Force radio receivers could decipher all but the most difficult of Russian codes. Milano had only one caveat: he insisted that the CIC give a thorough security clearance to each of the Austrians Wagner intended to employ.

Wagner, in turn, had a request to make. He wanted Milano to act as witness at a pseudomarriage with his Austrian mistress. He had applied to the Army for permission to marry her, but there had been delays and problems, chiefly because she had three children, each by a different man, each of whom had been killed before he could marry her. Wagner wanted to pledge himself to her, like Captain Pinkerton in *Madame Butterfly*, and needed a witness.

The ceremony took place the following Sunday afternoon. Milano presented himself at an apartment owned by a friend of the woman's family and found the two sitting snugly together on a sofa. It was an altogether surreal occasion. The blinds were drawn, and in the gloom the host distributed glasses of sherry. There was a table against a wall, with a white cloth over it, and two candles, a covered bowl, and a goblet. It looked altogether like an altar, though without any religious symbols. Bill Wagner then told Milano and his host that he and his fiancée, Maria, intended to pledge themselves to each other. When the legal problems and security clearances had been completed, they would be properly married. In the meantime, this ceremony would serve as a guarantee of their permanent commitment to each other.

Wagner removed the cover from the bowl, which contained small pieces of bread. He gave one to Maria, who ate it, and she gave one to him. Then he gave her wine to drink from the goblet, and she did the same for him. Then they held hands, faced the two witnesses, and repeated the oath from the marriage service. Wagner then announced that Maria and he were married in the eyes of God and before the two witnesses. The host then produced cold cuts and a bottle of wine, and the four of them had lunch.

Milano left afterward, reflecting on the curious duties that befell commanding officers in overseas assignments. Two weeks later, Wagner informed him that the new listening post was operational. The CIC had given Wagner security clearance for his Austrian employees and provided him with a particularly tall house on high ground in the American sector of Vienna. He had installed his B-17 radio receivers discreetly, so that no one in the street should suspect anything, and had immediately found that they could pick up all the radio traffic along the border. The operators recorded everything and turned their intercepts over to the cryptanalysts. The codes proved easy to crack, and within a few days the Wagner operation was providing a steady stream of invaluable intelligence to Pete Chambers. He now knew the dispositions of the Soviet patrols along the border and could send his agents safely across in the gaps between the patrols or during the intervals when the shifts changed. The intercepts served a further, and potentially very important, purpose. If ever the Soviets moved their troops into position for an attack on Austria, the radio intercepts would surely pick up the orders.

Milano was taken to the secret garret to see the team at work. He examined the carefully concealed radio receivers and inspected the monitors, with their headphones and notepads, who listened for every transmission. The analysts proudly showed him the grid paper on which they plotted the intercepts and started to explain to him how they set about breaking the codes. The method was based upon mathematical formulae and probability theory, and Milano hastily backed off: he knew all about radios and how the Soviet traffic was intercepted but understood nothing at all of the mathematical principles of cryptanalysis. He preferred not to try to understand something that was probably beyond him—and knowing which would be of no use to him.

When the program had proved a success, Milano disclosed it to his superiors. He sent a report to Colonel Oscar Koch, the new head of Army Intelligence in Vienna, who was delighted with the scheme and its results, and forwarded a copy to the Army Security Agency. It described the genesis of the program, how it had been set up, and how it had been hugely successful, at minimal cost. He assumed that the ASA, like Koch, would approve of his actions and was astonished at their reaction. The ASA responded instantly with a categorical demand that the operation be shut down at once. The cold war was at its height, tensions along the Iron Curtain were at fever pitch, and Bill Wagner had succeeded in penetrating Soviet methods and operations and breaking the Soviets' codes. But for the ASA, this was an intolerable invasion of territory. Agency headquarters in Frankfurt insisted that it alone had the right to conduct electronic intelligence in Europe. This upstart operation in Vienna must be stopped immediately, however useful the Army might think it.

Koch, reluctantly, had to comply. He admitted that he had not been consulted by Milano, whose modus operandi was always to get the job done and then worry about the consequences. It was a bureaucratic style that usually paid dividends, but not on this occasion. The ASA was too powerful and too well entrenched in Washington to tolerate a rival in Vienna, and Koch ordered the operation closed down. Wagner was devastated, and his team was out of work again. The ASA informed Vienna that it would set up a radio monitoring and decoding operation in Austria, and in due course did so at Wels, in the American zone. It did the job well enough, but with layers of bureaucracy between the people who made the intercepts and read them and the agents who needed the product. Pete Chambers, who had briefly had his own radio intelligence operation, which responded instantly to his requirements and kept him informed on a twenty-four-hour basis, now had to content himself with whatever information the ASA passed down the chain of command.

He and his colleagues had to console themselves with their other plans and programs, some of which were brilliantly successful. The best intelligence came from defectors, and a large part of his effort was directed at keeping up the supply. There were as many reasons to defect as there were defectors: the problem was contacting them in the first place and letting them know that they would be made welcome in the West and that a new home would be found for them in South America. In the early days, many were discovered in the DP camps and persuaded to stay. Operations Claptrap and Horsefeathers produced a steady stream of recruits, while other defectors presented themselves unsolicited to the Americans, usually to military units, which passed them along either to the CIC or directly to the operations staff of the G-2.

One of the more unusual captures was the work of a beautiful young Nazi, Trudi Schaaf. She had been the mistress of an SS general during the war, with all that that implied of loyalty to the Führer and the Third Reich. The general had been killed on the Russian front (Karl Brewer said acidly that the man had done Trudi a favor by laying down his life for the Fatherland), and she had then become the mistress of a senior Nazi in Vienna, thus continuing to move in the smartest circles. After the war, her social successes became a liability. Her lover was taken off to Nuremburg, and she was left one of the more notorious Nazis in Vienna.

It was not an enviable position. The Socialists had taken over the city government and had no sympathy for the tyrants who had oppressed them. Trudi could look for no help from any of the Allies. The de-Nazification policy was never rigorously applied and did not extend to mistresses, but still she concluded that she wanted to leave Vienna, and if possible to leave Austria altogether and start a new life somewhere else. As a Nazi, she would never be accepted in any of the international refugee programs. So she became a fisher-woman.

Her catch was a Russian captain, Yuli Andreyev, who worked in the secretariat of the Soviet Staff in Vienna. She hooked him and reeled him in, slowly and delicately. Sometime after they first met, she took an apartment in the building where he lived; it was more discreet that way. Then she made herself known to American intelligence agents. This was a further sign of her skills: she had to conceal herself from the KGB, which was of course monitoring the apartment building where Andreyev lived, but allow the Americans to find her. In due course, Brewer went to Milano to tell him about Trudi. She had suggested to Brewer that she would be willing to sell him whatever information she could gather from her lover. Brewer had a better idea. He thought that she might be able to induce the captain to desert.

They were under no illusions about Fräulein Trudi: Karl Brewer described her as a clever, ruthless, cunning bitch, as charming and as loving as a cobra. She was also very beautiful (SS generals had high standards), and the young Russian had evidently fallen for her. He would be in serious trouble if his commissar ever found out he was having an affair with a Nazi. Milano wanted to know whether she was reliable; he had no qualms about using Nazis to catch Communist soldiers or about Austrian women selling themselves for the purpose. This is what a "fisherwoman" does, and Trudi was not the only one he used over the years. Brewer proposed that she be invited to visit one of Park Hancock's safe houses and meet Milano and his colleagues there. The house was on the edge of the Vienna woods and very discreet, and Trudi and the Americans could get there without being observed. Milano's theory was that the Devil hates a coward, so he told Brewer to go ahead and set the meeting up.

When Milano reached the house he found his colleagues had already arrived and were setting up the inevitable Viennese coffee and cookies. Brewer had sent a driver to pick up Trudi on a street corner in an unmarked car, and she soon arrived, shepherded through the back door. She was just as beautiful as Brewer had promised, a striking blonde with great poise and self-control. She spoke excellent English, and the three Americans introduced themselves with a complete set of new names: Milano was Mr. Donnelly, Hancock was Mr. Simpson, and Brewer was Mr. Oberlin.

Brewer served coffee and offered cookies and cigarettes to everyone. Then Milano started the conversation.

"Miss Schaaf, we understand that you want to leave the country."

"Yes," she replied. "I chose the wrong side during the war, and there's no future for me in Austria. I have no wish at all to settle down as some nondescript hausfrau. I'm sure I can do better than that. The trouble is I can't do anything here, so it will have to be abroad. Can you help me?"

Milano asked, "Am I right in thinking that you want to establish a new identity, as well as a new country?"

"Yes, that would be better. I don't want to have my past dragged around with me. I want to make a completely new life for myself, start all over again."

"What about your family?"

"My father was killed in France, and my brother was killed in Russia. My mother has disowned me and says she will only forgive me if I become a nun. That's not one of my ambitions. I don't think a habit would suit me."

"Well, Miss Schaaf, I suppose we could help you, but there would be a price tag attached."

There was a long pause as Trudi drank her coffee. Then she said, "Look, I'm not stupid, Mr. Donnelly. I know perfectly well this isn't something you would do out of charity. Why don't you come out and tell me what you want?"

Mr. Donnelly was not about to be hurried. "Please," he said, "we've got plenty of time to get around to that. I'd like to ask you some more questions first, to clarify a few things. What about this Russian friend of yours? I understand you've moved into the same apartment building in the Soviet zone. Isn't that rather dangerous for a lady with your background?"

Trudi replied with some asperity, "I wanted to be near him and discreet. He would get into the worst sort of trouble if he were seen with me. Like this, he can come to see me whenever he likes. Besides, he's supporting me. I don't have any money, and he's able to give me enough to live on."

"What are your relations with him? Is he in love with you?"

"No, but he is very fond of me. He's a sweet man, and I'm very fond of him, too."

"Do you think he will miss you when he has to go back to Russia? Will you miss him?"

"Yes. We've talked about it. He says that he'll miss me a lot. As for me, I don't know. We'll have to see."

It was time for more coffee and *Kuchen* and another cigarette. They talked about life in Vienna, the hardships facing women in Trudi's position, the problems Andreyev was likely to encounter returning to postwar Moscow, their hopes that things would improve in Europe as it recovered from the war. This was all beating about the bush: Trudi was waiting for Milano to drop the other shoe.

"Tell me," he said, "do you think there's any possibility your Captain Andreyev might decide to stay in the West? Could you persuade him to desert if we guaranteed his safety?"

"Perhaps he would, perhaps he wouldn't. I could certainly try. What would you give me if I did?"

"We'd pay you. We'd get you silk stockings and cigarettes and some good brandy from time to time. If you carried it off, we would arrange for you to start a new life, with a new identity, somewhere far away from Austria."

"And what guarantee can you give me that you'll keep your word?"

"None at all. You'll just have to trust us."

Trudi looked at the three Americans. They tried to look trustworthy.

"But what if it doesn't work, if he won't come over? What happens to me then?"

"I'm afraid you would then be on your own."

Trudi was indignant: "I thought you Americans were big on chivalry," she said.

Milano grinned at her. "That all depends what you mean by chivalry."

Trudi considered the point for a while, concluded that it was not worth pursuing, and moved on to the next question: "If I can get him to come over, what sort of obligation will I have to him?"

"That's entirely up to you. Once you deliver him to us, we'll guarantee you both safe passage out of the country and new identities. He can go with you, or you can both go separately. You can travel as husband and wife or as friends. Whatever suits you best."

"And how long do I have to pull this off?"

"Well, the cutoff point will be when he's rotated back to Mother Russia. I can't guess how long it might take you to persuade him. Why don't you take a month to work on him and see how he might react? Then we'll see. We could always push things along by dropping a hint to the Russians. Then they'd recall him at once and he'd have to go—or bolt."

It was quite obvious that Trudi would agree to the Americans' plan and try to seduce her Russian lover into deserting. In fact, there had never really been any doubt. She asked how she should contact them and was told firmly that they would be in touch with her. Brewer gave her a package containing stockings, cigarettes, and some American cosmetics. Lipstick was a rare commodity in postwar Europe. They also gave her money, a first installment on her monthly allowance.

"Mr. Donnelly," she said, "tell me something. If I guess your real name, will you confirm I'm right?"

Milano smiled at her. "Certainly not," he said. "Good-bye, Trudi. The driver will take you back. He'll drop you off somewhere in the U.S. zone near your apartment." They would never take the risk, even in an unmarked car, of having the KGB spot her.

There was a long silence after she had left. Then Park Hancock observed, "The coffee's cold—so let's have a drink." He then remarked, "Jim, you may have met your match. That's one tough chick."

They heard little of Trudi for the next few months. Every few weeks Park Hancock would arrange for one of his Austrian agents to bump into her casually in a bar or some discreet corner of the city and slip her another package of hard-to-find goodies and a wad of money. They paid her well: if she succeeded in reeling in her Russian captain, he would be the most important capture they had ever made. She needed smart clothing and good American makeup, as well as brandy and American cigarettes for her Yuli. The Americans wanted her to be as beautiful and desirable as possible, and as suave and sophisticated, and in postwar Vienna a little money and useful contacts went a long way. Trudi used her gifts well. She was not only a beautiful woman but one with a good dress sense. She was stylish, cosmopolitan, worldly, and quite beyond anything Andreyev had ever met before. Stalinist Moscow was a dowdy, grim place, and Trudi was the first modern, sophisticated woman he had ever met. No wonder he was bowled over by her.

Trudi introduced him discreetly to the delights of a Western and affluent lifestyle. As the weeks passed, sweet memories of the girls of dreary Moscow faded, and the privations that would face him if he returned to his homeland appeared all the more daunting. Milano did not allow his operatives to hurry her, but at last, after several months of patient waiting, at one of those brief encounters, Trudi told her American sponsors that Andreyev was about to return to Russia. They passed the word to Milano, who alerted the Rat Line support group: they might be about to receive their most important customer.

Barely a week later, Brewer sent a cryptic message through to Salzburg: the fish had bitten. Andreyev was ready to defect, and the whole operation immediately swung into action. The plan was that the two fugitives would be hidden in the French zone until it was time to send them down the Rat Line to Italy. It was best not to hide them in the American zone: Milano wanted his superiors to be able to assure the Soviets that they had no knowledge of the missing captain's whereabouts. He had no intention of telling them of the operation, so their denials would be all the more convincing. He did not want to send the two fugitives out of the country immediately, either. It was too dangerous. The instant the defection was discovered, every agent and border guard would be alerted and Soviet representatives at every frontier post would look most carefully at every traveler. The French zone had many advantages. The Soviets paid it much less attention than they did the British and American zones, and it happened that Milano had the best of relations with his French colleagues and had the use of an ideal safe house high in the mountains. It belonged to a Jewish couple, the Newmans, who had escaped to Switzerland early in the war. Afterward, they had been befriended by the French agent Captain Muti Gillette, who had persuaded them to make the house available to French Intelligence, for a price. The house was near the Swiss border and the minute principality of Liechtenstein, which would give its occupants two escape routes if the need ever arose. It was in the country, a mile or so from the small town of Bludenz.

Milano sent two agents ahead, one a Russian specialist, one a German specialist, who were ready to interrogate the defector. He estimated that it would be necessary to keep him, and Trudi, in Bludenz for at least a month while he was exhaustively interrogated on everything he knew about the Red Army. Transcripts of the interrogations would be sent daily to the Pentagon, where the experts would study them and would undoubtedly have many further questions to put. Later, when the worst of the manhunt had subsided, the two fugitives would be moved to a safe house on the outskirts of Salzburg, where they would be prepared for the trip to Italy and the ship that would take them to the safe anonymity of South America.

The first step was also the most dangerous: getting the two out of Vienna. They were picked up separately and carried off to one of Brewer's secret residences. There they were disguised: getting out of Vienna meant passing directly under the noses of Soviet security and taking the *Mozart*, the train from Vienna that passed through the Soviet zone before reaching the comparative safety of Salzburg. The Russian was given a new name, Dexter, with passport and other papers to match. He was given an American sport jacket and slacks and a stick-on mustache. His blond hair was dyed black, and he carried bags and belongings that would make him appear to be just another American. He had a gray pass, papers that showed that he was a civilian employee of the U.S. Army. Trudi was renamed Josephine. She wore a dull red wig, a turtleneck sweater, and a long, pleated skirt. She looked positively dowdy, not at all the glamorous vamp who had seduced the Russian officer. Her papers, all perfectly in order, showed that she was an American citizen, Dexter's wife. She provided her own wedding ring. They were then driven to the station and put aboard the overnight train for Salzburg, accompanied by two of Hancock's agents. American officials, under Brewer's watchful eyes, waved them through, and the Soviet guards paid them no particular attention. Captain Andreyev had not yet been reported missing.

They arrived the next morning in Salzburg, tired but elated. The worst was over. The reception committee, consisting of Paul Lyon and Charlie Crawford, drove them straight to Innsbruck, in the French zone, where they were taken to the villa occupied by the CIC's liaison officers. They were given lunch and a room in which to spend the afternoon: they were to be driven to Bludenz after dark, and the Americans were determined that as few people as possible should see them.

Late that evening, a couple of cars drove from Innsbruck up into the Alps and delivered Dexter and Josephine, with their minders, to the safe house. The Newmans were there to welcome the party. The house was a large one, which was fortunate: there were eight or a dozen people there at all times, including Trudi and her lover, the two interrogators, the Newmans—and a couple of agents to guard them all. Mrs. Newman was delighted and busied herself in the kitchen to feed the crowd with supplies brought in from Salzburg or provided on a barter basis by the French intelligence office. No doubt the CIC would be able to return the favor at some later date. Trudi helped Mrs. Newman with the cooking, showing a quite unexpected aptitude. If she found it ironic that an active Nazi was being helped by a Jewish family who had barely escaped the Holocaust, she never revealed it. She was not needed by the interrogators, who were laboriously debriefing her lover in Russian, and was glad to make herself useful.

Three days after Trudi and Yuli fled Vienna disguised as Josephine and Dexter, Marshal of the Soviet Union Ivan Stepanovich Konev, commander of Soviet Forces in Austria, presented himself at American headquarters. Andreyev had been missed, and the Soviets wanted to know where he was. The marshal demanded to see General Keyes, who had replaced Mark Clark as commanding American general. He wanted to know if a junior member of his staff, Captain Yuli Andreyev, was being held by American forces anywhere in the American zone. Keyes replied that he knew nothing at all about the matter and would make urgent inquiries. The Russian was obviously upset and worried: if the man had deserted, it would be a serious matter for the entire Soviet headquarters.

Within hours, General Keyes was able to tell him that there were no Russian officers being held anywhere in the American zone, nor had any defected. He was telling the absolute truth, as far as he knew it: Milano had made sure that none of his superiors knew anything about Trudi and her boyfriend, and, when they asked, the CIC was able to reply truthfully that it had no one answering that description anywhere in the zone. The Soviets may or may not have believed the general. Certainly, when a U.S. general gives his word, it is bound to impress a Soviet marshal. On the other hand, the Soviet general staff did not necessarily know anything at all about the activities of the KGB, so at the very least they must have suspected the Americans of deceit. There was a general alert among all Soviet agents in Austria and on the borders, and the KGB made strenuous efforts to find the missing man, but without success. Milano and his team had been very careful.

The interrogation lasted five weeks. Andreyev proved a most useful source of information on the Red Army's order of battle, readiness, morale, and plans. He was a mine of information on the very topics that most interested the Pentagon. There was a constant stream of top secret coded communications between Salzburg and Washington before the captain was at last pumped dry and Milano judged that it was safe to move him and Trudi back from Bludenz. It was time to activate the Rat Line. Draganović had been told that the Americans required two refugee passes for South America for a man and wife. They would go directly to Rome, to be passed through regular refugee channels: Paul Lyon considered that his charges would be safer in Rome than if they were smuggled through Genoa or Naples. The priest replied that he would be delighted, merely, as usual, requesting that they bring their marriage certificate with

them. The Good Father assumed they were Catholic: the whole operation was based on the fiction that every client of the Rat Line was a
Catholic refugee.

Trudi was told that if she wanted to leave Europe it had to be as
Dexter's wife. Milano had promised her, months earlier, that she
would be able to choose whether to go with Andreyev or not, but circumstances had changed. It would be much safer for him to travel
as a married man. She agreed. Whatever her feelings for her lover,
she concluded that he would be useful to her in starting her new life
in Brazil.

First, they returned to Salzburg from Bludenz. Once again, they
took two days on the road, stopping for the night at Innsbruck. When
they reached Salzburg, they were put up in a villa some miles outside
town, staying with several American agents. They were not prisoners,
but they were not allowed out anymore than they had been in
Bludenz. Indeed, they had to hide more carefully now, even though
the Soviets were presumably despairing of finding their missing officer. They were to spend no more than a week in their new hideaway
before being taken across the border to Udine and Rome.

Milano's next task was to organize the wedding. It had to be a top
secret ceremony but also a properly legal one. The happy couple
would be traveling under new names and with new papers, but their
marriage certificate would be perfectly genuine. What is more, they
had to be married in a church, to satisfy Draganović, and by a mag-
istrate, to satisfy local requirements. Austria, like most European
countries, recognizes only civil weddings, which are carried out in
the local town hall and are usually followed by a church ceremony.

The Americans took it all most seriously. After all, top secret weddings were most unusual, if not unprecedented. Milano recruited a
local priest to perform the ceremony. He was known as Father Joe,
and he officiated at a small church near the villa where Dexter and
Josephine were to stay. Two of the American agents who used the
villa, Charlie Crawford and Paul Lyon, were Catholics and attended
Mass from time to time. They had made friends with Father Joe and
occasionally brought him back to the villa for dinner. They had an
excellent cook, and he appreciated their attention. When the time
came, he was quite ready to marry the two fugitives. Trudi was
Catholic, though she had probably not been inside a church for a
decade. Andreyev had been baptized into the Russian Orthodox
Church, though he had been brought up as an atheist in Soviet
Russia. Father Joe saw no impediment to their marriage, provided
that Yuli promised that their children would be brought up Catholic.
He raised no objection and cheerfully signed the Latin document
required on such occasions.

Milano asked his two secretaries, Eileen and Pat, to make all the
arrangements. They hired an accordion player, laid in a stock of

wine, and urged the villa's cook to spare no expense. The wedding was on a Saturday morning. Milano took Dexter and Josephine to the town hall with the necessary two witnesses and a number of his men to provide security. They were the first couple to be married that day, and the whole procedure took half an hour. Then the wedding party went to the church, where Father Joe was waiting for them. The two women acted as bridesmaids: Pat had found corsages for herself, Eileen, and for the bride. The MIS supply officer, Jim Alongi, acted as best man, and Jim Milano gave away the blushing bride. As he took her down the aisle on his arm, the accordion player played "Here Comes the Bride." Afterward, there was a party for them at the villa.

Everyone drank to the health of the bride and groom and to their future in South America. In the midst of the party, the villa housekeeper pulled Milano aside and took him into the room Trudi and Yuli had been using. One of the housekeeper's jobs was to check the bags of departing guests. Particularly after the incident of the defector who had concealed a pistol and used it in Chile, Milano wanted to be sure that the people he sent down the Rat Line were carrying nothing they should not. The housekeeper had examined Trudi's suitcase and had found a derringer pocket pistol with two bullets in it. Milano went back to the party and asked the bride if he could have a word with her. She came out into the hallway, and Milano asked her just what she was doing with a pistol. She was astonished.

"You don't miss anything, do you?" she replied. "I've had it for years. A friend of mine gave it to me during the war: I didn't know when it might come in useful. If you'd double-crossed me, I was going to shoot you and then use the last bullet on myself."

"That would have been a splendid end to everything," Milano replied.

"Can I have my gun back?" she asked.

"Certainly not."

Trudi looked him in the eye, laughed, and said, "You know, if things had gone a little differently, we would have made a splendid couple."

Milano was left speechless for a moment. Then he took Trudi firmly by the arm and back to the party. Late that evening, escorted by two of the most senior agents, Trudi and Yuli departed for Udine, Rome, and South America. Like all the other clients of the Rat Line, they then vanished from the face of history. The Americans never learned how they adapted to life in Brazil, whether Trudi joined the large German colony there, or even whether she and her Russian lover remained married. From Milano's point of view, she had amply earned her passage and her new identity.

16

The Rover Boys

Vienna was a dangerous place after the war. Gray, desperate people inhabited a dingy, run-down city strewn with the wreckage and rubble of war, barely recalling the glories of Old Vienna. There were spies of every nationality, black marketeers, profiteers, smugglers, criminals of every sort, and refugees from every country in Eastern Europe. There was a steady undercurrent of violence. Every Viennese appeared to be engaged in shady dealings of one sort or another or at least knew people who were. The whole grim and grimy city was controlled by aloof and intrusive Allied military governments. It was divided into four zones, one for each of the wartime allies, and the center of the city was administered jointly by the four powers. There was no wall dividing Vienna, and military personnel from all the conquerors moved freely throughout the city. There was a multitude of police forces and military security organizations, and in all this confusion the criminals and spies moved easily among the zones, hiding in one and operating in the others. Many people of dubious antecedents disappeared all the time, never to be heard of again.

Usually, none of this concerned the Special Intelligence Section of the Counter-Intelligence Corps. If people disappeared, that was their bad luck or their choice. People would surface in Vienna, working some racket or pursuing some phantom road to riches, and then vanish just as suddenly, either because they had found the crock of gold or to keep ahead of the police or the competition: remember Harry Lime in *The Third Man*. If bodies were found floating in the Danube or dumped in city parks or in any of the wilderness of bomb sites, that was only to be expected. Milano and his colleagues began to worry only when their own people started to disappear.

The first to vanish off the streets of Vienna, late in 1949, was a Polish refugee who was on the books as an interpreter. The CIC needed such people to help it cope with refugees from any of a dozen countries who had tales to tell, or might. There were many Poles among them, and the interpreter was kept busy. He was called to the door of his apartment late one evening, stepped outside for a moment, and was never seen again. Then it was the turn of an Austrian woman who worked for the Vienna station. She left for home one afternoon, and she, too, vanished without trace. Perhaps the first incident was a settling of accounts in the Polish émigré community. Perhaps, in the second case, the lady had found a new protector and wished to escape her current American boyfriend without explanation. But the third disappearance was an Austrian who worked in the riding stables Pete Chambers was using to spy on the Russian officer corps and to look out for possible defectors—Operation Horsefeathers. Two men wearing the uniforms of American military policemen called on the unsuspecting Austrian one evening and took him away. When his wife went looking for him in the morning, there was no news of him to be had in any of the police offices in Vienna. The disappearance in a short period of three people connected to American intelligence operations was highly suspicious. As a fictional spy once said, "Once is happenstance. Twice is coincidence. Three times is enemy action."

The Special Intelligence Section set to work to discover what had happened to its employees. Agents interrogated the missing people's wives, friends, neighbors, and acquaintances. They went to the riding stables in the Soviet zone, but discreetly. It was one of their own front operations, and they feared that its activities had been compromised or would be compromised by their inquiries. The stables were directed by an Austrian officer who had been a major in a prewar cavalry regiment. Every day, Soviet officers and officials would come out to the stables, located in a quiet, leafy suburb of the capital, and ride in the ring for an hour or two or take one of the horses for a ride through the Vienna woods. The Austrian major made friends with them, ran errands and performed services for them, supplying them with drink, special foods, cigarettes—and more sensitive services. There was no shortage of women hungry enough to befriend a Russian officer in exchange for cigarettes or money, and the major had plenty of contacts. Every so often he would approach a Russian he thought susceptible to seduction, usually a man who was about to be recalled home, and offer to arrange a safe refuge for him with his American friends. He was a man of excellent judgment and never made a mistake. Many of Milano's best sources were defectors recruited by the Austrian major. Later they were sent to South America down the Rat Line.

It would be a calamity if the Soviets discovered that the stable was an American intelligence operation. The missing man, Albert Youngman, had been an ordinary employee. He had kept the books and helped the major administer the place. He had played no part in clandestine operations and had known nothing of the major's role in the secret world, but it was always possible that he had suspected something or had discovered some significant piece of information that a Soviet agent would understand. The stables sometimes received hidden subsidies from American intelligence funds, and the bookkeeper might have noticed unexplained credits and suspected their origins.

There was another reason to be concerned. There had used to be constant kidnappings in Vienna: the Americans had not been averse to seizing people in the Soviet zone and spiriting them to the West, and immediately after the war the Soviets had regularly kidnapped people from the other zones, using the local police, who were heavily infiltrated by the Austrian Communist Party. The Americans and their allies had soon purged the police, and the regular kidnappings had come to an end. Now, suddenly, it seemed as though the Soviets had developed a foolproof method, with agents masquerading as American MPs. They would be very hard to catch, because they could so easily move back to the safety of the Soviet zone.

The story had in fact begun several months earlier. Sergeant Barney Nelson of the U.S. 297th Military Police Battalion had made a comfortable life for himself in Vienna. He had encountered the young widow of an SS officer, one of tens of thousands of soldiers' widows in Austria, who filled every sexual fantasy that a twenty-year-old from Coeur d'Alene, Idaho, had ever dreamt. She was older than he and far more experienced. She taught him everything she knew, and her every lesson was a revelation to the naïve and stupid young American. Her name was Elsa, and like many Viennese she added to her income by dealing in the black market. At the same time, she demanded all the money Barney Nelson could give her, extorting three quarters of his pay and constantly asking for more. He was the supply sergeant for his battalion, and he began stealing from its stores. That was a dangerous and difficult operation, and Elsa was not satisfied with his achievements.

He once bragged that he had an off-the-books radio transmitter in his store and suggested that she might sell it for him. He knew nothing of radio technology, and perhaps he exaggerated the set's qualities. Elsa was impressed and arranged for some friends to look at it. Barney got a buddy of his, Corporal Nicholas Roundtree, a farm boy from Louisiana who was also an MP, to help him load the transmitter into a small truck and bring it around to a spot near Elsa's apartment in the British zone. It was a desolate part of town, an empty street lined with warehouses and deserted lots, and Elsa guided the two MPs in their truck through a side gate into one of the warehouses. Three taciturn men were waiting to examine the transmitter. They used no names, and Barney was not told their nationality. One of them spoke English with a foreign accent, the others were silent. They looked the transmitter over carefully and concluded that it was worth nothing. They thanked Barney for his trouble and sent him back, disappointed, to return the machine to store.

Thus was Barney dragged into a new world of conspirators and spies. A few days after the aborted sale, Elsa told him that the English-speaking man in the warehouse, Mark, had a different proposition to make to him. Barney swallowed the bait at once and set off willingly, a fish reeled in by a master angler. This time the meeting was in Elsa's apartment. Mark, correctly judging the stupidity and greed of the young MP, now admitted that he was a Russian. He proposed that Barney should don his uniform and earn some money by arresting suspects wanted by the Soviets. For each arrest, he would be paid 3,000 schillings.

It would be easy. All he would need was another MP to help him: they always traveled in pairs. But everything else was ready to hand. They had their uniforms, a jeep, and all the weight of the U.S. Army. They would drive around Vienna unsupervised, like scores of other teams of MPs. They could arrest anyone with impunity and deliver their captives to Mark and his friends in that discreet abandoned warehouse in Elsa's street. Barney agreed at once. This sounded a painless way to make money—and Elsa always needed money. Mark gave him an advance on his first pay, and he flashed the money in front of his friend Nick Roundtree and invited him to join the operation. After an evening spent drinking the windfall money, Roundtree agreed.

The plan was simplicity itself. Mark told them whom to find, and where, and how to do it. A few days later, the two Americans set out to pick up the Polish translator. Their first effort at kidnapping ended in fiasco. They decided to drink to their success before they started, to get up their courage. By the time they reached the street where the Pole lived, they were completely drunk and wisely decided to postpone the effort. Mark was very understanding when they arrived, empty-handed and incoherent, at the warehouse. He sent them out again the following evening, and this time they stayed sober. They knocked on the door of the Pole's apartment and, when he answered, told him that an American officer wanted to see him briefly. He agreed at once, and they drove him to the warehouse, where Mark and two burly men in plainclothes were waiting for him. He vanished there for good, presumably carried off to the Soviet zone to be interrogated by Soviet intelligence on whatever he knew about American operations, methods, and personnel. He was then either shot or sent back to Poland to disappear into the Communist gulag.

The two Americans were paid their blood money and went out to celebrate. This was easy money. Their next hit, the Austrian woman, was easier still. They arrested her in their jeep as she was walking home one evening. She offered no resistance, was not at all surprised, until they delivered her to Mark and his friends. Then she learned that she had fallen into the hands of the enemy. She was luckier than the Pole: her captors released her after three days' interrogation.

The kidnappers' third victim, Albert Youngman, fell into their hands just as easily. They presented themselves at his apartment and invited him down to police headquarters. In Vienna in 1949, that was an invitation that no Austrian could refuse. But this time the two MPs did their work in the daylight. The door was opened by Youngman's wife, and other people in the building saw the kidnappers, too. Youngman was spirited off to Soviet Intelligence headquarters in the Austrian countryside, forty miles from Vienna. He was then subjected to a nonstop three-day grilling in which he was asked, over and over again, for every detail he knew or could dredge from his memory concerning the riding stables, the Austrian major, and the various Americans who rode there. The Soviets had photographs of every American and wanted to know their names, their units, and their life histories. How much time did they spend in the stables, whom did they talk to, what were they interested in? The interrogators wanted to know all about Youngman's boss. Where had he come from, where had he gotten the money to start the stables, what were his contacts, how did he spend his spare time, did he ever show any interest in politics or military matters? What did he and Youngman talk about, and did he carry American guests off for private conversations? They showed him pictures of Soviet officers who had frequented the stables: Did he remember these men, did the major devote any unusual attention to them? Had Youngman ever seen him take these men aside for private conversations in the seclusion of his office or go riding alone with them?

Albert Youngman was baffled by all these questions. He was no more than a simple bookkeeper and general manager. He was unobservant and rather stupid; these were qualities that had endeared him to his boss, a man who believed in taking every precaution. He had seen nothing suspicious and could remember nothing that now seemed suspicious, not even when the Soviet interrogators showed him photographs of officers who had defected and asked if they had behaved strangely at the stables. They pumped him dry and then set him free. He returned to his wife and recounted his experiences to the Austrian major—but resolutely refused to return to work for him. He had no wish to have anything more to do with so dangerous an acquaintance.

The sudden reappearance of the Austrian lady and Mr. Youngman gave American and Austrian police a clear account of the Soviets' methods of picking up suspects, but they still did not know whether the two MPs were genuine or fake. Stories appeared in Vienna newspapers about a mysterious pair of American MPs who were working for the Soviets and kidnapping Austrians off the streets of Vienna. They were nicknamed the Rover Boys, and there was a full-scale search for them. Sergeant Nelson and Corporal Roundtree soon heard about it: they had bragged of their exploits to other men in their unit, and before long some of their friends who read the German newspapers brought them the bad news. It would be only a matter of time before the counterintelligence agents caught up with them.

They could have escaped to the Soviet zone, but Mark was suddenly unavailable. The Rover Boys had worked well for a short while, but they had been indiscreet and incompetent and were bound to be caught sooner or later. The Soviets preferred to cut their losses immediately, and they wrote off the unfortunate Americans. Elsa vanished. She had taken her share of Mark's payments and had doubtless been paid separately and generously for introducing the two Americans to her Soviet friends. She vanished into the underworld, and the CIC never found her. Nelson and Roundtree tried to escape their fate by going to the CIC themselves, to claim that they had been approached by the Russians to kidnap people in the Western zones and had virtuously refused. Each swore a solemn oath to the other that he would never reveal the truth, that they had in fact succumbed to Soviet blandishments and used their uniforms to work for Soviet Intelligence. Their courage and firm resolutions lasted no more than a few hours. Each man was interrogated separately, by efficient and hard-faced cops who produced Albert Youngman, his wife, and other witnesses who identified the two as the men who had kidnapped him, and the Austrian woman, who was equally certain in her identification. Each broke down and confessed. They were court-martialed and sentenced to twenty years apiece.

17

The Goulash Connection

In the summer of 1948, an American agent, working temporarily in the U.S. Embassy in Budapest, achieved a remarkable double: he recruited a group of former German and Hungarian anti-Communist agents to work for the Americans, and he found and rescued a young Austrian who had been left there by his Jewish mother in 1938. The agent was Harry Klingensmith, who had been recruited by Park Hancock in Vienna. The U.S. Embassy in Budapest looked on Klingensmith's work with great suspicion, and its attitude was typical: Milano and his colleagues constantly had trouble persuading the Foreign Service to allow his agents to operate under embassy cover. This was before the days of the CIA and its establishment of residents in every embassy in the world.

Klingensmith had made contact with the remnants of the Abwehr network in Budapest. These were Hungarians who had worked for German Military Intelligence during the war. Some of them had been seconded from Hungarian Intelligence, and their loyalties must have caused the Germans many doubts: in the last year of the war, Admiral Miklós Horthy, the Hungarian regent, had tried repeatedly to get Hungary out of the conflict and escape from its alliance with Germany. He could see perfectly well that the Nazis were going to be defeated and had tried to save what could be saved for himself and his country. The Gestapo had been well informed, and in March 1944 Hitler had ordered his armies to occupy Hungary. Eichmann had followed the Wehrmacht to Budapest and had begun the destruction of the Hungarian Jews. Horthy had remained titular head of state but had been stripped of all real power. The following

October, as the Red Army had crossed the Carpathians and entered the Hungarian plain, Horthy had proclaimed an armistice and tried to surrender to the Allies. Hungarian Fascists had arrested him and shipped him off to Austria, then mounted a last, desperate defense of Budapest. It had finally fallen to the Red Army in February 1945.

The Abwehr had, of course, continued its intelligence gathering until the last. Its Hungarian employees had been left behind at the end of the war. They had supported Germany to the bitter end, some no doubt because they were Fascists, some patriotic ones because they feared for their country's survival if it fell under Stalinist control. In the three years after the war, they saw their worst fears realized as the most ruthless of all Eastern European Communist regimes, headed by Mátyás Rákosi, imposed itself upon the country. Rákosi coined a phrase to describe the standard Communist process in Eastern Europe: he called it the "salami tactic," the cutting away of one democratic or civil liberty at a time, slice by slice. Now, in 1948, Harry Klingensmith began cautiously making contact with one or two of the agents and proposed building a new anti-Communist intelligence network. At the height of the cold war, Milano and his colleagues in Austria, who supervised the recruitment and maintenance of the network, had no scruple in using former German agents for the purpose.

At the embassy, Klingensmith's official task, which was tolerated by the Hungarian government, was to try to discover the fate of the crew of an American bomber that had crashed near Budapest in the last months of the war. It had been on a bombing run from Italy against an oil field in Austria, at Zisterdorf, and had been hit by German flak. The pilot had radioed that he could not make it back to base and would try to land behind Soviet lines in east Hungary. The Soviets denied ever seeing the plane or knowing anything of its crew. Klingensmith reported that he had heard of a crash site near Lake Balaton, just north of Budapest. The Hungarians could not object to Americans investigating the reports, and they allowed Klingensmith to stay a month to complete his investigation. In the event, he failed to locate the crash site, but he used the time, and his ability to move around the country, as cover while he made contact with members of the Abwehr network and made arrangements to pay them and communicate with them. This was the most important and dangerous of all clandestine tasks; the best agent is no use if he cannot report to his handlers and if his handlers cannot contact him to ask specific questions.

One morning during this interesting period, while Jim Milano was sitting peacefully in his office in Salzburg, smoking a cigar and studying an agent's report, his secretary came in to tell him that there was a woman who wanted to see him on a private matter. She had given her name, Maria Torkey, but had declined to state her business. Milano, on the theory that anything would be preferable to analyzing an unreliable agent's report, had her sent in.

She was a handsome middle-aged lady who spoke excellent English with a slight accent. She said that she had been born in Hungary, which Milano had already guessed, and now lived in New York City. She had escaped there after Hitler had occupied Austria in 1938. Milano waited patiently to hear what this had to do with him.

"I'm Jewish," she said. "My original first name was Miriam; I changed it when I married. My husband was Christian. We were both from Budapest, and he had estates south of Vienna, so we lived in Austria. He hated the Nazis and didn't make any secret of the fact. He was killed by the Gestapo after the *Anschluss,* in the fall of 1938. We had a nine-year-old son, Johnnie, and I was terrified that he would be killed, too. So when my husband was murdered, I sent him with our maid, Sonia, who was Hungarian, to her village near Lake Balaton, in Hungary. I had to stay, to try to settle our affairs after my husband was killed, but then some friends in the government told me that I was about to be arrested by the Gestapo because I was Jewish. All my property would be confiscated. My friends told me I had to leave at once, that I couldn't get to Budapest to look for my son. So I just packed a few things and escaped over the border to Italy. I got to Trieste, where I managed to get a ship to London.

"I'd spent three years there as a child, so I had friends who took me in. I was desperate about my son, but there was no way I could contact him without giving him away to the government. Hungary was allied to Hitler, and he would certainly have been shipped back to Austria if they had found out about him. Then I met an American sailor who was stationed at the naval section of the U.S. Embassy. We got married, and he took me to New York when he was sent home just before Pearl Harbor. Unfortunately, the marriage didn't last: we were divorced five years ago. I've been working for the government in New York ever since.

"Now at last I've managed to return to Austria to look for my son. Will you help me?"

"Why do you think I could help you? Can't the consulate or the embassy in Budapest do anything to find the boy?"

"I've spent a month here trying. The embassy in Vienna says there's no chance at all that I can get a visa to Hungary, and I daren't write to Sonia. Anyway, I don't have a proper address for her. I've been staying at the Österreicher Hof here, and I saw you were also a guest. Last night, I had dinner with the consul in Salzburg, Peter Constant. I told him how discouraged I was and that I would probably have to go back to New York. He said I should speak to you.

"He said he didn't know exactly what you do, except that you are listed as an economic study group in the phone book. He didn't say much more, but he sort of hinted that you might be able to help me somehow."

Torkey was lucky. Milano had an agent in Budapest—Harry Klingensmith—and he was touched by her story. He thought he might possibly be able to help. All the same, he would have a word with Peter Constant about taking his name in vain, and especially dropping hints that he was in the intelligence business.

"I'll see if there's anything I can do," he said. "I seriously doubt it, so you mustn't get your hopes up. But we'll try. The Economic Development Office chiefly works in Austria, but we might have some contacts in Hungary. I'll see. Give me every detail you know about Sonia, her full name, last known address, any other contacts you might have. I'll get back to you in a week or two if there's anything to report. Or you can call here from time to time, to see if there's any news."

Maria was touchingly grateful. Her son was the most important thing in the world to her, and she had lost him for ten years. Milano was the first American, let alone Austrian or Hungarian, official who had given her any hope at all. She had come prepared with all the details she knew written out: she handed the paper over, thanked him profusely, and left.

Klingensmith had another two weeks on his visa. He had succeeded in setting up the essential communications arrangements for the reconstituted Abwehr network but had made no progress with the missing American B-24 crew. Milano sent a coded message, giving him all the details of the Torkey case and telling him to spend two or three days seeing if he could find the boy. Meanwhile, Milano noted that Maria was, indeed, staying at the hotel he used as his base in Salzburg and seemed to be spending a lot of time with a civilian employee of the Army, Frank Bozen, who worked as a translator at a base in Germany. Milano concluded that their interest in each other had nothing to do with intelligence matters.

A few days later, he had a coded message from Klingensmith. He had begun his search for Johnnie by checking the lists of local employees of the U.S. Mission in Budapest, looking for one from the town near Lake Balaton where Maria had sent her son. There were two, both middle-aged women who had lived in the place during the war. Klingensmith interviewed them both, after first checking their credentials: he had no wish to confide his concern to some spy of the Hungarian secret service. One of the women knew nothing of Sonia Zerka, Maria's former maid, but the other, a translator in the embassy who spoke good English, remembered her from the war years. She reported that Sonia had died a year earlier. The information was both encouraging and worrying: to begin with, there was no indication at all of what might have happened to the boy. Klingensmith would have to go look.

Milano decided not to report the news to Maria. She continued to call on his office every day or two and was always assured that the hunt for her son was continuing and that she should return again. Milano decided that he would tell her nothing until he had some concrete news for her.

Then Klingensmith sent another message that he had found the boy. He had gone to the village where Sonia had lived and had easily discovered that her son, a boy of about nineteen, was living with a relative of Sonia's nearby. The relative worked in the famous Tokay vineyards, and the boy had just finished school. Klingensmith went to see them and reported that there was no doubt of the identification. Johnnie remembered his mother perfectly, knew the family names, and remembered being taken away from home by Sonia—and that he had been forbidden ever to mention his real mother during all the terrible years since then. He was delighted that his mother was looking for him: he had assumed, after all the horrors of the war, that he would never see her again.

Milano replied that Klingensmith should look into the possibility of smuggling Johnnie into Austria. The Hungarians and Russians should not be informed: they would refuse to give the boy a visa and would certainly arrest him if he were caught trying to leave. Furthermore, Milano ruled that the U.S. Embassy should not be informed, either. The State Department resented and distrusted everything to do with clandestine intelligence and would certainly oppose any effort to get Johnnie out of the country. Milano and his colleagues had no such scruples.

Klingensmith was a resourceful, imaginative agent. He discovered that a large shipment of furniture was being sent from the U.S. Embassy in Budapest to the embassy in Vienna. The consignment consisted of the furnishings of the prewar embassy, which had been put into storage when Hungary declared war on the United States, at Hitler's behest, in 1941. The embassy had been closed and had been severely damaged during the fighting between the Wehrmacht and the Red Army in 1944 and 1945. Repairing it was going to take months, possibly years, and in the meantime the ambassador had decided to send the prewar furnishings to Vienna for safekeeping. The Hungarians had authorized an Austrian firm to send a number of moving vans to pick everything up.

Klingensmith brought Johnnie back to Budapest in the course of one of his trips into the countryside, where he had ostensibly been looking for the missing Air Force crew. Johnnie had bidden a hurried farewell to the family that had taken him in when Sonia died:

they blessed him and wished him luck. There was no trouble getting the boy into Budapest: his papers were in order, he was just a hitch-hiker picked up by a passing American diplomat. In the event, they were not stopped. Klingensmith persuaded a U.S. Embassy employ-ee who was in charge of packing up the furniture to allow him into the warehouse, and then they rolled Johnnie up in a carpet and stowed him in the front of the moving van. They carefully stacked furniture around and above the carpet, to conceal and protect the boy. He was told to stay where he was and above all to keep absolutely still when the van stopped at the Russian checkpoints.

The Austrian driver and the American official who accompanied him knew nothing about their unusual cargo. They simply drove the truck from Budapest to Vienna, stopped at Soviet checkpoints at the exit from Budapest, at the border, and then a third time as the van entered Vienna. Their papers were in order: this was a diplomatic cargo. They passed through every checkpoint without difficulty, and Johnnie managed to remain quiet and safe during the day-long trip. In the evening, the van arrived at the U.S. Embassy compound in Vienna, where Park Hancock was waiting. He sent the driver and escort off while he and a couple of his agents examined the van's contents and discovered Johnnie, safe and sound, rolled up in the carpet, just as Cleopatra had been delivered to Julius Caesar. He was taken to a safe house in Vienna, and Milano was informed that the operation had been successfully completed.

All that remained was to get him to Salzburg. He would take the Vienna–Munich train, the *Mozart,* which passed through the Soviet zone. It was the usual route: whenever Milano had to make a clan-destine transfer, usually a deserter escaping the Red Army and des-tined for the Rat Line, he was dressed in a U.S. Army uniform and given American papers. A day after Johnnie arrived in Vienna, he and one of Hancock's agents were aboard the *Mozart.* The boy was dressed as an American private, carrying the "gray pass" that American servicemen used when crossing the Soviet zone. The *Mozart* never stopped in the zone: the railroad's Austrian employees would check all passengers' passes before the train left Vienna and report the number at the Soviet control point as the train entered and left the zone. That was all. It was a simple system, as long as the Russians' suspicions were not aroused. The train left in the after-noon, and Hancock sent a message to Salzburg announcing that the package was on its way.

It was time to inform Maria. Milano summoned her to his office and announced that her son had been found and rescued and would arrive safely in Salzburg the following morning.

She was ecstatic, astonished, tearful, incoherent.

"Oh, my God!" she cried. "You've found Johnnie! Is it true? Where is he? When will he get here? How did you find him?"

Milano tried to calm her down. He explained how his agent in Budapest, by great good fortune and much skill, had discovered the boy and smuggled him out of the country. She wanted to telephone him immediately, but Milano firmly refused permission. All phone lines passed through the Soviet zone, and all calls were tapped by the KGB. Besides, the *Mozart* had already left the station.

"The train gets in at five every morning. I'll pick you up in the hotel lobby at quarter of and drive you down to the station."

He ushered Maria, still incoherent with gratitude and astonishment, out of his office. The business of intelligence was often sordid and generally dull. It was very unusual indeed that Milano or any of his staff could do anything completely altruistic, could help people for no better reason than that they needed it, and correct one of the ghastly wrongs and crimes of the twentieth century. This time, through good fortune and skill, Army Intelligence had succeeded in restoring a family that had been broken up by the Nazis and saving a young man from the Hungarian Communists. It was all most gratifying.

The next morning, when the *Mozart* steamed into the station, Milano and Maria Torkey saw a young man in American uniform get off the train, accompanied by one of Hancock's agents from Vienna. It had been ten years since mother and son had been separated. The tides of war had swept her west to America and had passed over the boy's head in Hungary. All the same, there was never any doubt. Each recognized the other immediately, and Jim Milano stood to one side on the platform as the two embraced and wept together.

In the days after that touching reunion on the station platform, Jim Milano assumed that he had heard the last of Maria Torkey and her family and that she would return to New York with her son. He was therefore much astonished a month or so later when she reappeared at his office and invited him to lunch—together with his senior staff. She announced that the civil authorities, who had been quite unable to help her in the search for Johnnie, had done much better on another front. They had returned to her all the property confiscated by the Nazis in 1938, including a large villa in the Austrian Alps at Bad Aussee. This was where the party was to be held: she had arranged with a local restaurant to do the catering.

"There's only one problem," she said, "and it will amuse you. After my husband was murdered and I had escaped to England, the Nazis gave the villa to a prominent composer, Johann Dustoff. He was a great favorite of Dr. Goebbels and used to compose marches, fanfares, and things for Party rallies, odes to Hitler, that sort of thing.

He moved into the villa with his wife and three children—and they're still there.

"Only in the meantime he got divorced and married another woman. That was during the war, when housing was a problem, even for senior Nazis, so the first wife got the divorce court to order the villa divided in two: Herr Dustoff got the upper floor, Frau Dustoff number one got the ground floor. She stayed there with her children while her ex-husband installed his new wife upstairs, and they've had a baby. Now they've given me my house back, but both families asked the court to let them stay for a while, to give them time to find new housing. It's even more difficult than it was during the war, and there's not much demand for Nazi composers these days.

"The court gave them six months and ordered Frau Dustoff One out of the ground floor of the villa. So she moved upstairs, with the children, and joined her ex-husband and his new wife.

"So the man is living with two wives—and four children."

Milano was entranced: "Sounds like the plot of a comic opera," he said. "I'm sure it couldn't have happened to a nicer man."

"Anyway," Maria continued, "the two parts of the house are quite separate, and I'll expect you all for lunch on Sunday. I'll have a surprise for you, so don't be late."

It was a pleasant break from the usual drabness of Salzburg on the weekend. Milano and several of his colleagues, together with their wives and girlfriends, all drove out into the Alps at the appointed hour. The villa was high in the mountains, near the Hallstätter See, with a magnificent view of the mountains. It was a beautiful house, and the ground floor had a superb living room, dining room, kitchen, bath, and three bedrooms. All the Torkey family furniture, silver, pictures, and porcelain had survived intact. Maria said that she had been astonished and delighted to discover that the composer and his wife had taken such good care of her possessions—though, of course, they had believed for years that everything belonged to them.

The party was a great success. There were ten people there, and Maria was an excellent hostess. The caterers had provided for everything on a lavish scale, and the wine and brandy flowed abundantly. Her friend Frank Bozen was there, too, and at the end of lunch Maria made an announcement. The two of them were going to get married and move back to the United States. They would live in Jonesboro, Arkansas, where the Bozen family ran a ham curing and bacon business. The whole party stood up, cheered, and drank to the happy couple—and to Johnnie, who would have to learn English in a hurry. Milano wondered how a cosmopolitan Jewish lady like Maria Torkey, who had lived all her life in Budapest, Vienna, London, and

New York, would adapt to the life of a ham producer in Arkansas. He kept his doubts to himself.

Then Maria made her second announcement: "I owe everything to Jim Milano and the rest of you, for finding Johnnie and getting him out of Hungary. So I'm arranging for you to have the use of this place for the rest of your time in Austria. You can use it for whatever purposes you want—and you'll have the whole of it in six months, when the Nazis move out from upstairs."

Milano protested that she was far too generous. Johnnie had been found by a series of lucky breaks, and he disclaimed all credit. Lending him the villa was quite unnecessary—she ought to sell it. Maria would not hear of a refusal. The villa was his for as long as he stayed in Austria: she would sell it when he left, unless Johnnie wanted to use it. Milano's colleagues were far less reticent than he. They praised Maria's generosity and insisted that he accept. The villa would be a very useful safe house for some of their clients, they said—and would serve admirably for R and R for the whole Operations Branch.

So for the next two years, Milano had the use of a luxurious, well-appointed villa in the Austrian Alps, a quite unexpected reward for a good deed. The house served as a hideout for a number of Soviet deserters and a useful conference center for planning sessions by the various departments of the American intelligence community. It was also very popular, as his colleagues had known it would be, among officers and agents in need of rest and recreation in the peace and tranquillity of the Alps.

Another incident that had little to do with intelligence occurred at this time. Milano's office first got wind of it from the daily press summary that was circulated to the various sections of the headquarters staff. The paper consisted of brief synopses of articles in the Austrian press. Pieces that caught the eye of one of the officers would then be produced and, if necessary, translated for him. No one had the time to plow through all the papers published in Vienna, but there was a constant stream of useful information to be gleaned from them. On this occasion, there was an item reporting that an American named Julius Hahn had been shot and killed by a Russian sentry. He had been driving near the border with the Soviet zone and had apparently taken a wrong turning. It had been pouring rain, and Hahn had failed to stop when challenged. The Russian soldier had then fired on the car, killing him.

The car had crashed, and a woman passenger, Emma Superina, had been injured and taken to a hospital in the Soviet zone. The article noted that she was a Yugoslav refugee living in a camp at Sankt Johann. There were several large camps in that town, and she was

housed in one chiefly occupied by Yugoslav royalists who had
escaped at the end of the war. The operations staff noted the incident with no particular interest. It was apparently an accident and
would be dealt with by the Allied and Austrian police forces.

Then John Burkel, the CIC station chief in Salzburg, got a call
from the American consul in Salzburg, Patrick Connelly. The consul
was most anxious for news of Frau Superina's health and safety. He
requested that the CIC should keep him informed of all developments. It was not an entirely unusual request: Burkel worked closely
with Connelly on the endless problems of refugees' visas. Burkel
asked if Milano knew of any connection between this Frau Superina
and any U.S. intelligence operation. There was none.

That afternoon, a second call came in concerning the lady. This
time it was the commander of American troops in Vienna, Major
General Robert Fredericks, who wanted to be informed of Frau
Superina's condition. He was most anxious that the Soviets be persuaded to release her immediately. Fredericks was a distinguished
soldier. He had commanded a division in Italy during the war and
had taken part with it in the invasion of southern France, Operation
Anvil, in August 1944. He had led his division up France and into
Germany in the last great Western offensive. He had been posted to
Vienna in 1948, when most of the American military brass had
moved to Salzburg during the Berlin Airlift. He had been given command of the garrison that was left to represent the United States in
the encircled capital.

Then a third request for news of Frau Superina came in, this time
from Colonel Bixell, the senior Army Intelligence officer in Vienna.
He had been asked by the CIA for any information he had on the
lady. The agency had just come into existence and was beginning to
establish itself around the world and had set up a bureau in Vienna.

Milano and his staff were greatly puzzled by all this high-level
interest in a Yugoslav refugee. There was a mystery here. They were
intelligence officers, and their curiosity was aroused. If no one wanted to tell them what this was all about, they would see if they could
find out for themselves. John Burkel was told to send one of his
agents to Sankt Johann to investigate Frau Superina, and messages
were sent to Allied intelligence operations in the British and French
zones and to the American outstations in Vienna and Graz, asking
them all if they had anything in their records that might be useful.

The first to report back was Burkel's man, who had been to Sankt
Johann and inquired there. He had found that Frau Superina was a
registered Yugoslav refugee at one of the camps. She was a royalist
and claimed that her husband had been killed fighting for Draža
Mihajlović's Chetniks, who had started as a resistance movement
against the Germans in 1941 but later in the war had been allied

with the invaders. In 1945, when Tito's partisans had started wreaking vengeance on the Chetniks, she had fled to Austria. She had obtained a job as a seamstress at a dressmaker's shop in Sankt Johann. The agent said that by all accounts she was a strikingly beautiful woman, aged thirty-nine, who was a model citizen in every way. No one knew anything more about her.

As for the unfortunate Julius Hahn, who had been killed by the trigger-happy Russian sentry, he was an ordinary enough American bureaucrat, a member of the International Refugee Organization. The two had been dating occasionally, and at the time of the accident had been returning to the refugee camp from an evening spent in a local restaurant. Burkel's agent could find no evidence that either of them had any connection at all with any intelligence service.

The French in Vienna and the American CIC in Graz reported that they had nothing on anyone named Superina. The British at Klagenfurt said they knew nothing of Emma Superina, but that in one of the camps in their zone there was a Yugoslav couple named Superina who were accompanied by a nephew, a boy of nineteen, named Michael. They were all ardent royalists, and the man had applied for visas to South Africa. The boy claimed that his parents were dead and that he had no relatives other than his uncle and aunt. Archie Morehouse, who was head of the British Field Security Service in Austria (the equivalent of the American CIC), reported that the U.S. Embassy in Vienna and the American consul in Salzburg had inquired as to the welfare of the Superina family. The consul, Patrick Connelly, had telephoned Morehouse himself and told him that he was particularly interested in young Michael Superina and would be most grateful if his application for a visa could be helped along.

Evidently there was some connection between Frau Superina and young Michael: it was quite beyond coincidence that the same high American officials should be interested in both of them if they were not related. Milano still had no idea what the solution to his mystery was, but he was making progress. Then came one of the most remarkable episodes of stupidity that he ever encountered.

His operations chief in Vienna, Park Hancock, reported that Frau Superina, whose injuries were not serious, had been moved from the country hospital where she had been taken after the accident. She had been sent to a civilian hospital in the Soviet sector of Vienna. Hancock informed General Fredericks of the transfer, and Fredericks promptly sent an official request to the Soviet High Command that she be transferred to an American hospital. After the usual delay, the Soviets denied the request, saying that they needed the woman for their inquiries into the shooting incident. The general immediately summoned Hancock to his office. When Hancock

arrived, he found Fredericks examining a street map of Vienna that
was spread out on his desk. He pointed to the hospital where the
woman was being treated and demanded that Hancock discover
what room she was in and what security arrangements the Soviets
used there. The general said that he was told that the building was
surrounded by a six-foot brick wall. Hancock was to have the wall
inspected and check that there was no barbed wire or broken glass
on the top.

Hancock promised to have the information within two days. He
had many agents in the Soviet sector and would have no trouble
checking up on a hospital. At the appointed hour, he was back in the
general's office, reporting that Frau Superina was in Room 102. She
had it to herself. It was on the ground floor, on a corridor on the
outside of the building, facing Währingerstrasse. The wall was two
meters high, and there were no other obstacles. The Soviets usually
had two sentries at the hospital's main entrance, apparently because
there were often prisoners or military cases there.

Hancock made his report and left. He was puzzled at the sort of
information the general had requested. He considered the possibility
that the man might be planning a rescue but concluded that the idea
was too preposterous. Even a Regular Army officer could not be that
stupid.

He was mistaken. General Fredericks had decided that Frau
Superina must be saved from the Soviets' clutches and had decided
to do the job himself. That night, equipped with Hancock's information and accompanied by his aide-de-camp, he set out for the
Soviet sector. He used his own staff car, clearly marked with the
two stars of his rank. The two officers and their driver were
unarmed and wore standard army fatigues, and the general had his
stars on his shoulders. There was no attempt at concealment. They
drove straight to the hospital and after some trouble discovered
Währingerstrasse. The driver parked the car in the middle of the
long wall that marked the boundary of the hospital, and the general
and his aide proceeded to scramble up. They intended to climb into
the hospital through a window, find Frau Superina, and bring her
back with them.

The Soviet sentries had seen them coming. They had observed a
conspicuously American car driving around the hospital, finally
turning into a side street. They therefore set out to investigate. As
General Fredericks pulled himself up on top of the wall, he encountered a Russian gun stuck in his face. His aide succeeded in scrambling across: in his case, the sentry stuck his gun in his stomach.
Both Americans noted the disparity of force and raised their hands.
The sentries marched them around to the guardhouse, where they
called headquarters for instructions. Then one of them walked

around the outside of the wall to arrest the general's driver, who was nervously waiting for his superiors where they had left him.

Between ten at night and four the following morning, the Russian and American commands were in turmoil over the arrest of a senior American general in the Soviet zone. Fredericks and his two men were taken to the Quadripartite Police Headquarters, where the senior U.S. Military Police officer, a colonel, demanded that they be released. The Soviet colonel refused. Both of them were on the telephone, rousting out senior officers—and each officer they reached promptly called his own superior. Finally, at four, word came from the commanding general of the Soviet Armies in Austria that General Fredericks might be released. The Americans were not told whether the question had been bucked back to Moscow, but there was no doubt that the general would have to answer for his follies. Throughout all the frenzied negotiations over his fate, he sat impassive in the MP's guardroom, showing no interest in the affair at all.

A week later, the Soviets abruptly informed the American command that Frau Superina was free to leave her hospital. An MP was sent to the hospital to pick her up, and she was put onto the train for Salzburg, where she was handed over to the CIC. John Burkel put her into one of his safe houses, in Fuschl in the countryside, with a registered nurse to look after her, while he and Jim Milano decided what to do with her.

One of Burkel's agents went to see her once she was safely installed. She stoutly denied that she knew the other Yugoslav refugees with the same name in the British zone. She had no children, had never had any children, and had never heard of Peter Connelly. She could offer no explanation as to why so many senior American officials were interested in her case, nor why an American general should try to rescue her from the Soviets. The agent who noted all her statements reported to Burkel that he believed she was lying. The deduction was confirmed by British Intelligence, who interrogated the Superina family in Klagenfurt. The aunt and uncle admitted at once that Frau Superina was Michael's mother. He was an illegitimate child, and, when she had married, her husband had insisted that the baby should be given to his brother and sister-in-law, who were childless. Connelly, meanwhile, went to see John Burkel about Frau Superina. He said that the South Africans had offered her an immigrant's visa and asked Burkel to expedite the security clearance she would need to take it up.

The pieces were falling into place, but the last detail came not from any of the high-powered sleuthing or the espionage networks that the CIC was so well equipped to provide, but from a much older system, the powder-room network. Patrick Connelly's secretary, Louise, a long-term Foreign Service employee, called on John

Burkel's secretary, Susan, with some documents. The two women, who had known each other for several years, then had lunch together. Over sandwiches in the park, Susan told Louise that her boss was having a great deal of trouble with a particular refugee in whom Patrick Connelly was showing a quite extraordinary interest.

Louise laughed at the puzzle. "You should have asked me," she said. "I don't think it's much of a secret: everyone at the consulate knows about Michael Superina. He's Mr. Connelly's son. He was stationed in Belgrade years ago, before the war. He had a torrid love affair with a local girl who worked in the consulate there. She was called Emma something, and they had this boy.

"He was married at the time. In fact he still is, and he and his wife don't have any children. I guess he came looking for Emma and the boy after the war. Ever since he found them in refugee camps, he's been pulling every possible string to get them safely off to South Africa."

After their lunch, Susan reported on her conversation with Louise to her boss, John Burkel. The only remaining mystery was why General Fredericks had gone to such lengths to help Connelly's former mistress, and Burkel and Milano concluded that that was none of their business. They closed the books on Frau Superina. In due course, she, her son, and the uncle and aunt set sail for South Africa to start a new life in a new world. No doubt Patrick Connelly was glad to see them go. As for General Fredericks, he was told to moderate his enthusiasm in the future. The Soviets could not dictate which general officer should command the American forces in Vienna, but, after a suitable interval, he was recalled.

18

The Major and the Hooker

The first security crisis to blow up in Salzburg after the arrival of the numerous and strong-willed military staffs from Vienna in 1948 was more farce than tragedy. The G-2, the staff officer in charge of security, was now Colonel Oscar Koch. Jim Milano, as director of operations, had reported directly to him while he was in Vienna. His arrival in Salzburg made the reporting and supervision altogether closer than Milano wanted, even though they had always worked well together and there were never any serious problems between them. One of the officers on his staff was Lieutenant Colonel Pope Blackshear, who supervised all intelligence matters except Milano's Operations Branch. He was a formidable chess player and used to wander around the office with a pocket set, looking for someone to play him. He also carried a thermos full of gin to the office every morning. He was yet another West Point man who had little sympathy for the unmilitary ways of the Operations Branch. His senior enlisted assistant was Master Sergeant Jerome "Shorty" Welch, who happened to be from Charles Town, West Virginia, and was therefore a neighbor of Jim Milano's. They had never met, but the coincidence instantly brought them together. Welch had been a jockey in his youth but had joined the Army in 1937 and had been co-opted into Intelligence.

A week or so after the move, first thing in the morning, Welch arrived in Milano's office and closed the door behind him. "Major," he said, "I've got something to report that I think you ought to know. But it's a bit embarrassing, and I don't want to get involved. Can you promise me you'll keep my name out of it?"

191

"I can't promise you anything of the sort," Milano replied. "I'll have to judge the situation when you've told me about it. Come on, Shorty, you must see I can't make any promises. But you can be sure I'll do my best for you."

Welch looked, and felt, distinctly uneasy. All the same, he plunged ahead. "You see, Major, I've worked hard for my stripes, and I don't want to lose them over this. That's why I came to you, not to Colonel Blackshear. He's a stuck-up West Pointer and wouldn't understand at all.

"Anyway, here's the deal. I was down in a bar in town last night for the first time. It's called the Splendid Bar—you must know it."

Milano indeed knew the place. It was a favorite hangout of the enlisted men from the various American establishments of the district.

"Anyway, I had a few drinks and started talking with a cute little Austrian girl at the bar. The hookers are much cheaper here than in Vienna, and a lot less stuck up. This one's called Hertha. She's blond and is very well set up, if you know what I mean. She doesn't speak much English, but we got along just fine. She quoted me a very reasonable price, much less than the girls in Vienna. So off we went to her place, which was quite near there. I didn't want a one-off quickie, I wanted to spend the night."

Shorty looked Milano defiantly in the eye. "She was okay," he said. "Then, in the middle of the night, I had to go to the bathroom. I didn't put the light on, I didn't want to wake her. So I felt my way to the door. She's got a big dresser there with one of those fancy German runners on the top. I was feeling my way along it when I felt something under the runner, like a document. So I pulled the material back, and sure enough, it was a whole wad of papers. I took them with me to the bathroom.

"Major, it was a secret document from your section. It's a report from one of your defectors' interrogations. I didn't know what to do, whether to wake her up and shake out of her where she got it from, or what. In the end I just went back to her room, found my pants, and stuck it in the pocket. Then I went back to bed. I'd paid for an all-nighter, so that's what I took.

"When I left in the morning, I didn't say anything about the document. Then, when I reported for duty this morning, I went down to the file room and asked Kathleen, the clerk there, to let me draw it out. I told her you'd asked me to work on it this morning. She told me Major Early in the Security Section had taken it a couple of days ago. She said he must have put it in his office safe overnight."

That was the rule in the intelligence world. All secret documents had to be kept in the central file room or locked away in one of three designated safes in the building. Shorty Welch had discovered a serious breach of security.

"Where's the thing now?" Milano asked.

"Locked in the drawer of my desk."

"Go get it right away, Shorty. I'll take charge of it."

The soldier went off and was back in five minutes with the incriminating document. He had taken the precaution of hiding it in a standard issue envelope. Milano examined it thoughtfully.

"Thank you, Shorty," he said, "You've done the right thing. I'll take it from here. I can't promise that you won't have to be called if there's a court-martial, but perhaps it won't come to that. I'll do my best to keep your name out of it, though it's against regulations to consort with hookers. Just keep your mouth shut—don't tell Colonel Blackshear or anyone else. Just leave it to me."

"Thank you, Major, I'm most grateful. I won't say a word. Is there anything else I can do?"

All Milano needed was the girl's name and address. Shorty Welch departed, considerably relieved, and Milano set to work. His first call was on the local CIC detachment. He drove over to its office in Salzburg to see the chief of investigations, John Berg. He repeated Welch's story, though without giving his name, and announced that he needed a rush security check on Miss Hertha Mauser. Two German-speaking agents were dispatched to see her to discover how she had gotten the papers, why she had hidden them, and what she had planned to do with them. Austria was still under Allied military occupation, and all the force of the U.S. Army was to be brought to bear on this one prostitute. The agents were to report back to Milano immediately.

Three hours later, the agents and Berg were in Milano's office. Special Agent Sherman Kahn made his report.

"I spent two hours with Fräulein Mauser. Her story is that the night before last she picked up Bill Early at the Splendid. She says she works the bar regularly. He was already very drunk and bought a half bottle of cognac to take with him. She says she took him straight back, and while he was undressing he dropped the report on the floor. She says he didn't notice and she kicked it under the bed, out of sight. The next day, she hid it under the mat on her dresser. You know the rest.

"She says that her idea was to sell the papers back to Major Early. She didn't know his name. She guessed he would be back in the Splendid in a day or two, and she'd just ask him what sort of present he would give her for the return of the document. She was going to tell him that she had found it in her room the morning after he left.

"We've no record on her, except as a local hooker. There's no evidence she can read English: she only knows a few words. I don't think she has any connection to the Soviets or is any sort of intelligence problem—now that we've gotten the document back.

"As for Major Early, from Hertha's description, he must have been so plastered he probably doesn't have the faintest idea what happened to the document, or even if it's missing."

Milano thanked him. "That's good work. For the moment, we won't need a written report, but keep an eye on Hertha, just in case. As for Bill Early, first thing is to see what he has to say for himself."

The agents and their boss departed. Milano then called Early in and asked him for the document. He needed it, he said, and the file clerk had told him that Early had drawn it out two days before.

"Sure, Jim," Early replied. "It's in my office, I'll get it right away."

The unfortunate man marched blithely off, quite unaware of the chasm that had opened before his feet. He reappeared a few minutes later, looking worried and nervous.

"I'm sorry, Jim," he said, "something stupid has happened. I've just remembered. The other night I was working late and I had this file in my office, and when I left the file room was closed. I couldn't find the duty officer to open the office safe, so I stuck the document into my jacket pocket and took it home with me. It's still there—I've been wearing a different suit since then. It was a real jackass breach of security, and I'm really sorry. I'll have to go back to my quarters to find the thing."

Milano played him along. "Okay, Bill," he said. "Go get it. I need it this afternoon."

A very chastened Major Early reappeared an hour later.

"Jim," he said, "I've been to my room, and I can't find the document. It's not in my suit, and I can't find it anywhere. Some of the hotel staff must have stolen it. What can we do?"

"Well, we can stop playing games. Sit down, Bill. You know damn well that document wasn't in your room. You got dead drunk two nights ago, carrying it around with you, and shacked up with a hooker you picked up in a bar. I've got the document in the middle drawer of my desk."

Early was white as a sheet. "If you had the damn document, why the hell did you put me through this torture?"

"I wanted to see how far you'd push the charade. I wanted to see if you were acting."

"Jim, I swear to you I thought the document must be in my jacket pocket. It's true I spent the night with a hooker a couple of nights ago. But what's that got to do with the missing document? Are you telling me she stole it?"

"I can only tell you you're in real trouble, Bill. I'm sorry. This whole episode is going to have to be part of the official record."

Milano reported the incident to Colonel Koch and his deputy, Lieutenant Colonel Glen Carey, who was a close friend of Milano. He told them that the incident had been discovered by an enlisted man, who had very properly reported his discovery immediately but had requested that his role be kept dark. He would be ready to testify if there were a court-martial. The counterintelligence branch had investigated thoroughly and had concluded that there had been no breach of security after the original loss of the secret document.

Early's superiors made him an offer he could not refuse: he was given the choice of resigning his commission immediately or facing a court-martial. He left for the United States the next day.

The follies of some members of the staff were not always treated so severely. It all depended on who was involved and whether the infraction involved security or was merely a breach of regulations. Bellezza fell into the latter category. The saga started when the time came for Dominic Del Greco to replenish the office liquor supply. Every two or three months he would go on a "spiritual trip," as he called it, to Benevento, behind Naples, to resume his profitable relationship with Lefty Spinosa, the retired Brooklyn bootlegger. The wine, gin, and brandy he brought back from Benevento and Trieste were an essential part of the Operations Branch's office equipment and a necessity for the purposes of commerce. Del Greco could trade his stock of booze for many favors from other units. He added a small surcharge to the price of every bottle sold and stored the money in a cigar box in the supply room safe. The money was used for various odds and ends the unit needed that it could not obtain through the usual channels, official or unofficial. The cigar box was now empty, and Del Greco intended to replenish it with the profits from the next spiritual trip.

His staff sergeant, Earl Brown, always went with him on these excursions. They loaded four empty twenty-five-liter glass demijohns, each carefully packed in a straw-and-wood frame, into the back of a three-quarter-ton truck: when they returned, the demijohns of liquor would be emptied into bottles for distribution. It was a two-day drive from Salzburg to Naples. They were well used to the journey and stopped for the first night, as always, in a hotel on the outskirts of Florence. Come evening on the second day, they reached Benevento, and Del Greco went off with Lefty for dinner while Brown checked in at the distillery. He was a happy volunteer, because on earlier trips he had made particular friends with a girl working there, Lucia Zeppio, known as Bellezza. As her nickname implied, she was strikingly beautiful. She was nineteen years old and shared a room with her older sister. The girls had moved to

Benevento from their ancestral village in the mountains, and Bellezza, at least, had discovered that there was more to life than the conventional round of church, family, and cooking that her mother had followed. Whenever Sergeant Brown was in town, the two moved to a local hotel.

On this occasion, Brown discovered that his girlfriend had been doing some thinking since his last visit. She started asking him difficult questions about his future intentions: she wanted to know when he was going to marry her and take her back to America. In the meantime, she wanted to leave boring Benevento and go to where the action was—Salzburg, for instance.

Brown, like many young men in such circumstances, replied that it was too early to make plans for the future. He had another year or so to serve, and when he was discharged he would have to find a job. Of course he loved her, he promised, and had every intention of marrying her, but for the moment it was not possible to make any firm plans.

Bellezza was not to be put off. She was tired of Benevento, and Earl Brown was asking too much to expect her to sit around placidly waiting for him to turn up for a night's dalliance every two months. She wanted to go to Salzburg with him.

He protested: "But I'd have to ask Dominic, and I guess he'd have to check with Jim Milano. I don't know at all what they'd say."

"Why do you have to ask them at all? Why not just take me? I could hide in your truck."

Brown was appalled. He protested that they would never get away with it, that they would be discovered and she would be sent back in disgrace. She was unmoved.

"Why can't I stay with you in Salzburg?" she asked. He had to admit that there were frequent visits to the enlisted men's barracks. There was a rule that, to keep up appearances, women were admitted only after dark and had to leave before dawn, but Brown conceded that the rule was seldom enforced. He insisted that he must consult Dominic, but in vain. Bellezza played her trump: either he promised to take her with him to Salzburg, or she would go back to her sister immediately.

Earl Brown capitulated, and the next day, when he and Del Greco set out for home with their load of liquor, Bellezza was comfortably ensconced among the bottles in a nest of blankets Brown had contrived for her. They drove west to Naples and then headed north toward Rome. Somewhere along the road Bellezza banged on the back of the cab and demanded that they stop. She needed to use a bathroom.

Astonished and enraged, Del Greco demanded an explanation. Sergeant Brown explained, with a careful mixture of contrition and impudence.

"It's Bellezza. You remember her. She insisted on coming to Salzburg on a visit, and I couldn't say no to her. I'm seriously thinking of taking her back to the States with me when I'm discharged, and I thought it was time she saw the world."

"But what on earth is Jim going to say? What about her papers? I'll bet she hasn't anything that would get her across the frontier, let alone let her stay in Austria. Anyway, she can hardly speak English."

Brown turned supplicating. "I thought you could help her. You know all about arranging false papers, and it shouldn't be too difficult to set Bellezza up."

"And what about Jim? What do you suppose he's going to say?"

"I guess that's a bridge we'll have to cross when we get there. How about it, Dominic?"

Del Greco had nothing of the regular officer about him, and Earl Brown was an old friend.

"Well, okay," he said. "First of all, we have to find a rest stop for the girl. If we don't have any papers for her, we'll have to hide her away again when we hit the border." He was rewarded by a brilliant smile from their passenger, who now moved into the cab of the truck. She sat between the two men on the long drive home, ducking back among her blankets for the border crossing and for their arrival in Salzburg.

Earl carried her off to his room in the hotel the enlisted men used, and Del Greco delivered the booze to the Civilian Censorship Detachment's supply room. He had originally come to Austria with that unit and had set up his laboratory there, with funnels, hoses, bottle-cleaning facilities, and, of course, a large supply of demijohns. When he had been transferred to the Operations Branch, he had left all his equipment in the Censorship supply room, keeping full control of it. No one in Censorship objected: they, too, benefited from his "spiritual trips."

Del Greco was always helped on these occasions by a temporary, unpaid supply officer, Louie Strubel, one of the most useful and colorful people in Salzburg. He was tall and slim, dressed elegantly at all times, and wore a monocle. He looked every inch the ambassador, which was not surprising: his father was a German diplomat who had been posted to Sofia as consul general, where he had married a Bulgarian woman. Strubel had been born there and had spent the first twenty years of his life moving from city to city as his father's diplomatic career dictated. Those postings had included London, and Louie had spent three years in an English school.

Later in life, he had become an exporter of bananas from the Canary Islands. His chief market had been North Africa, and he had spent the first part of the war in Algiers. He had left for Europe shortly before the Allied invasion. Milano and his friends could never get him to explain how he had managed to live out the rest of the war in Germany and Europe without being conscripted. Whenever they asked, he avoided answering, replying merely that it was too dull a story to relate. It may be that he had kept a Bulgarian passport for those occasions when he was in Germany and a German one to use in Sofia. At any event, he had been in Bulgaria until the Russians were at the gates, at which time he had prudently withdrawn. At the end of the war, he had been in Salzburg. He had acquired a large collection of stamps, especially those issued by Germany and its allies and satellites, and he had opened the first stamp shop in town. Dominic Del Greco and Jim Alongi were both avid philatelists and had soon met Strubel.

To begin with, they had bought stamps. But then they had discovered that Strubel had an uncanny ability to find things. All the usual trade patterns had been broken down by the war, and a man who could find his way through the ruins to lay his hands on that multitude of goods the U.S. Army needed was a treasure beyond price. He could locate glass, silver, porcelain, souvenirs, furniture new and antique; he could find masons, plumbers, and carpenters; he could discover tools and supplies, dressmakers and the fabrics and materials they needed to work. It was all most extraordinary, and the Americans also discovered that his researches, which extended throughout all the Western zones of Austria, could be greatly helped with a supply of booze.

This explained Strubel's presence in the supply room when Del Greco set about emptying his demijohns of booze into various-shaped bottles. It was all part of the trade pattern of postwar Europe. The operation took place the day after the return from Naples. Del Greco and Strubel spent a profitable morning. Strubel went forth with a few bottles to use for marketing purposes. Del Greco stashed away the rest in the appropriate bins, and his task ended there—though he had no doubt that he had not heard the last of Bellezza.

Jim Alongi, whose duties included a monthly inspection of the barracks, soon discovered Bellezza. He urged Del Greco to report her presence to Jim Milano before she was exposed, but for nearly a month Del Greco avoided the hard necessity. At last he could ignore her no longer. Everyone in the unit knew about her, and it was only a question of days before Milano heard of this new addition to his charges. Besides, Bellezza was being indiscreet. Alongi marched in to Del Greco one morning and announced: "I'm off to tell Jim about Bellezza. You'd better come too—or else you can wait for five minutes for Jim to haul you up."

When they entered Milano's office, Del Greco confessed, "Jim, I've done something dumb I ought to have told you about before."

"Does that mean I have to put on my chaplain's dog collar? Bless you, my son, for confessing. Now, what's the story?"

"When we came back from Benevento on the last booze run, Earl stowed away his girlfriend in the back of the truck. She didn't emerge until we were halfway home. I stupidly allowed her to come on to Salzburg, and she's been here ever since, living in the barracks. I guess I fell for it because he said he wanted to marry her and take her back to the States."

Then Alongi took up the tale. "I should have told you about this before, Jim, sorry. Anyway, things are coming to a crisis now. Bellezza has been cheating on Earl, and it's only a matter of time before he finds out."

Milano listened to all this with astonishment. Now he learned that not only was there an Italian girl hiding out in the unit, she was also spreading her favors around. "You're sure of this?" he asked.

"Yes, she's been seeing one of the other guys when Earl's not there. He's even given her a watch from the PX, which she wears when Earl's away."

Wristwatches were among the greatest treasures of postwar Europe. There was none available anywhere outside Switzerland, and a girl who managed to get her boyfriend to give her one was doing exceptionally well. Conversely, a watch would often buy the favors of the most virtuous lady. Bellezza, evidently, was far from virtuous.

"So brother Earl's a *cornuto*, as they say in Naples. Serves him right. Dominic, you should never have let her come along. You should have put her on the first train back to Benevento just as soon as you found her.

"Anyway, the thing is to ship her right back where she came from. We won't tell Earl about her playing around. Dominic, would you call Earl and tell him to come in to see me, and I'll try to talk some sense into him. I hope I don't have to tell him about his horns."

A few minutes later, Brown appeared, sheepish and embarrassed.

"I guess it's about Bellezza, Jim," he said. "I suppose you've heard the whole story."

"No, Earl, I haven't. You seem to have got into a first-rate mess, so why don't you tell me how you propose to get out of it."

"Well, you see, I was really thinking of taking her back to the States and marrying her. That's why I let her talk me into bringing her here. But after a month with her, I've changed my mind. She's not the girl I want to marry, and I just want to get her back to Benevento."

Milano professed to be sympathetic and understanding. "If that's your decision, Earl, then I'm sure it's the right one. What you must do is put her on a train for Benevento—and you can buy the ticket. Dominic can give her a passport. I think I'd better tell her the news. She won't argue if I order her home."

"Well, thanks, Jim. It's really good of you to tell her yourself. I was trying to nerve myself up to sending her home, but I didn't fancy breaking the news."

"One last thing: if you ever do anything as crazy as this again, I will personally break your neck."

An hour later, Milano's secretary brought in the famous Bellezza. She sat demurely on a chair opposite his desk, her knees pressed together, her feet tucked neatly under her chair. She was completely composed and evidently knew what was coming. They spoke, of course, in Italian.

"Are you going to send me back to Italy, Major?" she asked.

"That's right, signorina. There can't be any question, and no delays. Earl and Captain Del Greco will take you down to Bolzano and put you on the next train to Naples. You can get a bus from there to Benevento. They'll give you the price of the ticket and pocket money for the journey."

"Thank you, Major. I'm sorry for all the trouble I caused you."

"That's all right, Bellezza. Just be on that train—and *buona fortuna*."

First thing the next morning, Brown, Del Greco, and Bellezza departed from Salzburg for the long drive down to Bolzano on the Italian side of the frontier. They arrived in time to put her on the evening train for Rome and Naples, and she and Brown said a fond farewell. Del Greco noticed that as they left her, and as she settled into her seat, she produced a most elegant wristwatch from her purse and strapped it on.

19

The Butcher of Lyons

Jim Milano's tour in Austria ended in July 1950, and before he left he wound up the Rat Line (see Chapter 20). Six months later, it was reopened by his successors for one last client. The client was Klaus Barbie, a German officer, a Nazi, who was wanted in France for war crimes. Using the Rat Line for such a man was a complete break with the rules Milano had set. He had made sure that no Nazis, no war criminals, no former members of the SS, the SA, or the Gestapo could use it to escape Europe. With the one exception of the Nazi woman, Trudi, who had persuaded a Soviet officer to desert, the line had been used exclusively for refugees and deserters from the East.

Barbie had been head of the Gestapo in Lyons, France, during the occupation. He had murdered hundreds of people and deported hundreds of Jews to Auschwitz. At the end of the war, he had escaped arrest and then managed to ingratiate himself with American counterintelligence agents in Germany, giving them valuable intelligence on Communist agitators there. In 1950, the French were closing in on him. His American protectors, wanting to conceal the fact that they had employed a war criminal, sent him down the Rat Line to safety in Bolivia.

Thirty years later, when he was at last arrested and extradited to France, the fact that the Americans had protected him after the war and used his services was revealed. There was a great public outcry and a government inquiry. Jim Milano, who until then had known nothing of the Barbie episode, was brought out of obscurity to testify, and the history of the Rat Line became public.

Barbie had become police chief in Lyons in 1942. Earlier in the war, in 1940 and 1941, he had participated in the first anti-Jewish operations in the Netherlands. He had then joined the SS and had taken part in the invasion of the Soviet Union. The mass slaughter of

Jews by special units of the SS had begun then. These experiences had served as ample qualification for the post of torturer and intelligence officer in France. His task in Lyons had been to fight the French Resistance and to deport Jews to the death camps. He had been highly successful in both occupations. His greatest coup was infiltrating the highest councils of the Resistance and arresting Jean Moulin, General de Gaulle's chief representative in France and the greatest hero of the Resistance, in July 1943. In an excess of sadism over operational requirements, Barbie had himself beaten Moulin to death without extorting any useful information from him. (In 1964, Moulin's ashes were buried in the Panthéon in Paris.)

Barbie had continued his Gestapo work until the Liberation. He had personally tortured many of his prisoners, often killing them. In April 1944, he had raided a secret Jewish orphanage in the village of Izieu, in the mountains above Lyons, and arrested all the forty-three children there. They had been deported to Auschwitz, where forty-one of them were murdered, together with five of the teachers who were looking after them. He had supervised the trains loaded with French and foreign Jews that were sent east (the last left Lyons a few days before it was liberated). In the last months of the occupation, as Resistance activity increased, he had murdered hundreds of prisoners and led German units into the countryside in pursuit of the *maquisards*, burning villages and slaughtering their inhabitants. Barbie and the rest of the Gestapo contingent had escaped from the city on August 17, 1944, just before the Americans had arrived, and had destroyed all their files. It had taken several years after the war for the French police to discover Barbie's name and to establish the extent of his crimes. By that time, he had been introduced to the U.S. Army's Counter-Intelligence Corps in Germany and had been hired as an anti-Communist intelligence officer. He helped them by infiltrating local Communist Party organizations and also by spying on the French zone of Germany, on the pretext that France was riddled with Communists and the U.S. Army's security demanded information on their activities.

The French discovered that Barbie was living in the American zone and made repeated efforts to have him extradited to stand trial. The American High Command denied all knowledge of his presence, even though the CIC had produced him several times for French interrogators who were preparing the trial of one of the French traitors he had employed in Lyons. The CIC unit in Bavaria, the 66th, based in Augsburg, informed the American High Commission in Bonn and the army command in Frankfurt that they had lost track of Barbie, and those higher officials took care never to question the lie. The CIC justified its deception with the claim that Barbie was too valuable an intelligence asset to be lost. When this story became untenable, they told their superiors that they had never known that Barbie was wanted as a war criminal. They pretended that his anti-Resistance activities had been all part of the war effort, and therefore understandable, and denied all knowledge of his actions against the Jews. They offered the same defense twenty-five years later, when the matter was investigated by the U.S. Justice Department. None of their excuses is remotely credible: the Gestapo had been specifically ruled a criminal organization at Nuremberg, and various directives from Allied headquarters and the American political and military command in Germany forbade all contact with its officers.

In their favor, it can be argued that, at least after 1949, the Western Allies, as a matter of policy, suspended all war crime prosecutions and consciously allowed former Nazi officials, SS officers, judges, and others to assume senior posts in West German government and industry. Nazi judges, who had presided over "people's courts" and ordered the execution of all who opposed Hitler, returned to the bench as honored German judges (none of them was ever tried for his crimes). The advent of the cold war meant that West Germany had to be restored as an ally against the Soviet Union, and the new government had no wish to conduct a protracted and difficult purge of the tens of thousands of Germans who had participated in the crimes of the Nazi regime. Only those directly involved in the death camps were prosecuted, and even that concession to justice was a protracted and largely ineffectual affair. Why, then, should not the CIC in Augsburg avail itself of the services of a junior Gestapo official whose contacts throughout Germany were so good? Indeed, as former SS men were allowed to resume senior positions in German society, the network of comrades became a very valuable source of intelligence—and Barbie's chief use to the Americans was that he was a trusted member of the SS old-boys' network. Furthermore, he was an expert in anti-French intelligence gathering at a time when the Americans greatly feared the dangers of the French Communist Party, one of the organizations Barbie had fought during the war. Last, although Barbie was the "Butcher of Lyons," he was a minor war criminal. There were thousands of more dangerous men on the loose. He was no Eichmann or Mengele. General Heinz Lammerding, who had commanded the Nazi division that wiped out a French village, Oradour-sur-Glane, in 1944, was living openly in Germany despite every effort by France to have him extradited. Why bother with an SS captain who was actually useful to the CIC?

By 1950, this deception was becoming increasingly difficult. Various American officers lied repeatedly to the French about Barbie, first denying all knowledge of him, then pretending that he no longer worked for them and that his whereabouts were unknown.

Barbie himself lived in constant fear of arrest. He was by then listed as a war criminal by the German police, and they might stumble across him at any moment: the Americans could try to hide him, but by 1950 they could not protect him from the German police if he were discovered. At this moment, one of the 66th CIC officers paid a visit to the 430th CIC in Salzburg and learned of the existence of the Rat Line. Milano's simple and elegant method of disposing of troublesome "visitors," all of them (except Trudi) defectors from the Soviet Union or its satellites, had been suspended when the CIA began taking over the operations of Army Intelligence, and Milano himself had left Europe. The line could still be used, however. The "Good Father" still had access to travel documents and visas to South America, and the 430th agreed to make him available to their colleagues from Augsburg.

They were not, however, told anything about the clients who were to be sent down the line. They were merely informed that one Klaus Altmann, his wife, and his two children were "of very great interest" to the 66th CIC. The family was issued with travel documents and identity cards, either forged by the 430th CIC or (which is more probable) obtained under false pretenses by the 66th itself in Germany. "Altmann's" papers gave his place of birth as Kronstadt, Germany, which was rather odd: there is no such place. The only Kronstadt is a famous Russian naval base near Saint Petersburg. The Altmanns were driven by their American friends to Salzburg, where they were put onto a train for Genoa. All their documents were in order, and they arrived safely.

Draganović himself met them in Genoa, according to Barbie's own account of his travels, and took him to the various consulates to obtain the necessary Argentine and Bolivian documents. The family was lodged in a safe house, which, according to Thomas Bower's book on the subject, was already full of escaping Nazis, including Eichmann himself. Barbie was presumably the source of this sensational piece of information. It is entirely possible that Draganović helped Eichmann, but it would seem improbable that Eichmann took the same boat to Buenos Aires as Barbie. The Barbies were escorted to Genoa by George Neagoy, who had succeeded Paul Lyon with the Austrian CIC in Linz as chief operator of the Rat Line and had later joined the CIA. If, indeed, Eichmann was in Genoa, Neagoy missed the chance of a lifetime. American officials might have condoned the use of a minor Gestapo official like Barbie, but Eichmann was the most senior war criminal alive, Heinrich Himmler's top lieutenant, the man who had organized the "Final Solution," and, if he had been identified, he would have been arrested immediately.

Eichmann had passed through several American interrogation centers undetected after the end of the war and had lived for four years in the British zone of Germany, raising chickens. According to the Israelis who interrogated him after his capture and tried to reconstruct his movements after the war, Eichmann had been smuggled through Austria to Italy by one of the SS rat lines, perhaps the one known as "Odessa." In July 1950, he was in Genoa where he was hiding in a monastery. A Franciscan monk provided him with a refugee passport in the name of Ricardo Klement, and on July 14 he obtained an Argentine visa. He reached Buenos Aires in October. It is possible that Draganović's operation was involved in Eichmann's escape, but there were other rat lines and other Fascist priests in Europe at the time, and the case has not been proven. As for the possibility that Eichmann's and Barbie's paths crossed, it would mean that the dates given by one of them were wrong. Barbie reported that he left Genoa on March 22, 1951, and surviving American documents corroborate the date. That was nine months after Eichmann, by his own account, left Genoa. In 1960, Eichmann was discovered in Buenos Aires by the Israeli Secret Service, which sent a commando unit to kidnap him. He was taken to Israel, where he was tried for war crimes, convicted, and hanged. Most of the Nazis who escaped were more fortunate and lived out the rest of their lives, anonymously and undetected, in South America.

That was the future Barbie planned for himself. He and his family were put safely aboard a ship for Argentina. When they arrived in Buenos Aires, they took the train to La Paz, Bolivia, where Barbie made contact with other German exiles and eventually established himself successfully as a businessman and an adviser to a series of Bolivian presidents.

Barbie's name was known only to specialists in the occupation, even though he was the man who had killed Jean Moulin. He became famous in the 1970s, when two French anti-Nazi specialists, Serge and Beate Klarsfeld, discovered that he was living in Bolivia and devoted themselves to bringing him to justice. They stirred up the press and, through them, the French government. Finally, in 1983, they succeeded. A new, democratically elected president took office in Bolivia and was persuaded by the French government to deport Barbie to France. He was taken back to Lyons and tried and convicted for war crimes in 1987. He was sentenced to life in prison and died there in 1991.

By the time of his arrest, the climate of opinion had changed. In Europe and America a new generation had grown up that had never known the tensions and the absolutes of the early cold war years. They could not understand how a branch of the American government had knowingly employed a war criminal, had concealed him from the French, and had then smuggled him to South America—all the while denying knowledge of his presence. Numerous protests were mounted, and the Justice Department in Washington set up an investigation into the case.

A detailed report was presented to Attorney General William French Smith by Allan A. Ryan in August 1983. It concerned Jim Milano and his former colleagues in the CIC in Austria because their Rat Line had been used to smuggle Barbie out of Europe, and the Ryan investigation had thrown some light upon that operation. It is also striking how differently the two intelligence organizations, the one in Germany and the one in Austria, conducted their business. According to the documents and the recollections of the surviving case officers, the CIC in Germany never hesitated to use former Gestapo officials or SS men and never concerned themselves with their agents' past records. Milano and his colleagues, by contrast, were constantly worried about using former Nazis, even those who had spent the war behind desks in Vienna analyzing reports from the eastern front. As we have seen, former SS men and Gestapo officers were sometimes used, but always with discretion and for short periods. Barbie, by contrast, had been treated as a friend and colleague by the 66th CIC and had been one of its major assets for three years. That organization was deeply concerned with the dangers of communism in West Germany. The 430th CIC in Austria took a much more relaxed attitude to the Red Menace. It noted that the United States had several fully equipped divisions in Germany and the Communist Party was an inconsiderable risk.

After the Barbie incident the Rat Line was closed down again, and the CIA has always denied that it ever made any use of it. However, as various writers have pointed out, the CIC agent who shipped Barbie to Bolivia, George Neagoy, joined the Agency in 1951. Obviously, he took with him all the knowledge required for using the Rat Line. Furthermore, the agency made use of Draganović, in some capacity, at least until 1960. All that time, he continued to work for Croatian refugees and to take part in political activity among Croatian exiles. Some of the Ustashe war criminals whom he may have helped took part in the terrorist campaign waged against Yugoslavia, notably against Yugoslav embassies abroad. In those years, the Yugoslav embassies in Washington and New York, for instance, had armed guards at the door, protected from Ustashe attack by concrete shields. Draganović may also have been involved in currency smuggling. Then his career took a surprising twist: in 1967 he returned to Yugoslavia and ended his days peacefully in Zagreb, the capital of Croatia. Evidently he had made a deal with the Yugoslav authorities, and it is entirely possible that he had for many years been a double or triple agent, working simultaneously for Ustashe plotters, American intelligence, and Tito. He died of old age in 1983.

Two contemporary accounts of the Rat Line and the Good Father have survived, and they are given in full in the Appendix. They were both written by Paul Lyon. The first, dated 1948, refers to "a tentative agreement" with Father Draganović, which he described as "simple mutual assistance, i.e. [we] assist persons of interest to Father Draganović to leave Germany and, in turn, Father Draganović will assist [us] in obtaining the necessary visas to Argentina, South America, for persons of interest to this command.

"It may be stated that some of the persons of interest to Father Draganović may be of interest to the Denazification policy of the Allies; however, the persons assisted by Father Draganović are also of interest to our Russian ally."

This implied that G-2 operations was ready to assist Draganović in smuggling war criminals out of Germany. The Justice Department investigation in 1983 found no evidence that anything of the sort ever happened, and Milano and his friends are quite clear that the rule was always that no members of the SS, SD, or Gestapo or other potential war criminals would ever be allowed down the Rat Line. That prohibition explicitly extended to Croatian refugees: the services provided by Milano's Rat Line had never been made available to Draganović for his own friends and clients. They were reserved entirely for deserters from the Soviet army or former DPs who had provided useful information on Soviet dispositions. In Milano's view, the people qualified for the Rat Line were those who had risked their lives to bring useful information to U.S. Army Intelligence, people, in Lyon's ironic phrase, who were "of interest to our Russian ally."

Paul Lyon is long dead, and it is quite impossible to discover just what he meant by "mutual assistance." His colleagues understood that the deal was strictly financial: they paid Draganović $1,500 for each visa. One possible explanation, which was certainly discussed at the time, was that Draganović used the funds the Americans gave him to subsidize his own rat line, with which he smuggled Ustashes out of Europe. Milano certainly knew that this was a possibility and consciously turned a blind eye.

The Ryan report's conclusion, as far as it concerned Milano's Rat Line, is as follows:

> the evidence establishes that the 430th CIC in Austria had been using Father Dragonovic's rat line for several years as a means of providing defectors and informants with a safe and secret passage out of Europe.

This investigation yielded no evidence that the 430th CIC had used the rat line as a means of escape for suspected Nazi war criminals.

As the discussion of the rat line's operation makes clear, the 430th CIC and its parent command, G-2 United States Forces Austria (USFA), were operating on the edge of the law, if not over it: false documentation was obtained surreptitiously, information was withheld from United States agencies controlling travel, funds were transferred in unorthodox and perhaps illegal ways, and knowledge of the entire procedure was intentionally restricted to the persons actually involved in it.

The use of the rat line for informants and defectors raises troubling questions of ethical and legal conduct. The United States Army certainly had an obligation to protect from harm those informants who had assisted the Army at substantial risk, as well as defectors whose discovery in the American zone would have jeopardized their lives and safety. Furthermore, there was nothing inherently wrong in evacuating such persons from Europe to places of sanctuary in South America. But to carry out this obligation by relying on the intercession of a foreign national whose own background and interests were suspect, by concealing information from United States agencies, and by possibly violating lawful regulations on travel, currency and documentation, the Army did not act responsibly.

The proper course, when faced with the necessity of bringing such people to safety, would have been to arrange, with due authority, an approved and lawful mechanism for their safe passage. This mechanism could have been arranged to operate covertly; there is no inherent contradiction between lawful action and covert action. But there is an important distinction between lawfully establishing a covert escape route and covertly taking advantage of a secretive and unauthorized scheme.

In addition, the rat line procedure took unnecessary and ill-advised security risks by placing sensitive informants and defectors in the unsupervised control of a foreign agent. One cannot exclude the possibility that United States intelligence methods or information were compromised when defectors and informants were turned over to Dragonovic. It is abundantly clear that Dragonovic was not loyal to the United States; he simply accommodated United States requests to the extent they were consistent with, or could advance, his own objectives in assisting his compatriots.

But questionable as these actions may have been from a legal or security standpoint, they do not appear to have risen to the level of an obstruction of justice other than in the Barbie case. This investigation examined all materials known to exist on the operation of the rat line and interviewed all persons now alive known to have been involved with it. No other case was found where a suspected Nazi war criminal was placed in the rat line, or where the rat line was used to evacuate a per-

son wanted by either the United States Government or any of its post-war allies. *

The Ryan investigation and report were just the sort of thing that Milano and his colleagues feared when they built their Rat Line in such secrecy. They specifically did not seek legal approval for their actions because they were fairly sure that they would not have got it and had no faith at all in the State Department's ability to keep a secret. The report expressed Ryan's regret that there are no files giving the names of the people sent down the Rat Line, either their original names or the ones they had been given to start their new lives with. Ryan wanted to interview them to make sure that they were not Nazis or security risks. Milano had anticipated just such an official inquiry when he made sure that no traces of his "visitors" should be left behind, and the passage of thirty-five years had not given him any reason to think he had been mistaken.

---

*[Document footnote] Because there is no central file containing the names of all the persons who were assisted into the rat line by the 430th CIC in Austria, there is no way to retrieve the files of those who actually went through it. The conclusion that there is no reason to believe that anyone else with a Nazi background was placed in the rat line is based on a) the absence of any such evidence in files that do exist on rat line; b) the clear recollection of the agent [Neagoy] who took over the rat line for the 430th in 1949 [*sic:* Neagoy succeeded Lyon in 1950] that both he and, to his knowledge, his only predecessor (who is deceased) [Lyon], handled only defectors from the East (aside from Barbie); c) the clear recollections of the G-2 operations officer from 1945 to 1950 [Milano] that only defectors were put in the rat line; and d) the clear recollection of his successor [Dobson], who served from 1950 through the end of USFA's involvement with Draganovic, that Barbie was the only non-defector handled during his tour of duty.

20

The End of the Rat Line

Late in 1949, Jim Milano was told that his time in Austria was coming to an end. A successor chief of operations would be sent out from Washington the following summer, and at the same time the CIA would take over some of the Army's intelligence operations in Austria. Army Intelligence had carried the burden since 1945, when the Americans had first occupied the country, because there had been no regular spy agency: the wartime OSS had been disbanded. The CIA had been established by act of Congress in 1947 and had steadily expanded its activities since then. This was an opportune moment for it to take over responsibility for peering across the Iron Curtain into Central Europe. The Berlin Airlift had ended, with a signal Allied victory, in May 1949. The Communist offensives in France, Italy, and Greece had been turned back, and the split between Tito and Stalin had exploded into open animosity, which relieved some of the pressure on the West. NATO had been formed, and the Federal Republic of Germany had been set up. The heroic period of the early cold war, 1945 to 1949, was over. It was succeeded by the long years of cautious confrontation punctuated by occasional crises like the Korean War, the Berlin crisis of 1961, and the Cuban missile crisis. The new phase of hard animosity lasted until 1989. One reason that the Army had been left to conduct most intelligence operations in Austria for the four years after the war had been that everyone expected an agreement between the World War II Allies on the fate of Austria, to be followed by the departure of all the armies of occupation. By 1949, it was apparent that there would be no quick treaty. Prolonged diplomatic maneuvering had at last achieved an Italian peace and treaties with the other European Axis powers, Bulgaria, Hungary, and Romania. But the negotiations over the key issue, Germany, had failed utterly, and Stalin had also refused to give up the Soviet zone of Austria. The American and Allied armies remained in Vienna and in their zones of Austria far longer than they had ever anticipated: the Austrian State Treaty was not concluded until 1955. It was evident by 1949 that the provisional arrangements in force since the end of the war might continue indefinitely, and it was necessary to put them on a regular basis. As far as intelligence gathering was concerned, that meant calling in the CIA.

It was time for the pioneers, Milano and his friends, to move on. They had achieved outstanding success in observing the activities of the Red Army, measuring its capabilities and judging its intentions, and had also protected the West by their assiduous attention to counterintelligence. The Army accepted the transfer of its intelligence functions to the CIA with good grace. The Agency had already expanded the operations of its precursor agency, the SSU, and it had brought several case officers and headquarters personnel into Vienna. Army Intelligence networks and operations large and small, essential and marginal, would all be reviewed by the Agency, and the ones it deemed useful would be taken over. Those it did not want would either be wound up or kept by the Army until that distant day of its withdrawal from Austria. The two organizations would, of course, cooperate: the Army would still want to analyze the fruits of CIA operations, and the Pentagon would still ply the Agency with the questions it had regularly sent to Milano. The CIC would continue counterintelligence work, guarding the security of army installations and personnel. The MIS continued to direct civil censorship and the interrogation of returning Austrian POWs.

Milano had no personal concern in the matter. He was leaving anyway. He had only one question: What would happen to the Rat Line? It was the most secret of his operations, and he had a proprietorial interest in its fate. He was particularly concerned with its security: he wanted to be sure that the visitors he had sent off to their new lives in South America would be left undisturbed.

The question was tied up with a decision he had to make himself: the CIA had offered him a job, and he had to decide whether to accept or to remain in the Army. It was not an easy decision, and Milano was influenced by news coming out of Washington. In the course of 1949 and into 1950, the great anti-Communist witch-hunt was spreading like a plague across the face of American government and a great part of intellectual life. It affected the State Department and the military, and American agencies in Austria received ever-increasing numbers of peremptory demands for detailed background information on their personnel. President Truman, in a concession to the forces his secretary of state, Dean Acheson, called "the primitives," had agreed to institute "loyalty procedures" in the State Department and elsewhere in the government. The purge began immediately, and before very long scores of government officials were sacked because they had at some time shown sympathy for left-wing causes. The Army was particularly vindictive and obsessive in its hunt for soldiers whom it considered disloyal, frequently basing its judgment on such matters as a relative's leftist sympathies.

This was before Senator Joseph McCarthy got up at a meeting in Wheeling, West Virginia, in February 1950 and waved a piece of paper in the air, announcing "I have in my hand a list of two hundred and five men and women known to the secretary of state, Dean Acheson, to be card-carrying members of the Communist Party who are still employed in the State Department." It was one of the most audacious lies in history: the piece of paper was not a list. It bore no names, let alone the names of State Department officials. It was some scrap of paper the senator had found in his pocket. McCarthy had no information at all on Communists in the government. The number he offered was derived from a note by a previous secretary of state, James F. Byrnes, in 1946 and referred to "dubious cases" then under scrutiny. McCarthy produced different numbers on subsequent occasions. Under McCarthy's urgings, the witch-hunt spread through the American government, universities, and even Hollywood. It was at last brought under control when McCarthy attacked the Army and was condemned (not censored) by the Senate in 1954. By then, however, most of the damage had been done.

The intelligence community in Austria was a potential victim of the ever-increasing paranoia in Washington. Milano received repeated queries from the Pentagon on the backgrounds of his staff and colleagues, to the extent that, at one of his staff meetings, Jack Whitmore remarked that the Red Menace situation was becoming so ridiculous that it was becoming dangerous to use tomato ketchup on a hamburger. One man, for example, was under intense scrutiny because his sister's name had appeared on a list of members of a left-wing organization in the 1930s. The inquisitors wanted to know whether the man had ever discussed his sister's allegedly Communist activities and whether he was ever in touch with her. The wife of one of the interrogators was suspected of having been a member of the Industrial Workers of the World, the "Wobblies," in the 1930s. That was a militant union that had arisen during the Depression, and the idea that an intelligence officer's career might be ended because his wife had been a member ten years before was deeply troubling. Milano himself had a lucky escape. When he was a junior in college, a classmate had asked him, as an Italian American, whether he would like to join the college's Dante Alighieri Society. It was, he said, a national organization devoted to studying the arts, culture, and history of Italy. Milano had declined: he was a chemistry student and lacked the time for such things.

A decade later, he saw the society in a list of subversive organizations put out by the Justice Department. It had been a Fascist front, and although by 1949 a past association with it would have been much less serious than belonging to a Communist front organization, he was very glad he had never joined. He could easily have signed up. The narrow escape demonstrated how his colleagues' careers might be blighted by a thoughtless signature on some liberal petition at the age of eighteen. The suggestions of persecution and paranoia emanating from Washington contributed heavily to Milano's decision to decline the offer to join the CIA. He remained in the Army.

Then word came that the Army chief of intelligence, General Alexander Bolling, was coming to Vienna during a tour of the European Command. Milano and his superior, Colonel Oscar Koch, chief of intelligence staff for the U.S. Forces in Austria, were ordered to meet him. General Bolling was not merely conducting a tour of inspection: he was supervising the transfer of intelligence operations from the Army to the CIA. The conference he held in USFA headquarters in Vienna, therefore, marked a turning point in the history of American intelligence and the evolution of the cold war. It was the occasion for Milano to pass the torch to the head of the CIA in Vienna, John Ritter.

Bolling was the general who had summoned Milano to Washington a year earlier, when Patsy and Pete had nearly brought the Rat Line to ruin by shooting a Nazi war criminal they had recognized in Chile. He greeted Milano warmly.

"Well, Jim, it's good to see you again. Last time we met, I had you in my office explaining how one of your clients had been misbehaving, shooting a customs officer in Chile."

"Yes, General, I remember it well. I spent three days in a plane and two hours in the Pentagon. You told me you'd square all my problems with the State Department, and I'm very grateful. I never heard from them again.

"But I've always been curious how you did it. Now it's all water under the bridge, can you tell me how you managed to persuade State to forget the whole thing? It was quite a problem for us—and then it just disappeared."

Bolling laughed. "Jim, I told you it was a problem I would handle, and you didn't need to know how I was going to do it. I'm still of the opinion it's much the best for all concerned to leave what I said just between me and State. Also, I don't want you to sit in judgment on my abilities as a storyteller."

Milano could recognize a brick wall when he met one, particularly when it was built by a general. "I'm sure you're right, General," he said. "I certainly don't need to know. I was just curious."

"That's okay, Jim. You're meant to be curious. That's your job. But now we've got serious business to discuss."

The general then turned the proceedings over to John Ritter, the CIA station chief in Vienna, who had received some precise, and surprising, instructions from Washington.

"What we want to do, Jim," he said, "is to put one of our men into your operation undercover, with a secretary, to check things out. They could come in at different times, perhaps a week apart, so that it wasn't evident they were working together. We think it would be best if your people don't realize that the Agency is evaluating their operations, so we suggest our man be sent in as an analyst from the Pentagon. You could say he was reviewing your operations to use them as case studies for teaching purposes at the various Army Intelligence schools. He would be formalizing the documentation and writing them up, all very straightforward. You must have plenty of Department of the Army employees passing through.

"Then he would review all your files and operations, discreetly, of course. He would have to interact very closely with your staff and with the CIC and MIS agents who are actually conducting the operations. He's called Bill Johnson, and I think you'll find he will be very discreet. How do you react to the idea?"

Milano was astonished. It seemed to him quite absurd that the CIA should want to spy on the Army in this heavy-handed way. Why not come in openly and examine the files and talk to the agents and officers? It looked as though the CIA did not trust the U.S. Army, which he had served for eight years, or Army Intelligence, of which he was now a senior officer. It was all very odd, but clearly the matter had been approved by General Bolling and Colonel Koch, so Milano held his peace.

Instead of denouncing the whole scheme as nonsense, he merely observed, "I'm not sure reviewing operations on an undercover basis will work. This gang of mine is a savvy bunch of intelligence operators, and it won't take them long to see through the cover story."

No one responded to the warning, so Milano played the good soldier and acquiesced. If this was the way the CIA and the Pentagon wanted to play it, that was their affair. He was going home. There was, however, one piece of serious business left.

"What about the Rat Line?" The question was put to Ritter. "I realize you don't know all the details of the operation, but you know the general outline. Do you plan to handle it like the other operations?"

Ritter and his superiors had clearly given thought to the matter and had consulted Bolling and Koch. His reply was emphatic and not at all spontaneous.

"First of all, the Agency has no interest whatsoever in getting involved in the Rat Line. That's an Army show, and it's up to the Army to bring down the curtain. Our man need not be given any information at all on the matter. Secondly, we definitely want him to operate undercover."

So much for the Rat Line, thought Milano, and so much for an amicable transfer of duties. He was more certain than ever that he had chosen well in refusing to join the Agency. It evidently did not think much of Army Intelligence, its accomplishments, or its operations—or, probably, of its agents.

Years later, skeptics looking into the Barbie affair suspected that the CIA had in fact wanted to keep the Rat Line in existence, though there is no evidence it did so. However, Ritter was quite explicit in disclaiming all interest when Jim Milano offered to turn the operation over to him.

The meeting broke up amiably enough. Milano promised to provide every help to the undercover CIA man, Bill Johnson, and his secretary. He was given a desk in the room occupied by the regular analysts and was soon hard at work examining all the operations, past and present, and discreetly cross-examining the various case officers and field agents. He was the very model of a clandestine operative, and within a week Captain T. J. Strucker, one of the analysts who worked with Dominic Del Greco, put his head around Milano's door and said, "Come on, Jim, who do you think you're kidding? Bill Johnson and that secretary of his even *smell* like Agency employees. What are they doing here?"

Milano was secretly delighted. This was exactly what he had expected and what he had warned Ritter would happen. He kept a straight face, however, and told his visitor, "T.J., I didn't realize you were an expert at solving mysteries. I'll have to see if there's an opening for you with Bill Waggoner's code breakers."

Strucker just laughed. He was merely the first to let Milano know that Johnson's cover was blown. The secret was out. Everyone in the building knew it, and the embarrassed CIA man was forced to admit that he had been sent from Washington to evaluate the CIC and the MIS and all their works. The attempted, and failed, deception did not make his task any easier.

Milano followed instructions and kept Johnson well away from the Rat Line. He was informed that there would be a month's interval between his own departure and his successor's arrival, during which Dominic Del Greco would be left in charge. Milano wanted to send the last visitors down the Rat Line before he left Salzburg and then close down the line altogether. There were men on the waiting list, and he summoned the Rat Line support group to his office to examine their cases.

Paul Lyon was still the officer in day-to-day charge of the Rat Line, and he proceeded in his usual methodical way to brief the group on his clients.

"Major, we've got four candidates on the books now. There's Gimpy, who is in Steyr; Silas, in Gmunden; Tomahawk, in Zell am See; and Buster, in Sankt Wolfgang.

"Gimpy is a middle-aged former sergeant from Lithuania. He was drafted into the Russian army and was wounded in the leg during the war. He's got a permanent limp. He has been living with other Baltic refugees in Steyr and sometimes works for the CIC in Linz. They're always interested in what the refugees are up to, particularly in case the KGB tries to infiltrate them. He has been doing pretty well for himself. He's been here since the war, and we never had to put him into one of our training programs. He's got a job and has found himself a twenty-year-old live-in housekeeper to take care of him. Now he's got himself involved with other Lithuanians in working on the structure and problems of the government in exile. They want to be ready for the day when the Russian occupation collapses and they can return home. He is perfectly content to stay where he is: he has no wish to leave Austria until he can go home to Lithuania. I think he's in for a long wait, but I don't think we need to be concerned about Gimpy. I recommend that we stay in touch with him but don't try to relocate him.

"As for Silas, he also has been doing well in the private economy. He was a printer before he was drafted. He got to be a captain in the infantry and showed up at the Military Government Headquarters in Linz last year. We were able to arrange a job for him at a print works in Gmunden, where he has done extremely well. His boss wants to sell him a share in the business sometime in the future. He's trying to stay in Austria as a refugee and eventually apply for citizenship. He knows that could be dangerous but seems ready to take his chance. I wouldn't recommend it, but we can't force him to go to South America. I think we should leave him where he is and see what happens.

"As for brother Tomahawk, he's in a CIC house in Zell am See. He was a corporal in a Russian motor pool who turned himself over to our MPs in Vienna. He had an advanced case of gonorrhea, and I believe he deserted to escape being court-martialed. Besides, he probably guessed he'd get better medical treatment with us. Anyway, a course of penicillin has worked wonders and now he's as good as new. We put him to work with a motor mechanic, who rates his abilities not very high. He'll never be a master mechanic. He wasn't much of an intelligence source, and now he's mostly a liability. I suggest we ship him out on the next consignment, if there is one.

"As for Buster, he's a much more valuable catch. He's the artillery captain who was stationed with a unit near the Hungarian border. The Pentagon is still sending questions for him to answer, so we have to keep him here for the moment.

"That means we have just one candidate for the Rat Line immediately and one more farther down the road."

The group concluded that Tomahawk would have to wait at least until Buster was ready to go to South America. The two would be the last candidates for the Rat Line, but it was too early to make detailed plans for their future. In the event, Milano left the two men to his successor, Lieutenant Colonel J. W. Dobson, who eventually shipped them safely to South America, the last regular clients sent down the Rat Line. The other two remained in Austria.

The same evening as Milano held his last meeting on the Rat Line, he had dinner with an old friend, Maria Torkey. She had returned to Austria from her new home in Arkansas, to sell her villa near Bad Aussee, the house she had lent to Milano two years earlier. She invited him out to the house for a last dinner together and described her new life in the backwoods selling cured hams. She told him she had found a purchaser for the villa, a businessman who had contrived to transfer most of his fortune to Switzerland when the Nazis occupied Austria in 1938. He was therefore able to pay for the house by depositing Swiss francs into a Zürich account, an arrangement Maria found most useful.

She had another tale to tell: this was not just a social occasion.

"I've been in the house for the past week, making the last arrangements for the sale. I've spent a lot of time in the village, and I've come across some really interesting things. Perhaps you could explain them to me.

"First of all, that Nazi composer, Herr Dustoff, who was given the house by Goebbels and lived upstairs with his wife and his ex-wife: now he's disappeared. The wife and the ex-wife are still sharing the apartment with their children, but he vanished about two months ago.

"I took some goodies for the children, and while I was having tea with the wife, she confided that her husband was in Buenos Aires. He's written to her. He told her that when things returned to normal, he would send for her and the children. She said she was absolutely astonished to get the letter. She had no idea where her husband had gone and couldn't imagine why he had gone to South America. The only thing was that for months he had been vanishing in the evenings to attend meetings in the village. He wouldn't tell her what these meetings were all about, except that they were special and important. Then one day, without warning, he packed his bags, gave her some money to live on, kissed her good-bye, and vanished.

He said that he would write to her in due course, and she wasn't to worry.

"Now, I found this most suspicious. Do you suppose some Nazi group is smuggling people out of the country? I don't suppose Herr Dustoff was any sort of a major war criminal. So far as I know, he was just a composer. But he certainly had lots of friends in the Party and the SS. I've known the chief of police here for thirty years, so I paid him a visit and asked if he had any idea what had happened to Herr Dustoff. He said he had heard informally that our famous composer had left the area. He also said that various other residents had vanished lately, including two former SS officers, and no one knows where they have gone. At least that's what their wives told their neighbors. I got their names for you, in case you're interested. He said that none of the wives of the missing men had reported them gone or started any inquiries into their disappearances. He had concluded that this was probably not a police matter—which means he thinks they've left the country. I didn't tell him Frau Dustoff had gotten a letter from her husband in Buenos Aires.

"I guess the composer went to Argentina because there's a Fascist government there. That's one reason I'm concerned that my son Johnnie is living and working with my relatives there. I'm not sure that it's very safe. Do you know anything about this? And is there any chance that any of these people could get into the United States?"

Milano had not at all expected to be questioned about anything so sensitive, let alone to hear from Maria of the possibility that the Nazis, too, were running a rat line out of Austria under his very nose. He was about to leave the country and she was in town for a few days only, so he was judiciously indiscreet. He wanted to calm her fears, and the best way to do that was to reassure her about some American security procedures.

"You're quite right to tell me about all this, Maria," he told her. "It could be a serious problem if the Nazis are smuggling themselves into the United States. But I don't know if they are. My section is concerned with all intelligence and security questions, and I'm not certain whether the disappearance of these people is a security question. I'll look into it. But you can be sure that we keep as close an eye as we can on these characters.

"So there's nothing much I can tell you about what may have happened to Mr. Dustoff or the other two. But if I hear anything, I'll let you know. Of course, if there was any sign of Johnnie getting into any sort of danger, I'd tell you at once." He did not tell her that he had a particular interest in rat lines.

In fact, there was a mechanism that might have helped uncover the Nazi rat lines, but it was not being given a high priority. All mail between Austria and Argentina was monitored by the Civilian Censorship Detachment and by the British and French censorship operations. So was all mail between West Germany and Argentina. This had been going on since the war. The Censorship Detachment put together a monthly report to the Pentagon and Colonel Koch on everything it discovered from censoring mail to and from Argentina. A curious thing was that they never found in any of the letters any discussion of how the writers had gotten to Argentina in the first place. They had just turned up, without explanation. It was assumed that many of them were using aliases and perhaps using a pre-arranged code to convey messages.

Later, Milano discussed the case of the disappearing Nazis with John Burkel. Burkel said that he had never been given any orders or guidance in such cases. His superiors apparently did not consider such questions a matter of local security, which was the CIC's chief mission, or of gathering intelligence on the Soviets.

As his time in Austria ran down, Milano began to worry about the records he might leave behind him. He had never had the slightest doubts about any of his actions, which, in any event, had always been covered by his superiors—though sometimes they had been notified after the fact. The problem was that times change, and what appeared perfectly normal and correct in 1950 might look quite different to someone examining the files twenty or thirty years later. The abrupt changes in official attitudes caused by the rise of McCarthyism in the United States were proof enough that no one could ever be sure what future attitudes might be.

Milano was worried that at some future date his files might be opened and mishandled. He was particularly concerned about the security of the Rat Line. If the files were opened, would the identities of the people who had gone down the line to South America be exposed? Would he and his colleagues be protected from accusations that they had bent the law, or even broken it, in the pursuit of their intelligence mission? There was nothing seriously criminal hidden in the records, but Milano came to the conclusion that actions taken in good faith in 1946 might appear questionable in the cold light of 1966. He had no faith that future investigators would always judge events in the light of the times and circumstances in which they had taken place.

He discussed the issue with his superior, Colonel Koch, who recommended that the Department of the Army be consulted. Milano drafted a memo, which Koch sent to the Pentagon, outlining his concerns and proposing that selected files be destroyed. This was the Army, and Milano and Koch decided they needed permission from Washington before proceeding.

Within a week, a reply came authorizing the destruction of the files. However, the intelligence staff at Army Headquarters ruled that two officers would be sent out from Washington to supervise the bonfire and would review the files before they were destroyed. Milano, Lyon, and Del Greco sorted through the files to select the documents they considered should be destroyed. They chose everything relating to the Rat Line, files concerning the purchase of clandestine interests in local firms, and documents mentioning clandestine operations against other American organizations, such as the abstraction of Milano's file from the U.S. Embassy in Rome after the Patsy and Pete affair. They were very thorough. The only documents that have survived are copies of memoranda sent to other organizations. Everything else was consigned to the flames.

Two weeks before Milano left Austria, Lieutenant Colonel John Jacobs and a civilian employee of the Department of the Army arrived from Washington. They were given all the files to review and spent several days immersed in the history of intelligence in Austria and the Rat Line. Jacobs proved to be an urbane and well-informed officer. He told them that he had been warned before leaving Washington not to be surprised at anything he might discover—and added that, all the same, it was an astonishing story. He said he was surprised to find no evidence that the Operations Branch had ever attempted to buy a banana republic. It seemed to have tried everything else. Dominic Del Greco immediately suggested that the colonel keep his wild ideas to himself: Jim Milano had another two weeks to go, plenty of time to carry them out.

The ever-practical Del Greco converted a fifty-gallon oil drum into an incinerator, by cutting off one end and punching a few ventilation holes in its sides. He set a grate on some bricks in the bottom of the barrel, and then for two days the two visitors from Washington and Milano, Lyon, and Del Greco burned their files. The white smoke rose into the air like the smoke from the Vatican chimney when a pope is elected, as the fire consumed a small part of the history of their time.

Appendix

All the files concerning the Rat Line held in Salzburg were destroyed when Jim Milano left Austria (see Chapter 20). He had made sure that as few of his superiors as possible knew of the line's existence. However, two memoranda on the Rat Line survived and were discovered by the Ryan investigation. They are published in his report. They are top secret reports by Paul Lyon, dated 1948 and 1950, that survived in the files of the U.S. Forces in Austria.

The first memorandum, dated July 15, 1948, was addressed to Lieutenant Colonel George Schrantz, at his request, by Lyon and Charles Crawford. Schrantz was not informed of all the activities of Milano's Operations Branch, and apparently wanted a document in the file to protect him from any possible future criticism. Milano was shown the memorandum after it had been sent to headquarters and registered his disapproval. Lyon was notably circumspect.

The memo read as follows:

SUBJECT: Rat Line from Austria to South America.
SUMMARY OF INFORMATION
1. In accordance with instructions from the Office of the Director of Intelligence, USFA, these agents have attempted to establish a safe means of resettlement of dependents of visitors and VIP personalities.
2. Through the Vatican connections of Father Draganovic, Croat, DP Resettlement Chief of the Vatican circle, a tentative agreement was reached to assist in this operation. The agreement consists of simply mutual assistance, i.e., these agents assist persons of interest to Father Draganovic to leave Germany and, in turn, Father Draganovic will assist these agents in obtaining the necessary visas to Argentina, South America, for persons of interest to this Command.
3. It may be stated that some of the persons of interest to Father Draganovic may be of interest to the Denazification policy of the Allies; however, the persons assisted by Father Draganovic are also of interest to our Russian ally. Therefore, this operation cannot receive any official approval and must be handled with minimum amount of delay and with a minimum amount of general knowledge.
4. On 3 July 1948, these agents contacted the Austrian representative of Father Draganovic in Salzburg, as prearranged. Through the assistance of CIC Salzburg, transportation was obtained and the representative was escorted to Bad Reichenhall, Germany, where he was to meet the

223

German representative of Father Draganovic's organization. However, due to unforseen circumstances, the German representative did not appear. The Austrian representative was escorted back to Salzburg to await developments.

5. On 4 July 48, these agents received a telegram from the U.S. contact in Rome (Fred Martin) that the German representative was arrested while crossing the German-Austrian border on or about 1 July 48. It was the desire of these agents to go to Bad Reichenhall, Germany, to make the necessary investigation, however, due to transportation difficulties, this was not deemed advisable.

6. The status of subject rat line is not settled at this time, however it is felt that with CIC connections in Germany, these agents can assist the German representative and continue their progress as outlined above.

NOTE: It is suggested to the Chief, 430th CIC Detachment, USFA, that a reassignment of jeeps be made, and that two detachment jeeps be assigned to headquarters. These jeeps could be stationed and utilized by Land Salzburg and Land Upper Austria but be prepared to move upon call from representatives of CIC headquarters. In this manner most of the difficulties in obtaining transportations for such operations can be avoided. Also, the responsibilities for incorrent use of such vehicles, i.e., police violations, utilizing Government vehicles for pleasure, will be the responsibility of the driver and not the Land Section to which the jeep is originally assigned.

It is believed that in this manner considerable time, personal difficulties, and personality differences could be avoided and assist in the speedy completion of similar missions.

(Signed) PAUL E. LYON S/A, CIC

CHARLES CRAWFORD S/A, CIC

The second of the Lyon memoranda was written two years later. It is rather franker and certainly more informative. It was drafted at Milano's request and is addressed to him, dated April 10, 1950. It reads as follows:

1. ORIGINS.

a. During the summer of 1947, the undersigned received instructions from G-2, USFA, through Chief CIC, to establish a means of disposition for visitors who had been in the custody of the 430th CIC and completely processed in accordance with current directives and requirements, and whose continued residence in Austria constituted a security threat as well as a source of possible embarrassment to the Commanding General of USFA, since the Soviet command had become aware of their presence in the US Zone of Austria and in some instances had requested the return of these persons to Soviet custody.

b. The undersigned, therefore, proceeded to Rome where, through a mutual acquaintance, he conferred with a former Slovakian diplomat who in turn was able to recruit the services of a Croation [sic] Roman

Catholic Priest, Father Dragonivich. Father Dragonivich had by this time developed several clandestine evacuation channels to the various South American countries for various types of European refugees.

2. HISTORY OF OPERATIONS.

a. During 1947 and 1948 it was necessary to escort the visitors physically from Austria to Rome from the standpoint of security and to avoid any embarrassment on the part of the US Government which could arise from faulty documentation or unforseen border or police incidents.

b. Documents to assist in the journey of these people from Austria to Rome were secured through S/A Crawford, Reference IRS, Subject: "Debriefing of S/A Crawford", dated 6 April 1950.

c. Upon arrival in Rome, the visitors were turned over to Dragonivich who placed them in safe haven houses being operated under his direct supervision. During this period, the undersigned then actively assisted Father Dragonivich with the help of a US citizen, who was Chief of the eligibility office of IRO in Rome, in securing additional documentation and IRO aid for further transportation. This, of course, was done illegally inasmuch as such persons could not possibly qualify for eligibility under the Geneva IRO Charter. However, after several months, the American suddenly lost his mental stability, through overindulgence in alcohol, and disclosed some of the details of the arrangement to his superiors and other official agencies in Rome which required the undersigned to realign the operation and to discontinue contact with the IRO office. Thus Father Dragonivich was forced to turn to other sources in the National Catholic Welfare Organization. He also secured permits for residence of those persons from the Italian police, permits to travel from Rome to Genoa or Naples, as the case might be, and permits from the Italian Foreign Office for various visas. In short, it can be stated that Dragonivich handled all phases of the operation after the defectees arrived in Rome, such as the procurement of IRO Italian and South American documents, visas, stamps, arrangements for disposition, land or sea, and notification of resettlement committees in foreign lands.

d. As the operation continued, Dragonivich's possibilities for the necessary means, documentation, travel and permits expanded and it became possible to ship the visitors from Austria, thus eliminating personal escort by CIC agents to Rome. A new phase was thus established and an employee of Dragonivich proceeded to Austria, picked up the charges and took them to Genoa where they were placed in safe haven houses to await disposition to South America.

3. DIFFICULTIES ENCOUNTERED.

The following difficulties and problems may be expected by those who may become engaged in rat line operations:

a. Frequent changes in travel documents necessary for movement in European countries.

b. Changes in the Italian border control and police supervision of DP's in Italy.

c. Land and sea transportation facilities or lack thereof.

d. Opening and closing of immigration quotas by the various countries of South America.

e. The physical condition of visitors and dependents. It may be stated here that it is desirable that all persons be examined for TB, syphilis or other contagious diseases and that the female dependents be cautioned during the evacuation period relative to pregnancy, inasmuch as pregnant women or small children are acceptable only with grave difficulty and at great expense.

f. Marriage Status. In view of the fact that Dragonivich is a Roman Catholic priest and the National Catholic Welfare is involved, the marriage status of male and female must be clearly established, inasmuch as the personalities associated in this operation will not condone any acts contrary to the Church, such as common law marriage, illegitimate children not baptized, etc.

g. Although it might be advantageous to have absolute "control" of Father Dragonivich and his means of evacuation, it may be categorically stated that it is not possible and in the opinion of the undersigned not entirely desirable. Dragonivich is known and recorded as a Fascist, war criminal, etc., and his contacts with South American diplomats of a similar class are not generally approved by US State Department officials, plus the fact that in the light of security, it is better that we may be able to state, if forced, that the turning over of a DP to a welfare Organization falls in line with our democratic way of thinking and that we are not engaged in illegal disposition of war criminals, defectees and the like.

4. COMPROMISES.

a. As stated above, the US citizen, Chief of the Eligibility Office, Rome, was one (Robert Bishop—deleted in Ryan report) who was allegedly a member of OSS during World War II, and who fancied himself as a top intelligence operative in Italy. After his breakdown due to alcoholism, [Bishop] imagined himself as the savior of Italy in view of the danger of a Communist victory during the elections of 1948, thus told stories of how the undersigned could assist in providing large numbers of underground troops, military supplies, sea evacuation, air evacuation and the like. This, of course, caused inquiries as to the exact nature of the work in which the undersigned was engaged. This was explained away successfully in a personal interview with Admiral Mentz, Chief of IRO, Italy, and a full report was submitted to G-2, USFA.

b. The Brazil Expedition was, again, a compromise which was not the fault of operational technique. A female visitor who was inclined to be rather frivolous in her attentions became a public nuisance while under protective custody in Austria and was, therefore, evacuated as a married woman in custody of her amour of the moment. During the voyage, the lady in question changed her mind and upon arrival in Brazil sought assistance and protection from both the Brazilian authorities and the US Embassy. They, of course, were uninformed, inasmuch as it is impossible, due to lack of knowledge of transportation dates, visa quotas, etc., to give prior information as to when the shipments are to be made. The affair was made a matter of official investigation and necessarily other innocent people were involved and returned to Europe.

5. RECOMMENDATIONS.

a. It has been the experience of this organization that only one man should be assigned the mission of disposition when dealing with Father Dragonivich. Inasmuch as he, although reliable from a security standpoint, is unscrupulous in his dealings concerning money, as he does a considerable amount of charity work for which he receives no compensation, it is not entirely impossible that he will delay one shipment for one organization to benefit another organization who pays higher prices.

b. Due to the background of Father Dragonivich and the nature of his work, it is not believed practical that the MA's in foreign countries under diplomatic status should become involved with the DP's who land through his channels of his operation.

c. Each visitor should be thoroughly and properly briefed and preparations for his movement be made in the light of his cover story. Each should be furnished sufficient clothing, some travel money, and advance notice sent through Dragonivich channels to assist in his rehabilitation in the country where he lands.

d. The facilities of Father Dragonivich should be handled as a single operation by one agency and no attempt should be made to control him or his sources for reasons set forth in this memorandum.

> *FOR THE COMMANDING*
> *OFFICER*
> *(signed) PAUL E. LYON*
> *IB Operations Officer*

(There is an MS annotation: "Copy No. 2 burned 14/4/50—RW.")

Index

About the Authors

An intelligence officer during World War II, COL. JAMES V. MILANO, USA (Ret.), commanded the Military Intelligence Service in Austria for a year and a half after the war. From 1947 to 1950, he was chief of operations for all U.S. forces stationed there. He retired from the Army in 1966. PATRICK BROGAN is a Washington correspondent for *The Herald* (Glasgow). His previous books include *Deadly Business: The Story of Sam Cummings and Interarms*, *The Fighting Never Stopped*, and *Captive Nations: Eastern Europe, 1945–1989*. Both authors live in the Washington, D.C., area.